First published in 2018 by Barrallier Books Pty Ltd, trading as Echo Books

This revised version published in 2025 by Echo Books

Echo Books is an imprint of Superscript Publishing Pty Ltd, ABN 76 644 812 395

Registered Office: PO Box 669, Woodend, Victoria, 3442.

www.echobooks.com.au

National Library of Australia Cataloguing-in-Publication entry.

Creator: David Tough

Title: 212 Soldiers for the Queen. Fijians in the British Army 1961—1997

ISBN: 9780648202523 (paperback)

A catalogue record for this book is available from the National Library of Australia

Book design and layout by Peter Gamble, Canberra.

Set in Garamond Premier Pro Regular, 13/17 and MinervaModern and Trajan Pro

www.echobooks.com.au

Front cover image: *Fledgling paratroopers. Jake Tulele (left) and Eroni Koroi, circa 1963*
Photo: Tom Morell

Back cover image: *L to R Watisoni Rogose, Asiveni Lutumailagi and Kasiano Qaduadua (both squatting) with Talaiasi Labalaba.and an unidentified comrade, Ballymena, early sixties.*
Photo: Asiveni Lutumailagi

212 SOLDIERS
FOR THE QUEEN

Fijians in the British Army 1961-1997

David Tough

echo))
BOOKS

Dedication

For David Rowe, soldier-philosopher, raconteur and inspirational leader; citizen of Adelaide and Sarajevo, but for whom I would never have met any of the subjects of this book.

For Mirza Moazzam Beg, without whose encouragement, assistance and support over twenty years this book might never have been completed.

And the late Dr Teresia Teaiwa, a distinguished Banaban and generous mentor, lost to the Pasifika community in March 2017.

CONTENTS

FOREWORD

The present government of Fiji insists that now all citizens of Fiji, whatever their ethnic origins, are Fijians. This replaces an understanding whereby only those of the indigenous Pacific Island race were Fijians—all others were Indians, Chinese, Europeans etc. This book is about those earlier times when the term 'Fijian' meant for the adult males of Pacific Island blood a generally strong, robust and active person, even intimidatingly so to some strangers.

Before contact with Europeans the Fijians led dangerous and precarious lives. For centuries they lived in villages. That word can summon up a vision of peace and harmonious contentment, but every family lived in a village group, and their safety and very existence depended on the strength of their group and the alliances which could be arranged with the chiefs of other groups. Cannibalism was commonplace, and life could be short and violent. The young men of all employment 'clans' were available for fighting and the *Bati* or warrior clan was under constant training and preparedness for war. And, as was said to Queen Victoria at the time of cession, the law was the club.

Fiji in those early days had an abundance of fine food, a healthy climate, a lack of western diseases, and an admiration for large-bodied people both male and female. Over the centuries the population became large, robust and vigorous. Fighting was a common activity and successful fighting a necessity for survival.

In the early years after Cession, there was a need for a force to settle reactionary groups and this was provided by the 'Armed Constabulary'— really, an organisation to demand conformation by the most unruly. But there was no army in those early years.

During World War I, there was Fiji enthusiasm for service but the British, in a policy which seems ridiculous today, declined, stating that it was a war between European nations and that the dark races were not required. They imposed the same strange restriction on the Maori volunteers of New Zealand although they agreed that the Maoris could provide a 'Pioneer' unit—really, just a battalion of labourers—a restriction soon overcome once in the field.

Fiji provided volunteers from the European population, but from the Fijians only individuals such as Ratu Sukuna and Ratu Tiali escaped to serve other nations. At the very end of hostilities, a wharf labour battalion was accepted to work in southern France.

World War II saw something of the same attitude by the senior partners. New Zealand had defence responsibility for Fiji and, as the Japanese offensive developed, made plans to counter it—but without Fijians. Citizens were enlisted and trained, but it appeared that they were for local defence whilst the Kiwis and others prepared for offensive operations.

When the American forces came to Fiji to train, they saw how useful Fijians could be in tropical warfare, and two battalions and two commandos of local troops went with them to the Solomons. There, their value was quickly and thoroughly proven, and they became known and universally accepted as first-class operational soldiers. Fiji society was also affected by this experience, in that Fijian officers and NCOs had shown that they were the equal of any others in the Pacific Theatre and were able to demonstrate their leadership in peacetime Fiji when opportunities arose.

From 1946 armies in non-critical countries were diminished and often disposed of. Fiji, proud of its Pacific experience, kept a tiny force—a company of regular Infantry, a Territorial (i.e. reserve) Battalion, a band, some logistic support elements and an 'employment pool'. The pool was instituted by New Zealand commanders of the RFMF who knew how difficult it was for New Zealand to recruit sufficient numbers from within their own population especially in trades such as catering, motor servicing and other support categories.

So, Fiji provided fifty men to serve various periods in New Zealand in trades where there were deficiencies. They also played Rugby! These fifty were paid by New Zealand and, where there were vacancies, they attended formal Army courses. The arrangement was good for both countries. It continued until 1977 when it was changed so that Fiji could have free training in New Zealand for 18250 man/days per year—an excellent arrangement for Fiji and only ended by Steve Rabuka's coup.

By 1951-52, the RFMF was feeling the lack of an operational outlet, as the Commander of the day phrased it. When Britain found herself strained by the insurgency in Malaya, she invited Fiji and perhaps other colonies to contribute forces. This suited Fiji and the RFMF. The 'Fiji Battalion' as it was known was a fabulous unit. Not only was it supreme in the jungle operations against communist terrorists but was undefeated at rugby, at amateur and professional boxing and at all track and field athletics up to one mile.

The first commanding officer was a New Zealander, as was the third incumbent, but the second and highly-successful last commanders were Fijian chiefs with World War II experience who produced from their battalions remarkable and unsurpassed operational results. Both Fijian Commanders later became national leaders at home—Ratu Sir Penaia Ganilau, the last Commander, became Governor General and the first President.

1961 saw the recruitment of the 212 Fijians into British Army service—the story of whom has so ably been told by David Tough in this book.

But the tale of the 212 did not end Fiji's overseas military adventures. In 1978 the United Nations was assembling a force to separate Israel from South Lebanon (UNIFIL) and Fiji expressed her willingness to provide a battalion. The UN mandate was for 6 months, and both Australia and

New Zealand advised the UN that Fiji could meet the obligations for the first six months but no longer. In fact, Fiji was in South Lebanon holding the critical coastal sector for 25 years. FIJIBATT, as she was known in the theatre, was highly successful and often known as the battalion to be emulated.

In 1983 a peacekeeping force was established in the Sinai Peninsula, and Fiji was chosen to join the Americans and the Colombians in providing units of which the Fiji Battalion in 2016 is still serving in the critical coastal sector.

In 2016 there is also a Fiji Light Battalion in the Golan Heights between Israel and Syria, a UN guard force of several hundred as the principal UN security element at UN headquarters in Baghdad and Fijian elements and individuals wherever UN military security and peacekeeping are called for.

It seems certain that for a nation of only 800,000, Fiji is quite the most active nation in providing operational soldiers for peacekeeping. In 1961 Fiji sent 212 men and women to Britain. In recent years. British recruiting of Fijians has resumed and there are now some 1340[1] serving wherever British forces are found, and many more who have been recruited by overseas private security organisations.

If this book relates how returnees from overseas service have taken leadership roles in the homeland, consider the future of the nation. So, Fiji is a continuing source of tough, reliable and skilled soldiers who bring respect and, of course, funds to the homeland. What makes the Fijian such a good soldier?

He comes from a village society where discipline and communal obligations rule existence. His housing and feeding seem frugal to a Westerner but are healthy and, often being on a Pacific shore, breed youngsters who know swimming and fishing as they know rugby football. After school in a village one may see children, perhaps 20 a side, of roughly

---

1   Figure provided by British High Commission, Suva, 2016—author.

the same age playing rugby, unsupervised, unrefereed, barefooted and with a plastic bottle rather than a ball. Mud, blood and noise!

There are those who criticise the militarisation of the country and point towards the coups which have taken place since 1987. They are concerned that a powerful military may again some day stretch its muscles. They are not reassured that the recently approved Constitution states:

> It shall be the overall responsibility of the RFMF to ensure at all times the security, defence and well-being of Fiji and all its residents.

Brigadier Ian Thorpe, CBE
Rotorua
June 2016

PREFACE

The most interesting three years of my working life were spent in Fiji from 1989-92. Throughout that period and subsequently, the country attempted to come to terms with the consequences of 'the events of 1987', as many citizens euphemistically referred to the county's first military coups led by Lieut Colonel, later Major General, Sitiveni Rabuka.

In my first few weeks working in the political section of the then Australian Embassy in Suva, I met the first of many of the 200 men and 12 women who enlisted together in the British Army in November 1961. It quickly became apparent that the '212', as they have come to be known, were a remarkable group and in 1961 a talented cross section of colonial Fiji's youth. Almost all the '212' served the full period of their initial enlistment, and about a third of the men extended their service for up to twenty-two years or more before returning to Fiji, remaining in the UK, or settling elsewhere. The army did very well out of the latter group in particular. Towards the end of my posting to Fiji, I met many more of the '212' and concluded that their collective biography was worth recording as a contribution to the social history of Fiji.

Several of the '212' were of special interest because of their obvious or apparent involvement in the events following the 1987 election in Fiji, Rabuka's first coup, and the aftermath military interventions. Ratu Meli

Vesikula had retired from the British Army as RSM of a line regiment and became involved with the indigenous *taukei* movement agitating against the elected Coalition government dominated by ethnic Indians. Four of the '212' contested seats for the successful Coalition parties. George Chute and Sam Pillay were successful, and Sam was among the new government members sitting in parliament when Rabuka entered the chamber, accompanied by a carefully selected group of trusted soldiers. Ilisoni Ligairi was widely, but erroneously, believed responsible for training the latter group, and groups supporting Fiji's next two coups, but denies any prior knowledge of either Rabuka's first coup or the Speight coup in 2000. Mike Yasa had returned to Fiji after six years in which he earned a Short Service Commission in the Royal Green Jackets, resumed his career in Fiji's civil service, and had successful tours with the Royal Fiji Military Forces (RFMF) on peace keeping operations with the United Nations in Lebanon and the Multinational Force and Observers (MFO) in Sinai. Mike also found time to write plays in Fijian. In May 1987, Mike was Fiji's Consul General in Auckland and publicly denounced the RFMF's intervention in politics. He resigned his post when it became apparent that Rabuka intended to stay in charge.

Collectively, the '212' served their Queen throughout the world in almost every minor conflict with which Britain became involved after 1961, and had in Jim Vakatalai's words, 'adventures on the crumbling fringes of empire'. Four of them finished their service in the Falkland Islands.

The men in particular were welcomed for their sporting prowess, and in later years many British officers lamented that their regiments had received too few or none of these Fijians–and thus did less well in rugby and other sporting tournaments.

Seven of the 200 men successfully sought selection into 22 SAS Regiment and fought in various declared and undeclared wars with great distinction. Talaiasi Labalaba died heroically in 1972 at Mirbat, Oman, and many believe he would have been awarded the Victoria Cross if the action was not part of a conflict kept secret at the time. 22 SAS remember him with a statue outside the Sergeant's Mess at Stirling Lines in Hereford. Tom Morell led one of the assault teams against terrorists holding hostages in the Iranian Embassy in London in 1980, in an action that brought 22 SAS out of its closet. Seconaia Takavesi was awarded a Distinguished Conduct Medal for his assistance to Laba at Mirbat and followed Tom through the windows of the Iranian Embassy. This spawned a legend in Fiji that the reason the SAS assault team wore balaclavas and gas masks was to conceal the fact that many of them were Fijians. Two of these seven had sons who later served for many years with 22 SAS.

Several other '212' had distinguished careers after their military service. Fred Dewa took advantage of the Open University scheme and was one of the first graduates. He later acquired a PhD in mathematics, taught in Papua New Guinea and at the University of the South Pacific, and was elected to Fiji's parliament after 1987. After their army service, Sam Tamata and Mike Yasa were ordained as ministers of the Free Church of Scotland and the Methodist Church, respectively. David Lelo twice served as a Mormon bishop in New Zealand. Two others also became men of God in their later years and several became lay preachers. Many prospered in businesses, including Bob Dass who ran two very successful Indian restaurants in Melbourne, and Pramod Tikaram, whose army service led to senior management in one of the early Vodafone companies in England. Others faded away, but they all had interesting anecdotes to relate. Two of the more colourful '212' who spent all or most of their subsequent working lives in England, claim titles as England's 'first black shepherd' and her first Fijian coal miner.

When I returned to Australia from Fiji in 1992 with the list of 212 names published in the *Fiji Times* of 6 November 1961, I also had contact addresses for many of them. I spent my evenings of the following two years with my first computer, writing to those for whom I had (or later found) addresses, to secretaries of regimental associations, and others such as the Army Pensions Board. Most of the twelve women returned to Fiji in the first instance, as did many of the men who served terms of six to nine years or less because of medical or other early discharges. Many of the longer serving men married women from Singapore, Malaysia, Israel, the UK, the USA, Germany, Norway, Finland and Denmark. They elected to stay in those countries or not return to Fiji because of greater opportunities for themselves or their children. Others decided to settle in Canada, Australia or New Zealand.

Unfortunately, the project then foundered for many years through a combination of my frequent changes of address, and many correspondents' lack of enthusiasm for 'snail mail' in the days before the internet was in common use.

My enthusiasm was re-ignited by Roger Cole's *Operation Storm*, purchased while transiting Tullamarine airport in 2012. What follows is an account of my interviews and correspondence with the surviving '212', relatives of those deceased, and those who served with them or encountered them in unlikely places such as Borneo and Brunei.

Fiji's military had received very little attention from historians or others until 1987. In particular, a reference that caught my eye after this project was reinvigorated illustrated this neglect. In Bayly and Harper's *Forgotten Wars*, discussing the service of the King's African Rifles in the Malayan Emergency, the authors noted 'Askaris were poorly paid compared to Gurkhas and Fijian soldiers, the latter mostly volunteers from the poor lesser islands'. A great number of the '212' came from those same islands and I thought such Fijians worthy of a better epitaph than that!

I found my subjects a very modest bunch. A frequent early query from them was: 'Why are you doing this?' They needed persuading that they had interesting individual and collective stories to tell. Even Fred Marafono, one of the more colourful individuals, with probably several potential books in his repertoire, considered this project 'an Honour for us who were/are 'no body', just young men and women who had the opportunity to start a new life with the added adventures overseas'. I rest my case.

Any attempt at a composite biography of 212 people is likely to contain errors of fact through the passage of fifty years, and the problem of 'the older we get, the better we were' complex common to many professions, but not least that of arms. I hope the following is an accurate rendering of my exchanges with the '212' themselves or their widows, children or other family members and I accept responsibility for any errors of fact and licence with interpretation. To this collective latter group, I extend my thanks for their trust, hospitality and much laughter. Individuals are acknowledged wherever possible for their contributions.

David Tough
Narrabundah
July, 2018

ACKNOWLEDGEMENTS

The research for this book would have taken infinitely longer without the patient and protracted assistance, advice and support of Mo Beg over twenty years and for his generous hospitality in July 2014 in particular. Mo was one of a select few who were kind enough to respond to my initial 'snail mail' overtures of 1992-94, and whose initial acknowledgement that I had identified a worthwhile project, and his subsequent encouragement, sustained my belief in the project, intermittently, for two decades. Keith Zoing, Seci Drika, Asiveni Lutumailagi, Ted Ledua and Jone Buakula provided early encouragement in 1992-94 before their untimely deaths. Kim Yabaki was another early correspondent. Bob Dass, Atunaisa Laqeretabua, Jake Tulele, Ann Rosa, Bryan Tichborne, Tom Morell, Pramod Tikaram and Jim Vakatalai also deserve special thanks.

Ratu Meli Vesikula, the first of the '212' I was privileged to meet, provided advice, encouragement and assistance over many years.

The 'Flames': Miriama Vuiyale, Mere Ratunabuabua, Samanunu Vaniqi, Sau Naceva, Kayby Ledua and Margaret Vuiyasawa, six daughters of the 200 men who helped Ratu Meli and other RBL Fiji staff compile a spreadsheet that decoded the list of names which appeared in the *Fiji Times* in November 1961, on the fiftieth anniversary of the '212''s recruitment. This list was an invaluable guide to exactly who did serve and under their correct names, or those they chose to be known by during their army service.

Numerous '212' who entrusted precious surviving photographs of aspects of their service to me for copying, all of whom are acknowledged herein but especially the first few: Torika Canano (Laba's mother), Sam Pillay, Vaciseva Tabua and Betty Foster/Hansen. Sam and these wonderful women and their photographs convinced me that here was a story that needed recording, and could be illustrated, for all Fijians, not just for those who served, and their families.

My late mother-in-law, Margaret Bradshaw, for her efforts locating some of the '212' in the UK in the early days of this project. Seci Drika gave her a four-digit telephone number at Maiden Bradley for Peni Levaci but it took another twenty years to locate 'England's first black shepherd', by then retired in Savusavu.

Tom and Rosalind Morell for the warmest welcome any Australian ever had in New Zealand. And Tom for his encouragement for recording as much as possible of every individual '212'.

Pastor Epi Ligairi, conscripted by his great uncle to assist me on my November 2013 visit to Nadi.

Dr Guy and Kathryn Hawley for their hospitality and assistance during the 2013 visit to Fiji. I credit Guy with saving the sight of my left eye after an accident on a squash court in November, 1989.

The late Dr Teresia Teaiwa, of Victoria University of Wellington, for her encouragement and assistance with contacting some of the twelve women.

Dr Dominik Scheider, University of Siegen, for his encouragement with a project paralleling his research into expatriate Fijian communities in Japan, Romania and elsewhere.

Dr Stewart Firth and Dr Paul D'Arcy of the Australian National University for their encouragement and suggestions regarding the outline of the narrative.

Dr John Nation for advice on the Fijian language and for analysing Mike Yasa's play.

Eric Roper, editor of the newsletter of the *Kings and Royal Lancastrian* regimental newsletter, and John Shannon MBE, for their assistance with recollections of deceased former Kingsmen, Jimmy Vanessa (aka Jemesa or James L Naivalu) and Kiniviliame Navusolo ('King Billy'); and through whom I was contacted by Jimmy's mate Joe Challoner.

Rarm Naga-Lingam and Grant Odell, uber geeks extraordinaire, for assistance with recovering a card index program from Windows 3.1 on my first computer and making it run in a 'virtual box' on a Macbook.

Rob Lellmann for assistance with finding Fijian names in German telephone directories, and to his family for providing an ideal location in which to break the back of the initial draft of this text.

The late Lt Col Sam Mallet MBE for his guided tour of Stirling Lines.

Brigadier Ian Thorpe, CBE, for his recollections of his time as the last New Zealand Commander of the RFMF and his post-1987 appointment overseeing RFMF training.

Rasheed Ali, CBE, for his vetting of my observations on the role of the Girmitiyas and other aspects of Fiji's sugar industry and for critiquing several key chapters.

Marsali Mackinnon for permission to reproduce an extract from her 1998-9 Fiji Oral History Project—the interview with the late Sir Len Usher's recollections of Ratu Sir Lala Sukuna's travel to Yacata in 1944 and subsequent presentation of Sukunaivalu's VC. Mars knows far more than I about Pacific Islanders and her critiques of the early chapters were very useful. I am most grateful for her subsequent patient and painstaking editing of my manuscript and owe her many bilos.

And to Mbak Ifa Barry for her patient support in recent years and her hectoring over the potential use of Facebook that took me a long time to recognise.

GLOSSARY OF TERMS

AC	Companion of the Order of Australia
ACS	Adi Cakobau School
ACT	Australian Capital Territory
AD	Air Defence
AKA	Also known as
ALTA	Agricultural and Landlord Tenant Act
AOG	Assemblies of God
APC	Armoured Personnel Carrier
AWOL	Absent without leave
BAOR	Briish Army of the Rhine
BEM	British Empire Medal
BOAC	British Overseas Airways Corporation
CBE	Commander of the Most Excellent Order of the British Empire
CO	Commanding Officer
CP	Commissioner of Police
CPL & L/CPL	Corporal, Lance Corporal
CSR	CSR Ltd is a major Australian industrial company, originally The Colonial Sugar Refining Company, the major sugar producer in Fiji and Australia

CT	Counter Terrorism
DCM	Distinguished Conduct Medal
DERR	Duke of Edinburgh's Royal Regiment
DO	District Officer
DOMCOL	Dominion and Colonial Leave, a remnant colonial benefit enjoyed by the '212' who served six years or more and were unmarried
DPRK	Democratic People's Republic of (North) Korea
DWR	Duke of Wellington's Regiment
EEC	European Economic Community
EOD	Explosive Ordnance Disposal
ERE	Extra Regimentally Employed
FCO	Foreign and Commonwealth Office
FDF	Fiji Defence Force (pre-Independence)
FFI	Fiji Forest Industries
FIR	Fiji Infantry Regiment
FLP	Fiji Labour Party
FMF	Common abbreviation for RFMF
FRNVR	Fiji Royal Naval Volunteer Reserve
Girmit/Girmitya	Indentured labour agreement and those contracted
GM	George Medal
GSM	General Service Medal
HMG	Her Majesty's Government
HMTQ	Her Majesty the Queen
KBE	Knight Commander of the Most Excellent Order of the British Empire
Kerekere	Fijian custom of making demands on relatives, friends or employers which must be met with no expectation of repayment
KIA	Killed in action
KINGS	The King's Regiment

KORBR	King's Own Royal Border Regiment
KRRC	King's Royal Rifle Corps
LAD	Light Air Defence (RA) or Light Aid Detachment (REME)
Lt	Lieutenant
Lt Col	Lieutenant Colonel
LPS	Levuka Public School
LSL	Long Service List
MA	Master of Arts degree
Mataqali	Fijian landowning social unit (Fij.)
MBE	Member of (the Order of) the British Empire
MFA	Fijian Affairs Department
MFO	Multinational Force & Observers
MBHS	Marist Brothers High School
MID	Mention in Despatches
MM	Military Medal
MOD	Ministry of Defence
NAAFI	Navy, Army and Air Force Institutes
NFP	National Federation Party
NRPS	Non-Regular Permanent Staff
NSW	New South Wales, Australia
OBE	Officer of (the Order of) the British Empire
OC	Officer Commanding
OIC	Officer in charge
PhD	Doctor of Philosophy
PKO	Peace Keeping Operations (UN)
PM	Prime Minister
PSI	Permanent Staff Instructor
PWD	Public Works Department
QC	Queen's Counsel
QEB	Queen Elizabeth Barracks

QGM	Queen's Gallantry Medal
QOH	Queen's Own Hussars
QVS	Queen Victoria School
RA	Royal Artillery
RAF	Royal Air Force
RAOC	Royal Army Ordnance Corps
RAR	Royal Australian Regiment
RASC	Royal Army Service Corps
RBL	Royal British Legion
RCT	Royal Corps of Transport
RDG	Royal Dragoon Guards
RE	Royal Engineers
REME	Royal Electrical & Mechanical Engineers
RFMF	Royal (later Republic of) Fiji Military Forces
RGJ	Royal Green Jackets
RKS	Ratu Kadavulevu School
RLC	Royal Logistics Corps
RMP	Royal Military Police
RN	Royal Navy
RNZAF	Royal New Zealand Air Force
ROK	Republic of (South) Korea
RRW	Royal Regiment of Wales
R.Signals	Royal Signals
RTR	Royal Tank Regiment
SAS (22)	Special Air Service Regiment
SEATO	South East Asia Treaty Organisation
SF	Special Forces
SGS	Suva Grammar School
SGT	Sergeant
SNCO	Senior Non-Commissioned Officer
SPCA	Society for the Prevention of Cruelty to Animals

SQMS	Squadron Quarter Master Sergeant
SQN	Squadron
S/SGT or SSGT	Staff or Colour Sergeant
SWB	South Wales Borderers (24th Foot of Rorke's Drift fame)
TA	Territorial Army (Reservists)
Tanoa	Large wooden bowl for preparing kava
Taukei, iTaukei	The possessor of a thing (Fij.); term used by indigenous Fijians to describe themselves (Fij.)
UAE	United Arab Emirates
UN	United Nations
UNDOF	United Nations Disengagement Observer Force (Syria)
UNGOMAP	United Nations Good Offices Mission in Afghanistan and Pakistan
UNIFIL	United Nations Interim Force in Lebanon
USAF	United States Air Force
USD	United States Dollars
USP	University of the South Pacific
WO 1 & 2	Warrant Officers, Grades 1 and 2
WRAC	Women's Royal Army Corps
Yagona	*Kava* (Fij.), traditional ceremonial drink of Fiji and other Western Pacific cultures, made from the pounded roots of the kava plant. *Kava/yagona* has sedative, anaesthetic, and euphoriant qualities.
2IC	Second in Command
2Lt	Second Lieutenant

CHAPTER 1: FIJI, 1961

Anyone old enough to have read newspapers in 1961 can only marvel at the changes since then—it was a very different world. The 'Cold War' between the two superpowers of the time was a threat to humanity but had yet to reach its apogee during the Cuban missile crisis the following year. In April the new US President Kennedy and the CIA were humiliated by the botched Bay of Pigs invasion of Cuba. Elvis had completed his voluntary military service in a divided Germany. *Wooden Heart* did well for him on the hit parades and no one had heard of the Beatles, the Rolling Stones or the internet. Bill Gates was only six years old.

Colonial, pre-Independence Fiji was much different to contemporary Fiji. There was no tourism or manufacturing industry of any consequence, and the economy revolved around sugar produced by Australia's Colonial Sugar Refining Company (CSR), or by mainly Indo-Fijians on small holdings sub-leased from CSR or indigenous Fijian landowners. Their ninety-nine-year leases under the Agricultural and Landowner Tenant Act, or ALTA, as it was known, were administered by the colonial government. The ethnic Indians were mainly the descendants of indentured labourers from Madras and Calcutta imported into Fiji between 1879 and 1916 to support CSR, directly from agents in India or via the company's interests in Australia.

The Indian community had thrived since the first indentured labourers arrived. Industrious individuals and families dominated the business sector. By 1961 their numbers exceeded those of the Fijian community, leading to anxiety from the indigenous population that they might eventually lose both political and economic control of their country.

The experience of indigenous populations in Australia, New Zealand and the Americas was not lost on the Fijians, and there had been race-based rioting over different issues in the previous two years.

Almost a century earlier in 1874, Christian missionaries were already well-established in Fiji when the *Vunivalu* or High Chief of Bau, Ratu Seru Cakobau, ceded sovereignty over the islands to Queen Victoria. The Church followed the Royal Navy, with Methodists and Roman Catholics claiming most of the early conversions. The Indian community was largely Hindu, but Muslims were also well-represented. A small number were Christians. Tensions between the indigenous and immigrant communities were inevitable but rarely erupted in violence. Intermarriage was discouraged in both communities and by the authorities. When intermarriage occurred, it was usually Indian men taking Fijian wives and rarely the opposite.

Most schools were segregated, either by community or government design. The colonial government recognised the need to educate and prepare Fijians for a role in government and created a tax on Fijian villagers to fund the attendance at boarding schools, with scholarships for boys from outer islands and the interior of the main islands of Viti Levu and Vanua Levu. Levuka Public School on Ovalau, and Queen Victoria and Ratu Kadavulevu schools (QVS and RKS, respectively) near Suva became the alma maters for the Fijian elite, particularly the sons of Ratus, or traditional chiefs, to whom the colonial administrators pandered. Even church-run schools such as Marist Brothers College had separate campuses for those of European, or part European descent, and for ethnic Fijian or Indian immigrant children. Many years passed before these schools accepted a racial mix of students, usually beginning with accepting students with European names, regardless of maternal input.

Some schools run by Hindu community groups accepted Fijian students who were ineligible for QVS or RKS or could not afford the fees charged elsewhere. Suva Grammar School, however, accepted only students of European or part European descent until after 1961. Neither Suva Grammar nor Levuka Public School in their early years accepted students with Fijian names. The education system was not a building block for national unity. In government high schools such as the Agricultural College, Fijians from outer islands often had their first contact with Indians and the exchanges were not always constructive.

The late Don Dunstan AC, QC, former Labour premier of South Australia and one of Australia's more colourful and innovative legislators, spent his formative years in Fiji, including a couple of years at Suva Grammar School around 1936. According to Dunstan's biographer, Dino Hodge, the social and racial rankings of colonial Fiji left a lasting impression on Dunstan, influencing much of his subsequent legislation in South Australia.[2] Dunstan practiced law in Fiji for a couple of years prior to 1951. Little seemed to have changed in Fiji a quarter century after Dunstan's schooldays.

St Felix's School in Suva Street in the capital's suburb of Toorak was run by the Marist Brothers. It was one of two Primary Schools on this site, the other being St Columba's School. St Felix was for children of European or part European parentage. The two schools have long since merged and are today known as Marist Primary School.

By 1961, a century of intermarriage within Fiji's main communities and with their colonial masters, with dashes of Chinese and Japanese blood from the inevitable immigrant trading communities, had produced a polyglot population of Fijians, Indians and 'Others'. The latter often included descendants of immigrants from other Pacific islands, or those of European seafarers and traders who had married women from Fiji and elsewhere in the Pacific. Fijian anxiety was heightened by the more vocal elements of the Indian community demanding the full political enfranchisement that Mahatma Gandhi and the independence movement had achieved in India.

---

2   *Don Dunstan—Intimacy & Liberty*, Wakefield Press 2014.

Fiji's infrastructure was minimal in 1961. The road from Suva to the international airport at Nadi along the south coast of the largest and most populous island, Viti Levu, was unsealed and the journey took six hours. Trains were limited to a small-gauge railway line serving the cane fields to get harvested cane to the sugar mills in the west of Viti Levu.

On the other side of the world, in the heart of what remained of Victoria's empire, the Chief of the Imperial General Staff was advised that the recruitment of volunteers was not providing the numbers that an army dependent on conscripts had provided since the 1939-45 war. More were needed to keep the Soviet and allied armies behind their 'iron curtain' and to keep the peace in an increasing number of colonies restless for the independence claimed by India, Burma and others in the immediate post war period. War Office files dealing with this issue were closed until 1995 and those dealing with the recruitment of Fijians do not record who first

MBHS Junior Under 9 Stone Rugby Team 1960 with their coach, Rev. Brother Eugene. Robert Kumar (Dass), rear row in centre and Jim Vakatalai in centre of middle row. Second left in middle row is Mo Beg's younger brother, Firoze Beg, who followed his father into medicine and is now a physician at Toowoomba hospital. Photo: Bob Dass

suggested supplementing the shortfall of volunteers from the UK with volunteer warriors from colonies such as the West Indies, the Seychelles and Fiji. Two things, however, are clear from these files. The first is the potential sensitivity of recruiting 'coloured' men into the armed services at a time when immigration of non-Europeans from Britain's colonies and former colonies was a political issue. The second is that whenever the decision was taken, it was well before the possibility was raised in a small article by *The Times* military correspondent on 19 July 1961, under the headings 'Army Drive To Get Recruits' and 'Effort to attract coloured men'.[3] The article noted that the army had particular problems in attracting medical orderlies, technicians and drivers. It speculated that the West Indies and Fiji were potential sources of recruits and noted 'The difficulties are obvious, but the War Office believes that more coloured men can be absorbed into British units without upsetting the balance'.

The 'balance' referred to by *The Times* was an arbitrary maximum of 2% of the establishment of those units deemed suitable for accepting 'coloured' soldiers from the colonies. The Household Brigade, Highland Brigade, Intelligence Corps and RMP were specified as unsuitable for the proposed initiative. Several MPs wrote to the War Minister, John Profumo, expressing concern about the proposal and hoping that *The Times* article was kite flying or 'inspired comment'. Sir Henry Studholme, first Baronet of Perridge and MP for Tavistock, considered the proposal 'would certainly be a mistake in my opinion, in the county regiments. It might work in the R.A.S.C or R.E.M.E'.[4]

The Times article was clearly 'kite flying', probably by Profumo or his advisers, as a memorandum on another file makes it clear that recruiting in the Seychelles had been completed by July, 1961.[5]

A War Office cable of 15 August 1961 advised addressees in Wellington New Zealand, Fiji and the Colonial Office that the proposed recruitment

---

3   National Archives file WO 32/20374 folio 28.

4   WO 32/19455.

5   WO 32/19455 folio 16a.

of Fijians had been approved by the Governor, Sir Kenneth Maddocks. A recruiting team headed by a Major was to be selected from Far East Land Forces (FARELF), Singapore.

Precisely why the War Office selected Jamaica, the Seychelles and Fiji as the most likely sources of suitable recruits to meet the shortfall is not clear from the War Office files that have been released. Indigenous Fijians, however, were well recorded as capable jungle fighters, both within their own units and supporting US, Australian and New Zealand forces in Bougainville and Guadalcanal in WWII. There, they earned the description 'death with velvet gloves' for their ambush tactics. Asesela Ravuvu[6] and Robert Lowry[7], among others, have recorded the exploits of the units involved and of one remarkable individual. Rev Usaia Sotutu was a Methodist missionary who performed outstanding service supporting Australian coast watchers and commandos of 1 Independent Company on Bougainville and later served as a Sergeant with the RFMF. He had won the trust of Bougainvillians and won support for the British Empire of the day in the course of his missionary work over preceding years. He showed gallantry under enemy fire well before joining the RFMF. Lowry has noted that nothing came of an Australian officer's nomination of Rev Sotutu for a gallantry award, and the belated award of a BEM for 'gallant and distinguished services in the South West Pacific' was, as Lowry notes, 'one of the most understated presentations of one of the most deserving BEMs ever awarded'.[8]

Sam Berwick[9] recorded that Usaia Sotutu was ordained as a Methodist minister in 1933 and was appointed a chaplain in the RFMF with the rank of Captain, before returning to Bougainville from 1946-49. Berwick also noted that Usaia was also qualified, or was recognised, as a 'sharp shooter'—an unusual qualification for a man of the cloth.

---

6   *Fijians at War 1939-1945*, 1988.

7   *Fortress Fiji* 2006.

8   Ibid Chapter 6, Footnote 185.

9   Sam Berwick, *Who's Who in Fiji.*

Arrival of the Recruiting Team

On 16 September 1961, the *Fiji Times* announced that an army recruiting team would shortly arrive seeking 100 single men with an elementary education and fluent English. Standard British Army pay scales were offered, together with a return passage to Fiji after each five years of service. On 28 September the paper reported the arrival of the recruiting team who were to be based at the RNZAF station at Laucala Bay. The following day the OC of the team, Major G.H. Worsley, RASC, held a press and radio conference advising that interviews would be conducted at the Masonic Hall in Gladstone Road. Major Worsley said that the British Army had not recruited men from Fiji before, but 127 men had been recruited in the Seychelles and a third recruiting team would go to Jamaica.

Major Worsley was supported by Captains B.C.B Pickles, also from FARELF, and S.H. Hardcastle, RA, from London. The team also included two senior NCOs and three other ranks to assist with interviews, medical and intelligence tests. The latter included a S/Sgt Williamson, Sgt Dunn, Cpl Daniels and Pte Moody. Worsley and others clearly under-estimated the degree of interest the recruiting team would attract. Initial selection began on 2 October, geared to processing forty recruits a day, and was overwhelmed by the 200 applicants presenting themselves on each of the first three days in Suva. The recruiting team moved to Nausori on 7 October, and thence to Nadi-Lautoka, Labasa and Savu Savu before returning to Suva on 31 October.

On 2 October 1961 the *Fiji Times* editorial queried an earlier claim by a Fijian politician that young Fijians 'exported on military duties' would ease unemployment in the colony. Against a background of criticism of the manner in which a Fiji battalion was deployed to Malaya in the 1950s to help quell a communist insurrection, the editor noted archly that 'most people believe that the clear and somewhat rigorous terms offered by British Army service will not discourage Fijian applicants, though non-Fijians without a military tradition may be less enthusiastic'. The latter statement was a thinly coded reference to the fact that few descendants of Indian labourers who migrated to Fiji under the Girmit scheme had been inclined to volunteer for service with Fiji's Defence Force in the two world wars or the Malayan campaign. This reluctance to serve in the Empire's conflicts was associated with agitation for parity in employment terms and conditions with Europeans in the Defence Force ranks, as well as political recognition.

Throughout the weeks that the recruiting team spent in Fiji, the leading newspaper was largely concerned with domestic developments, such as the appointment of Mr R.N. Nair as the first Indian District Officer, and the forthcoming Hibiscus Festival. Foreign news items reflected the precarious state of the world at the time. The USSR and the US were testing nuclear weapons, work had started on the wall that divided Berlin for the next three decades, and Indonesia's President Sukarno was a source of concern to his neighbours. The future looked gloomy for Australia's sugar industry as Britain negotiated to join the Common Market in Europe and 'gambling mania' was causing 'grave worry' in New South Wales. Decades later only the last concern remains.

The recruiting team's siren song appealed in particular to the eldest children of widows and the youngest children of large families whose fathers had served in WWII, or their elder brothers in the Malayan 'Emergency'. Some final year school leavers or young apprentices, such as Jim Vakatalai, Meli Vesikula and Dave Rosa, had a clear idea of what the British Army could offer as opportunities in various regiments. Others such as Alex Kubu were fortunate to have mentors in their workforce who could see how they might prosper in the British Army. Some, such as Fred Dewa, were frustrated by a lack of opportunity to further their education and either hoped, or believed the recruiting team's spiel, that the army or England would provide that opportunity. The oldest of those who did not lie about their age, however, was Mike Yasa, the only one of the 200 men eventually recruited with a tertiary qualification, who was identified as exceptional early in his army service by a future Field Marshal of the British Army. Yasa confirmed that judgement by winning the Sword of Honour at Mons Officer Cadet School when he qualified for a short service commission.

Tom Morell as a Special Constable in the Fiji Police Force, circa 1960.
Photo: Tom Morell

Pramod Tikaram's best friend Dennis Davendra Singh (right) was also accepted for
enlistment but accepted a scholarship from the Mormon church to study at the University
of Hawaii. They never met again and Dennis died in Salt Lake City in the early 2000s.
Pramod treasures this 1961 photograph and a tie Dennis gave him when he enlisted.
Photo: Pramod Tikaram

At least three young men had a clear idea of what enlistment might involve. Two of them, Asesela Waqairoba and Ilisoni Ligairi, were already serving in the Royal Fiji Military Forces (RFMF) at the time. Jim Vakatalai was a final year student at Marist Brothers High School and had a singular ambition—he wanted to enlist in the British Army and attempt selection for the Special Air Service (SAS) whose WWII exploits had been a mainstay of his varied reading. All three were to serve the maximum of twenty-two years for enlisted men that the recruiting team encouraged, with Ligairi and Vakatalai serving twenty of those years with 22 SAS.

Some, including Pramod Tikaram, were desperate to escape family or other pressures in Fiji. Other young men were already on their way to establishing themselves in the limited environment of the time. Tom Morell, at the ripe old age of twenty-two, had served in the RFMF's Naval Reserve, was a Special Constable in the Fiji Police and, having qualified in accountancy and Morse Code, was the youngest postmaster in the country at suburban Samabula. At the time, proficiency in Morse Code was mandatory for postmasters, who maintained high frequency radio links between Fiji's more than 300 islands.

A common motivation was a desire to see the England and the British Empire they had studied at schools dominated by expatriate teachers, and usually headed by a Principal from England. Some had a particular ambition to again see their Queen, who had visited Fiji in 1952 when most of this cohort were barely ten years old or young teenagers. Several nominated the Duke of Edinburgh's Royal Regiment as their first preference for service because they thought they might be part of a royal guard force for Prince Philip!

Some were influenced by fathers or other older family members who had served with the Fiji Battalion in the WWII Solomon Islands campaign, where Sefanaia Sukanaivalu won a Victoria Cross posthumously (Fiji's only VC to be awarded to date). Talaiasi Labalaba, who died heroically at Mirbat in 1972, in circumstances worthy of another VC, lost his natural father in the Solomons.

Some of these fathers and many older brothers served with the Fiji Battalion that helped defeat the Communist insurgency in Malaya (the 1948-1960 'Malaya Emergency.')

Ben Temo recalls being interviewed at Yaroi village in the provincial administration office outside Savusavu. George Chute was interviewed in the Majestic Theatre in Labasa and had his medical at the local hospital. The recruiting team's arrival, however, was not universally welcomed in each town. Tom Sorby was a junior shift boss at the Emperor Gold Mine in Vatukoula at the time, and the mine's General Manager banned the recruiting team from interviewing at Vatukoula.

Eager young men made the most of opportunities presented by the confusion that resulted from the massive response. Maciu Vatu was advised that his answers to the questions posed as part of the initial interview and intelligence test fell short of the required standard. He then interrogated those who had been told they had passed the test, deduced the correct answers to questions he had failed, and was successful when he re-joined the queue the next day. His high score got him selected for the REME.

Others took advantage of the confusion to lie about their ages, with both eager school leavers and older men using friends' birth certificates (thus frustrating subsequent efforts to identify exactly who had enlisted) and were accepted, despite being outside the 18-24-year-old age limit imposed by the recruiting team. Mike Yasa scraped in because his 24th birthday was not due until 24 December. Fulton College schoolmates Eroni Koroi Turaga and Jesse Maimanuku applied together. Eroni was accepted and served in the Royal Signals but Jesse's eighteenth birthday was not until 31 December and he was rejected. Jesse subsequently had a successful career in the Fiji Police.

Some of the confusion was fuelled by 'emotional and specious' criticism (according to Major Worsley) of the Government Secretariat's handling of the recruitment.[10] The Fijian District Officer for Suva expressed concern

---

10 Paragraph 5 of Major Worsley's report of 21 November 1961.

at the large number of dissatisfied Fijians in the Suva area who had applied, or claimed to have applied, to enlist and had been given no kind of test or interview. The DO feared that a situation was developing not unlike that in 1959 when an apparently trivial dispute between the management of the Shell oil company and its Fijian and Indian employees led to rioting. The following year had seen more rioting arising from a dispute in the sugar industry. Sir Kenneth Maddocks had briefed Worsley on the political sensitivity of the situation and the need for a balanced outcome of 'about 60% Fijian, 30% Indian and 10% part European'. Maddocks had spent most of his career in Nigeria. His governorship of Fiji was marked by industrial disputes which led him to invoke his emergency powers and call in the military in support of the civil power in 1959. His tenure in Fiji from 1958-1964 cost him his health although he survived in retirement until 2001.

The Spate and Burns Reports

Maddocks' predecessor Sir Ronald Garvey (1952-58) had spent sixteen years of his early British overseas civil service career in the Colonial Office in the Pacific, including two previous postings in Suva. Garvey commissioned Professor Oskar Spate, head of the Australian National University's geography department, to report on the economic and political prospects of the Fijian people. Garvey's previous experience of the country must have caused him grave concerns for the future, given his terms of reference for Spate's report:

1.   To assemble and assess such data as can be obtained on the economic activity of Fijian producers, with special attention to the effects of their social organisation on that activity, and

2.   To consider how far the Fijian social organisation may be a limiting factor in their economic activity and to suggest in what ways changes in that organisation might be desirable.

Spate's methodology involved extensive interviews in villages throughout the main islands, forty-six on Viti Levu, twenty on Vanua Levu, Taveuni and Kadavu and another six villages on smaller islands. His detailed report, submitted in April 1959, included dozens of recommendations for change.

It focussed frankly on the need for the Fijian administration and Fijians themselves to accept the need for cultural change, the modernisation of administrative practices initiated by Fiji's second governor, Sir Arthur Gordon (1875-79). Seeking to protect Fijian society and culture in the country's early years as a British crown colony, Gordon introduced policies that limited the Fiji peoples' involvement in commerce and politics. Through the early to mid-20th century, Ratu Sukuna and other ruling chiefs maintained this status quo, rigorously upholding Gordon's founding policies (albeit with the best of intentions).

By the late 1950s, Spate found problems of ineffective land use by Fijians, and even the tiny proportion they cultivated was not returning the welfare it should. He was concerned by very serious soil erosion and exhaustion, especially in western Viti Levu.

Garvey also commissioned another Colonial Office[11] administrator, Sir Alan Burns, to report on the problems posed by population growth and economic development. The Fiji government accepted the less controversial recommendations of these reports and passed legislation to implement them in the years that followed, in preparation for Fiji's eventual independence in 1970. Little of the proposed liberalisation in these reports was evident in late 1961, however, and the opportunity presented by the army recruiting team was too good for hundreds of young men to ignore.

Some Fijian leaders were pessimistic about the likely racial mix that would be accepted, fearing that Indian applicants would be favoured. One member of the Legislative Council declined the opportunity to be associated with the recruitment team on political grounds. It is not surprising that the racial mix in the eventual selection of the 200 men closely adhered to Maddocks' suggested formula. Nor is it surprising that rumours inevitably developed around the decision to double the number of male recruits from

---

11 Garvey published an entertaining account of his career in 1984 but omits any reference to either his specific concerns at the time or of either Spate or Burns. Maddocks' memoir of 1988 makes some reference to Burns' report.

one hundred to 200; to this day at least one of the men still believes that the reason the intake doubled was because most of the first hundred selected were of Indian descent! The final group of 212 men and women represented a fair cross section of indigenous Fijians from throughout the country, grandsons of the Girmitiyas of the nineteenth century, and others descended from European, Japanese, Chinese and other immigrants. Inevitably, many of the indigenous Fijians acknowledged a family link of some sort, usually through their mothers.

Several brothers were among those who served longest, but the most polyglot family mix was that of Mo Beg, Charles Giblin and Fred Maybir who shared a common grandfather, one Charles Andrew Maybir. The Maybir family originated in India and had Anglicised their name from Mahabeer by the time of Charles' birth in the Clarence River district of New South Wales. With Federation of the Australian states in 1901, and passage of an immigration act which produced the notorious 'White Australia' policy, the Maybirs and many other non-Caucasian Australian residents were obliged to emigrate[12]. In Fiji Charles Maybir married Adi Virisila Tikoigau from Saweke, Gau, and the couple had five children. All three of his grandson volunteers married English women and chose to remain in the UK on completion of their army service.

Rotumans

Several of the men and women volunteering came from Rotuma, the tiny northernmost island of the Fiji group. Rotumans, who are ethnically Polynesians rather than Melanesians, were given particular recognition in Fiji's first Constitution in terms of electoral representation. In the past century they have maximised opportunities for their children within Fiji and abroad. Rotumans put a premium on education and the professions, and the Fatiaki family, to take one example, includes a High Court judge, a medical practitioner, a geologist and a dentist within Fiji or scattered around the Pacific. Fred Marafono's father

---

12 Geoffrey Blainey has noted that this decision left Australia's sugar industry without the cheap labour it had enjoyed until that time, resulting in a need for subsidies in subsequent decades.

was a farmer, and Fred was a student at Navuso agricultural school, Nausori, with hopes of becoming a veterinarian prior to his enlistment.

Sefton Erasito was awarded a Rotuman community scholarship, was the first Rotuman to study science at Sydney University and was encouraged by his doctor father to enrol in medicine. This did not appeal to Sefton who wanted to study arts. He returned to Fiji after two years, an academic failure but recognised for his prowess on the rugby field.

His father was livid and lobbied the recruitment team to take his second son and make something of him. At the time, Sefton gave his occupation as 'reporter, Levuka' but the family historians have lost track of which newspaper may have employed him. Sefton's grandfather was chief of the Malhaha district of Rotuma and descended from one of the Rotuman chiefs who ceded the island to Queen Victoria on 13 May 1881. Sefton's grandfather had attended QVS and was one of the first three Rotumans to qualify as a doctor.

Four of the twelve young women selected were either born on Rotuma or had a Rotuman parent. In 1961 the Hibiscus Festival was a major event in Fiji's social calendar. Two of the twelve young women whose applications were successful were candidates for the 'Miss Hibiscus' title but Laurayne Thurley won the title.

Prior to their departure, the new recruits attended a function addressed by Maurice Henry Scott, son of Sir Henry Scott, KC, QC of an established white settler family. During WWII Maurice Scott was one a small handful of RAF pilots from Fiji. He was awarded a DFC for his courage piloting Hurricanes and Spitfires on photo-reconnaissance missions in the Western Desert and Italian campaigns. Scott impressed upon his young audience the need for *Tabu Soro,* literally 'don't give up', in the face of challenges they would face. Some of Scott's audience thought that *Tabu Soro* was the name of one of Scott's fighters but the aircraft were named 'The Flying Fijian' and 'Suva Sal'[13].

---

13 Advice from Scott's younger son in 2016.

Like his father and his brother Henry Milner Scott, Maurice Henry Scott did well at law and became both a knight of the realm and a successful barrister and Queen's Counsel. He became well-known for his *Tabu Soro* advice to the young recruits. This fame may have been because of his speech to the recruits, or his significant win in court defending Fijian fishing rights threatened by Tongan interests. Maurice Henry Scott was later appointed Speaker of the Legislative Council of Fiji and President of the Fiji Rugby Union. He was awarded a KBE in the Queen's Birthday Honours list in 1966. Sir Maurice's elder son, the late John Maurice Scott, became the Director of the Fiji Red Cross and played a significant humanitarian role during the Speight coup of 2000, discussed in Chapter 8. John Scott was murdered the following year and the eventual prosecution of his killer revealed many of the shortcomings of Fiji's post-1987 coup culture.[14]

At the time, and subsequently, the recruitment of the '212' aroused much criticism for the removal of some of the most talented young men from the colony.

It became known at the time that Governor Maddocks had exercised a veto on the recruitment of twenty-two young men who were considered too valuable for the future development of the colony to be let go. Seeking clues to the identities of these men was like the proverbial search for a needle in a haystack and, as Teresia Teaiwa has noted[15], Maddocks' eventual memoir[16] provided no reliable insight into the recruitment of the '212'. It is clear, however, is that these names were not on the list published by the *Fiji Times* on 6 November 1961, which is misleading in many respects and includes about twenty names of men who did not leave Fiji. What is surprising is the inclusion of Mike Yasa on the published list. Mike, who was a civil servant at the time and the only university graduate in the group, has no recollection of

---

14 John Scott's younger brother, Owen Scott, documented these events in *Deep Beyond the Reef* - Pelican, 2004.

15 *Intersections: Gender and Sexuality in Asia and the Pacific,* Issue 37, March 2015.

16 *Of No Fixed Abode,* published in 1988, mentions 'several dozen were recruited...(who)... had all done well' on p. 143.

anyone attempting to dissuade him from enlisting.

In April 2017 however, a chance telephone call revealed Vernon Yen, younger half-brother of David Whey (enlisted as 'John Whey alias David Michael Yen', later recorded by the RE as D. M. J. Whey) as one of those selected but dissuaded from leaving by his employer.

While at MBHS, Vernon developed strong interests in physics and economics, neither of which were on the school curriculum. His mother was a devout Roman Catholic and Vernon was initially attracted to the priesthood, but his mother's interest in grandchildren outweighed her enthusiasm for her second son becoming a priest. The MBHS principal, Bro Cassian, helped him get a traineeship with the Cable & Wireless Company. Vernon was involved in forming a trade union among C&W employees and was later appointed to Fiji's Labour Advisory Board, together with Apisai Tora.

After applying with David to the army recruiting team, Vernon was advised that he and a young Fijian were the top-rated applicants according to the assessment/intelligence testing process and he had the possibility of being considered for officer training at Sandhurst Royal Military Academy. The following day, however, Vernon was given the bad news by Captain Hardcastle that he was considered so valuable to Fiji's immediate future development that the recruiting team could not accept him. This exchange took place well before the Governor removed twenty-two men from the initial preferred intake list of 200 names submitted by the recruiting team.

Through his labour activism, Vernon was later given a scholarship under the British Technical Aid Scheme to study industrial relations for six months in London, Birmingham and Brussels. He returned to Fiji and remained with C&W until he emigrated to Australia for the sake of his young family in 1967 and joined OTC Australasia as a systems developer.

Vernon thought at the time that any senior positions he might aspire to in Fiji would probably be dominated by Fijians or Indians with few opportunities for 'Others'. Vernon became involved in the introduction of satellite technology in the early seventies, then graduated into video communications, spending many years with the Nine Network in Australia before accepting senior management positions with Telstra at the time of the Sydney Olympics and finally with British Telecom. The army evaluation of him in 1961 was clearly correct.

There were other bright young men who stayed and were not attracted to the army or were elsewhere at the time. Rasheed Ali, for example, was born in 1940 at Samabula in Suva, the son of a school teacher born in Nausori and grandson of one of the first Girmitiyas born in Fiji. Rasheed's great grandfather died in an influenza epidemic in the early 20th century. In November 1961 Rasheed was studying accountancy in Sydney, and the following year took himself to London and worked for London County Council for a year before returning to Fiji where he had a very successful career with CSR. Later, he joined the Fiji Sugar Corporation and retired as its first Fiji-born Chief Executive. Another bright young man in this age cohort, born in 1942, was Mahendra Chaudhry who became a leader in Fiji's labour and sugar politics, was thrown out of elected office in Rabuka's coup of 1987, and again as elected PM by George Speight's coup attempt of 2000.

The former RFMF Commander, diplomat and later President of Fiji, Ratu Epeli Nailatikau, was born in 1941 and in 1961 was school captain at QVS where the principal, Mr Gibson, mistakenly advised the boys who were interested in enlisting of the wrong day to present themselves in Suva. Ratu Epeli eventually followed his father (Ratu Sir Edward Cakobau, who served in the FDF Battalion in the Solomons) into the RFMF via the New Zealand military academy. Ratu Epeli suspects that the twenty-two names vetoed by Governor Maddocks were probably all civil servants at the time.[17]

Major Worsley's report to the War Office, dated 17 November, makes no mention of subsequent difficulty in ensuring that 200 men actually boarded a plane and arrived in London for their service. His report mentions drawing on a reserve list to make up for the twenty-two names vetoed by the Governor,

---

17 Ratu Epeli Nailatikau's advice to author, 2015.

but his staff had to draw on the list again to make up the shortfalls for the first group of ninety-three to arrive in London on 23 November, the second group of ninety-five and finally the group of eleven schoolboys and an older leader. It is possible that there may have been a shortfall of one or two men as the best efforts of this study have accounted for only 198 men, and the War Office files do not include a comprehensive list of the 200 who landed in England.

Eroni Bale Raturaga, later known as Eroni Bale, was an assistant customs examiner at Nadi airport in 1961 and listed by the *Fiji Times* as accepted for enlistment.

Eroni was talked out of leaving, however, by his father and E. T. J. Mabbs, the then Comptroller of Customs. At the time there were only four Fijians in the total of fifty to sixty officers in the Fiji Customs and Excise department. Eroni recalled years later that he had tears in his eyes as he watched the first contingent board the plane for Honolulu, San Francisco and New York enroute to the UK. Eroni's decision to stay seems to have been overlooked by the army's records, as he was apparently allocated to the Royal Armoured Corps and a War Office file noted that he 'did not report' to the depot of the 4/7 Royal Dragoon Guards as expected.[18] Eroni retired as Deputy Comptroller of Customs in 1991, having featured in the enquiry into the 1988 Khan arms shipment.[19]

The '212' were thus transported from meridian to meridian in four groups.

The first two groups, with Ilisoni Ligari and Mike Yasa designated as leaders, travelled to Hawaii and then to New York and London via either San Francisco or Colorado. In New York these groups were well looked after by the United Services Organisation which arranged tickets to Broadway shows and a boxing match at Madison Square Gardens. The volunteers were

---

18 WO32/19455 folio 193. Elsewhere the same file recorded the details of the loss and recovery of a wallet belonging to Mikali Baleitilagica!

19 A curious business initiated by Australian Customs interception in Sydney of a 12-tonne container load of weapons of Czech manufacture. Similar weapons had earlier arrived in Fiji and were recovered but exactly who initiated the shipments and why was never revealed.

Farewell lunch for MBHS friends Bob Dass (seated left at head of table) and Tim Bukasoqo, on Bob's left, December, 1961, at the home of Tim's father, a retired RFMF Major. The two proud fathers at rear. Photo: Bob Dass

fascinated by their first exposure to television with twenty-seven channels, and the experience of staying on the 32nd floor of the Governor Clinton Hotel in particular.

Jim Masuwale's expulsion from the forestry school in July 1961, resulted from him losing his temper with one of the instructors, a Mr Paul, who had a broad Scots accent. Jim's exposure to Mr Paul made him one of the very few recruits who understood the broad accent of Captain Hardcastle of the recruiting team. When Jim was selected to depart with the first contingent of recruits on 21 November, Hardcastle asked him to sit with him at the front of the BOAC Type 175 Brittania and relay Hardcastle's announcements ahead of each landing. These included projected turbulence and the need for fastened seat belts, and any other notable developments. Jim had to relay them in either Fijian, or English that the recruits would understand. Jim took it upon himself to relay Hardcastle's polite advice in a stern tone of voice befitting the senior NCO he later became. His tone of voice, however, alienated him from many of his cohort who wondered why this little bloke, whom few knew, thought he could assume such authority. After returning from his army service Jim spent several years as a broadcaster for Radio Fiji where he used his variously modulated tones to good effect.

The recruiting team had agreed to a suggestion that it was in the army's interest, and that of the individuals themselves, for twelve of those in their last year at school to complete their examinations for the Senior Cambridge Certificate.

This group included Jim Vakatalai, Bob Dass, Tom Waqabaca, Sotia Ponijase and Meli Vesikula. With the older Peni Koroituku, who had served in the FMF, as 'minder', they arrived at London's Stansted airport on 10 December.

Jim Vakatalai has vivid memories of the culture shock he first experienced on a stopover in Sydney:

> The cultural shock for me was at Sydney Airport, two hours (sic) after leaving Nadi. The telephone box was totally foreign. We arrived overnight and slept in an Army Barracks, the next morning was a Sunday. And the Aussie sergeant took us sight-seeing—Sydney Harbour bridge etc. etc. and around about the time I would have been attending Mass in Suva, he took us for a walk down King's Cross which was another world all together, as you can imagine. We started walking down an empty street... about half way down the doorways started to fill up with flimsy negligees, flashing alabaster thighs and hot smouldering looks. I made an excuse and fled back to the bus. Honest!!'

The twelve women travelled by commercial flights via stopovers in Sydney and Singapore, transiting Istanbul to arrive at Gatwick Airport on 31 December. Their move to Hobbs Barracks near Lingfield, Surrey was delayed by snow.

In 2015 Felipe Ravuoco recalled that the '212 generation' had some sense of identification with Australia and New Zealand, home to most of their teachers, but the prospect of going to England was 'like going to the moon'. He also recalled the sense of being in another, exotic, place on arrival at Gatwick with the second detachment. They were amazed by their first contact with snow, either because no one had warned them about it or they'd dozed through the part of their orientation briefing that mentioned it.

The twelve young women photographed while transiting Sydney
en-route to Singapore and London.
L to R: Tausia Cakauyawa, Vaciseva Tabua, Lily Pirie, Doreen Petersen, Munivai
Aisake, Edwina Eyre, Vicki Grant, Frieda – guide/chaperone, Fane Sivoki,
Emma Heffernan, Louisa Peckham, Betty Foster, Laurel Bentley.
Photo: Betty Foster

Felix Lockington recalls the first taste of what was to come with northern hemisphere winter cold during the stopover in San Francisco.

The last leg of the journey for many of the men was the train journey from London to training depots at Catterick in Yorkshire. David Lelo recalls:

> The journey from Euston station to Catterick was on the Flying Scotsman, much faster than the cane trains in Fiji! In the fields alongside the railway were the first sheep the boys had seen, wearing coats, and at first they thought the sheep were dogs.

A half century later, George Chute liked to reflect on his life through poetry and one of his poems recalls aspects of the village life in Fiji that many of the '212' had left behind.

Time

As I grow old I often see
The changes day by day
Just to survive our family had
Just two sound meals a day

Our kitchen was a thatched roof hut
No windows and no door
Our stove was made of three large stones
Built on a muddy floor

Our family owned a cast iron pot
Not many could be seen
And for a pot so many used
A four-pound biscuit tin

Our first meal of the day was like
What brunch is called today
For all our food was often cooked
In pots made from red clay

The evening meal was much the same
But now included fish
And banana leaves were often spread
To hold food like a dish

Flour sugar even tea
Was not seen in the week
But often came on Sundays
As a very special treat

As we grow old we now can see
That time has changed our way
That eating habits change a lot
With three sound meals a day

by George Chute

CHAPTER 2:
ENGLAND, 1962

The '212' arrived in England in the middle of a very cold winter for which most were totally unprepared, having very little concept of 'cold'. The recruiting team or some sensitive soul in the War Office arranged for a supply of army greatcoats and 'woolly pullies' (sweaters) for distribution on arrival. The subsequent winter of 1962-63 was worse and judged the coldest in a century, with twenty-five or more air frosts almost everywhere in southern England and South Wales in January 1963. This was extreme culture shock of a kind that western baby boomers later became fond of writing about for themselves in other environments for *Lonely Planet* and related travel publications. The late Norman Bradshaw was Headmaster of Tiverton Grammar School, Devon, where some pupils did not attend school until after Easter of 1963 because of impassable roads. The family's new Labrador puppy could not be trained properly and returned from infrequent walks wanting to relieve itself on old newspapers because it was unused to relieving itself outdoors.

The cold was something few of the '212' had imagined before they arrived in London. The novelty of snow initially attracted them; Mike Vuli recalled a half century later that few of the '212' had any real idea of a British winter, with its frosts, sleet and snow. Local newspapers and Pathe newsreels of the day recorded images of the Fijians in their 'South Seas' ceremonial costumes

Four of the twelve women rugged up against the cold outside the Catterick NAAFI in the winter of 1962. L to R: Fane Sivoki (Morell), Louisa Peckham, Vaciseva Tabua and Lillian Pirie. Photo: Vaciseva Tabua

of grass skirts and bare feet dancing in the snow. These images came at a cost as some of the Fijians contracted influenza, including Pramod Tikaram and Fred Dewa. Fred developed pneumonia and discovered that he had brought TB with him from the hinterland of Naitasiri, was seriously ill and hospitalised for nearly a year, losing most of the capacity of one lung. Isikeli Maravu survived the performance for Pathe and nine years in the army but was badly injured years later, on a North Sea oil rig. A small number were medically discharged for a variety of previously undiagnosed conditions in the first year.

Most of the huts used to accommodate the new recruits were sparsely heated, some with a small coal stove in the centre of the hut. The Non-Commissioned Officers in charge of the recruits' basic training became used to the sight of the Fijians' cots being dragged from their regimented ranks along the walls to as close as possible to the stove in the centre of the hut. Only one, however, is remembered as finding the cold so intolerable that he was given a medical discharge from the Royal Tank Regiment and a ticket home.

Guided tour of London immediately after completion of basic training, 1962.
L to R: Lote Kaitani, Romano Naceva, Aminiasi Ratuloaloa, Mick Silivale (rear), Bill
Vodo, Felipe Ravuoco, Ralph Lalabalavu and Etuate Qio Ledua.
Photo: Ulaiasi Ravela.

Mo Beg recalls his basic REME training at Arborfield, where the Barracks consisted of wooden huts mostly grouped in 'spiders', each spider being made up of six huts joined by corridors to central ablution and utility rooms.

Pramod Tikaram would have preferred one of the 'spiders' any day as they had proper central heating. Recalling the brick accommodation at RAOC Blackdown fifty years later, he said:

> Our brick block accommodation was cavernous, most basic and extremely cold most of the time, with one huge coal fire in the middle of the room which had to be put out every morning. We had to light this damn thing every day after training and we were forbidden to keep the fire going during the daytime; cruel or what?

The Fijians missed their homeland. Multicultural Suva boasted Indian and Chinese restaurants which were uncommon in the towns and small cities close to the army bases where the '212' did their basic training in 1962.

Allan Swanson was unimpressed, recalling that 'even (provincial) Ba had a Chinese restaurant' and was exotic by comparison to West Moors, Wimborne and even Aldershot where Allan did his initial training.

L to R: Harold Naidu, Mahendra Vijaynand, Sam Pillay and Michael Thoman appropriately dressed for their arrival in England, winter 1961/2.
Photo: Sam Pillay

The impressionable young '212' were used to holding all Europeans in respect from their schooling and colonial experience. Many of the British soldiers they first met and trained with at Catterick and elsewhere came from poor backgrounds and broken homes, were often less educated and many had very different moral values without the strong religious influences the young Fijians had brought with them. Army service had been 'suggested' to many British recruits by judges or magistrates, as an alternative to prison. Officers of the day are remembered as exhibiting the expected standards of European behaviour with which the '212' had grown up. Bob Dass quickly learned to loathe the class system and discrimination in UK society, but did not encounter these prejudices in the Army. Very few of the '212' seem to have been bothered by the class structures the British had preserved from the Victorian and Edwardian eras.

Older baby-boomers may remember 1962 as the year in which Marilyn Monroe died, Sean Connery gave James Bond a screen presence in 'Dr No' and the Beatles played together for the first time in clubs. Elvis had a good year with four more number one hits in the UK. Bob Dylan released his first album. Decca management decided against giving a contract to the Beatles, perhaps thinking that the Rolling Stones were a big enough risk. But the glamour of the 'swinging sixties' took time to develop. Cilla Black, who rose to fame as an early sixties pop star, later recalled:

> My first trip to London to promote the single, I stayed at the Russell Hotel on Russell Square. I was just so excited because there was a phone by my bed. Most people didn't have phones in Britain in those days because they were very expensive, and I remember picking the phone up to call someone, but everybody that I knew or that I wanted to talk to didn't have a phone. [20]

Times have changed!

The Second World War had bankrupted the country which was coming to terms with its loss of wealth and influence as Victoria's empire (on which the sun supposedly never set) gradually crumbled. In a 2012 biography of the Rolling Stones Christopher Sandford noted:

> For most young people in early-60s Britain, life was barely distinguishable from the 1940s. While the war may have ended seventeen years previously, there were still reminders of it everywhere in the capital's bombed-out streets as well as in the pinched appearance of many of its citizens. [21]

This was not the *Bolatagone* the '212' had learned about at school. But most adapted very well.

Syd O'Fee remembered doing duty as the blanket storeman at Catterick where he was stationed with 4/7 RDG when the first Fijians arrived in late 1961. He took pity on the new recruits and issued several more blankets on request than was usual. Thirty years later he recalled with great affection several of those he befriended during his service.

---

20 Morgan, Robin and Leve, Ariel *1963 - The Year of the Revolution.*

21 Sandford, Christopher, *The Rolling Stones,* pps. 7-8.

Tom Morell recalls that:

> The Royal Signals lads arrived in Catterick in late November 1961 and were given two weeks to acclimatise as it was pretty cold up there. The basic training started before Christmas; half way through we had three weeks break for Christmas (and) most of us went to the old Union Jack Club in Waterloo, London for the duration where we met lads from other regiments.
>
> 'We came back to Catterick in January 1962 and completed the basic training; six weeks in total. We were posted to 8 Signal Regt for technicians' trade training, 24 Signals Regt for operating trades etc.
>
> 'I went to 24 Sigs from Feb to April. In early May I was posted to 2 Div Signal Regt in Bunde, near Herford in W. Germany. In November 1962 I left Germany to do P Company with the view to joining 216 Para Signal Sqn (16 Para Bde Gp) which I passed in early December. The basic para course started before Christmas, we had two weeks break for Christmas and back in January. In 1963 we did about four jumps before it was postponed due (to) thick ice on the DZ until end of March. I got my para wings and joined 216 Para Sigs. Jake Mateyawa was already in 216—he came straight from Catterick after trade training in August 62 and did P Company.'

Racism in 1962 Britain

In late July 2014, Apakuki Nanovo illuminated comments made by a number of British officers beforehand comparing the cumulative qualities of the '212' with their fellow recruits of 1961 from Jamaica and the Seychelles. 'Kuki' said that while some of the younger Fijians (and Seconaia Takevesi admitted to this) had difficulty accommodating the British NCOs' parade ground banter and abuse, most Fijians accepted this assault on their egos as part of the British/colonial culture they had grown up with in secondary schools largely staffed by Australians and New Zealanders. Kuki maintained that the Jamaicans in particular took offence much more quickly, both on training and after hours in the NAAFI and the pubs. One 'took the Mickey' out of Jamaicans at one's peril! Pearl Bradshaw, who was born in Jamaica and migrated to England with her parents at this time, has pointed out in defence of the Jamaican soldiers that the Fijians did not grow up with the stigma of a slave background, which may have made the Jamaicans more sensitive to jibes about colour and race.

The '212' and other colonial recruits from the West Indies and the Seychelles arrived in a Britain struggling to assimilate large numbers of immigrants from Caribbean countries and deal with the reactionary racism of the 'Teddy Boys' and 'Alf Garnetts' of the day. Few of the '212' recalled racism in the army beyond the parade ground banter of their NCOs, but a couple of incidents reflected the aftermath of the Notting Hill riots of August-September 1958.

Bob Dass recalls an occasion in central London where a small group of '212' were taken to a police station for questioning because the constables on the beat did not believe that they were serving in the army.

On another occasion a small group were returning to the Union Jack Club late one night, full of beer and bonhomie, when a van disgorged several 'Teddy Boy' types keen to test their martial qualities against a group they supposed to be immigrants from south Asia or the Caribbean. The Fijians rose to the challenge, telling the Teddy Boys to 'bring it on', and there may have been references to their cannibal ancestors. Whereupon all but one of the challengers quickly got back in the van and sped away. The remaining thug probably soiled his underwear when surrounded by a group of well-nourished Fijians and begged forgiveness for his mistake. He was told that Fijians believed in fair play and he was offered the handicap of a hundred-yard start and his choice of his captors to pursue him and teach him some respect for British soldiers from Fiji. Unfortunately for the thug his choice was the shortest member of the group, Nat Ledua. Nat may have been shorter than the average '212' but he was an above average sprinter at school and a competent boxer who became a physical training instructor in the Cheshire regiment.

The thug took off with his hundred-yard start but was so nervous he kept looking back for his pursuer, collided with a cast iron lamp post, and knocked himself unconscious. The Fijians declined to 'put the boot in' to a defeated foe but emptied a nearby rubbish bin over him and repaired to the Union Jack Club to drink to the folly of Teddy Boys.

The next morning, however, a couple of the lads had pangs of conscience, wondering if their would-be aggressor had killed himself or died of exposure. They were relieved to discover when they returned to the lamp post to find just the contents of the empty bin and no corpse.

Few of the '212' recall racist attitudes within the army itself during their service, but a half century later George Chute remembered an early form of today's 'political correctness' during filming of an army promotional film involving the Royal Tank Regiment on exercises in 1965. The producers indicated that their first preference for footage of a tank commander emerging from his vehicle after the exercise was that it not be film of a black/coloured tank commander.

Rasheed Ali was gaining experience in accountancy with the London County Council in 1962, and after a few months of sharing accommodation with a school friend in Camden Town he sought a flat of his own. He recalled in 2016:

> The starting place was the shop fronts in news agents and I was shocked to see the number of notices that said: 'Sorry no coloureds'. Anyway, I overlooked these and telephoned some of the others which I was invited to come over to inspect only to be told on arrival on that the place had just been let. I became suspicious and on one occasion went around the corner to call again after just having been turned down and was told that 'yes please come over and inspect'.

> That single incident cemented my resolve that a racist place like the UK was not for me. In fairness I must say that the people I worked with in LCC were great.

In 1962 the future Prime Minister of Fiji, Ratu K.K.Mara 'had a most unpleasant and humiliating time finding accommodation in London as a graduate student at LSE until supported by a friend in the Colonial Office.'[22]

---

22 1988 memoir of Sir Kenneth Maddocks, p.140

The expatriate managers of the Fiji that Rasheed returned to a year or so later took a long time to evolve from their colonial ways:

> Working for CSR was also a challenge as there was strong segregation practised between expatriate and local staff. There was a huge bachelors' mess at Labasa which was occupied by a few expatriates but as a local I was not allowed to live in it. Instead I stayed at company expense at the Grand Eastern Hotel at Labasa for fourteen months until a new smaller complex was built for the expatriates and the old place was vacated for occupation by us locals.

> Some months later when a visiting Inspector from CSR's Sydney Head Office invited me over to join him for lunch in the 'Expatriate Mess' the white occupants walked out in protest, leaving me to enjoy a sumptuous meal with the visiting Inspector. I could not blame them for their actions because I was aware that several had been shipped back to Australia for 'consorting' with locals. Times were changing fast, but the message had not filtered down from the top of the hierarchy to the lower echelons.

Rose-tinted memoirs of the Fiji of the pre and post-war years, such as those of Beverly Angas and Patricia Page, conveniently ignore this aspect of expatriate attitudes of the day.[23]

The world was a very uncertain and dangerous environment for HMG and her soldiers in 1962. A wall was under construction to separate the Cold War protagonists in Berlin, the Koreas were as divided then as they remain today, and a nationalist leader with regional ambitions in Indonesia had analysts worried in London, Washington and Canberra. To finish off a year of living dangerously, the Sino-Indian conflict coincided with the Cuban missile crisis! That was more than enough to keep world leaders and their foreign ministries focussed. Many of the Fijian recruits found themselves pawns in the great game of Western superpower attempts to contain these challenges.

Reflecting on his early career decades later, the 'Poet Laureate of Siberia, Labasa', George Chute, summarised the transition he made from a plantation on Vanua Levu to a barracks in Catterick in a poem.

---

23 Angus, Beverley M, *My Colonial Fiji.*

Army Life

When I begged dad to let me go
To join the British Army
He looked at me tears in his eyes
And then said to me clearly

I really hate to see you go
But if I make you stay
You'll curse me to the day you die
I heard him to me say

Go my son he said to me
But remember mum and me
Your life is in your hands today
For what you are to be

We left Fiji late Monday night
For a land we didn't know
What a shock for everyone
To be greeted there by snow

In London where we all found out
What we had to be
Confusion came when I found out
Posted to the RAC

The sand and sea was now long gone
Homesickness was now rife
And tears of sorrow freely came
As I started my new life

In Catterick where it all began
A life we came to dread
Was how to start and drive a tank
And how to make your bed

Yorkshire pudding beans on toast
Was now our daily food
Uto bele lolo fish[24]
Had now left us for good

Training now was almost done
We travelled coast to coast
Sometimes it took us many weeks
Land's End to John O' Groats

---

24 *Uto* is breadfruit; *bele* a leafy vegetable; *lolo* is coconut cream.

Kingsman 'Jimmy Vanessa' aka Jemesa Vanaisa, a long way from Moala, on his first posting, to Berlin, 1962. Photo: Joe Challoner

The four Fijians who served with the KRRC/Royal Green Jackets meet the museum curator at Peninsula Barracks, Winchester, 1962. They are examining a sacred whale's tooth tabua and a tanoa (kava bowl) presented to the museum after WW1 by the late Ratu Sir Lala Sukuna, commemorating the association between the KRRC and the RFMF. L-R: P. Rakanace, M.M.K.Yasa, S.Ratini and S. Vuetibau. Photo: Mike Yasa

CHAPTER 3:
EARLY YEARS, 1963-67

The officer in charge of the Fiji recruiting team, Major G. H. Worsley, wrote an excellent summary report of the team's experience and included some very sensible advice to army officers who might find themselves commanding units to which the Fijians were posted. Worsley also addressed the lack of analysis by the colonial government of the potential the recruitment of the '212' had to cause local unrest. Governor Kenneth Maddocks had had his fill of civil unrest in the previous two years and provided sensible guidelines to Worsley but made no reference to the recruitment in his memoirs.

One assumes that Worsley's report received the same distribution as earlier War Office advice to the command and training establishments to which the '212' were initially allocated. Worsley's recommendations for care in the initial handling of these recruits, and the need to consider their very different backgrounds compared to those of the army's usual recruits (and those from other colonies) would have been invaluable to commanding officers and their training staff. Worsley's report is reproduced in full as Appendix K.

An exhaustive examination of Fiji Government files might reveal evidence of documented concerns echoing some of the newspaper reporting of the day. However, the extensive interviews on which this study is based revealed little evidence that the '212' themselves, especially those who signed up for the maximum of twenty-two years, had any clear idea of how they would be affected by their forthcoming experience. Nor could they have much idea, as their knowledge of army service and warfare derived largely from discussion with relatives who had served in the Solomons campaign in WWII or the subsequent Malayan 'Emergency'. Service in those conflicts, while often deadly, was at least limited to a maximum of two or three years away from Fiji. The only other input probably came from Hollywood and Pinewood movie studio accounts of how the US and the UK defeated the Nazi menace.

Thus, it is not surprising that many of the ethnic Fijians, not least those with some chiefly or acknowledged *bati* (warrior) status in their villages, either expressed a preference for the infantry in the first instance or for were seduced by suggestions that armoured or artillery regiments were acceptable alternatives. Several of the '212' who served in the Royal Artillery recall Worsley's 2IC, Captain Hardcastle, suggesting that the RA also involved 'real soldiering' or some other suggestion favoured by Gunners, to the effect that the RA 'adds some class to what would otherwise be an unseemly brawl' between combatants.

While the recruiting team may have considered the expressed preferences of their recruits, this was clearly secondary to the army's pressing need to address the shortfall in suitable volunteers for training in skilled trades. An annexure to a War Office file dated September 1961, entitled 'Enlistment of Coloured Personnel Overseas' specified minimum 'R' Test scores for specific trades within each corps, rising from 17 for a basic infantry soldier to 34 or 35 for REME technicians or radio technicians in the Royal Signals. Only three of the 200 men scored below 20 and the highest score of the '212' was earned by 'Ratumeli Basu', the earliest record on the War Office files to Ratu Meli Vesikula, later known as Sam Basu in REME and 1DWR.[25]

Some of the new recruits seemed predestined for service in Royal Signals because of their employment prior to recruitment. Seci Drika was a 'wireless

---

25 WO32/19455.

operator' with the Posts and Telecommunications Department, according to the *Fiji Times*. Tom Morell was listed as 'clerk, Suva' but was in fact the colony's youngest Post Master at the time, having mastered the requisite accountancy and Morse Code skills. At the time of his enlistment John Riley was a trainee Post Master. John wanted to serve in an armoured unit and drive a tank. Initially he was disappointed to be allocated to Royal Signals where his initial trade was that of 'Radio Technician, Light' supporting VHF and UHF communications. He later transferred to REME, serving twenty-two years, and was discharged as a Staff Sergeant.

John's cousin Alex Kubu was listed as a 'teletype trainee' by the newspaper but this rather understated the case. Alex was recruited into the Civil Aviation Administration at Nadi Airport by a New Zealander named John Horsefield. When the recruiting team arrived in 1961 he was training as an apprentice technician maintaining communications to aircraft in the Pacific region. Horsefield brought the recruiting team to Alex's attention and encouraged him to apply. Keith Zoing was a trainee technician with the Fiji Broadcasting Corporation.

Harry Powell was employed as a clerk/salesman and indicated a preference for Royal Signals as he hoped to become a radio technician. Isimeli Degei, who enlisted under the name Vuknuki, was a trainee wireless operator who also served twenty-two years with Royal Signals, retiring as a S/Sgt. Sailosi Soqo was a telephone mechanic in 1961 and left the army two decades later as a Sergeant instructor at the School of Signals. Seci, Tom, Alex and Keith also served the maximum period and the army clearly got an exceptional return on its recruitment investment with this group alone.

Tom Morell expressed a wish to serve with the Royal Green Jackets but his allocation to Royal Signals was perhaps preordained by his mastery of Morse Code. As soon as he finished basic training at Catterick he applied, and was rejected, for selection to the Parachute Brigade. He was then posted to Germany from May to November with 2 Div Sig Regt, in Bunde, Westphalia, learned German and married Fane Sivoki, one of the twelve women who had enlisted with him. Tom and Fane produced four fine sons, three of whom eventually followed their parents into the British Army, serving with the 2 RGJ and 22 SAS.

After eight months service. Tom applied again for transfer to the Parachute Brigade and was 'fronted' to his squadron commander, who sought an explanation. Tom told the Major: 'I signed up for nine years and one is almost gone. I did not come half way around the world to serve without proper soldiering'. The OC approved his application for 'P' Company and Parachute Brigade selection.

Those who elected for an initial enlistment of nine years received slightly more pay and those who passed selection for airborne units and qualified as basic parachutists received an extra six shillings a day or two guineas a week, a significant amount in 1962. Either the lure of the extra money or the lunacy of leaping out of 'perfectly serviceable aircraft', as the RAF would note, appealed to at least four of the '212', including Roi Koroi and Jake Tulele, ahead of Tom Morell's qualification in late 1962.

Ratu Meli Vesikula used Morell's ploy and a rugby connection to secure his transfer from REME to 1 DWR, a recognised 'rugby regiment'. Jim Vakatalai was obliged to complete the first two years of his army service in REME before attempting selection for 22 SAS and his determination ensured that he was successful.

A significant number of the volunteers were apprentices pursuing trades in government departments such as public works and ship building, or with larger commercial employers such as CSR and the Vatukoula gold mine. Many of these young men were obvious candidates for service in the Royal Engineers, who were probably steered in that direction by a Sapper corporal on the recruiting team. Of the twenty-one men who eventually served in the RE, fourteen had been apprentices in various trades. Another four men claimed employment as tradesmen when they enlisted. Sappers (or combat engineers) of any nation will quickly assure interlocutors that they are the backbone of their army. Those '212' who served with the RE were a talented and colourful group whose significant contributions included involvement in the construction of an airfield in north eastern Thailand in the mid-sixties and oversight of mine clearance in the Falkland Islands in 1982-83.

The recruiting team naturally 'cherry picked' the best of the more than 800 volunteers who presented themselves, and it seems likely that the full impact of this selection on the emerging workforce of the colony was not recognised until a year or two after their departure. The high proportion of the longer serving men who became senior NCOs and were decorated for their contributions to their regiments suggests that these were men who would have made significant contributions to Fiji's development had they not volunteered or been dissuaded from enlisting. A closer examination of Fiji's records than has been possible here might reveal the names of those Maddocks removed from Worsley's initial list, and an indication of why a follow up recruitment tentatively agreed between these men did not eventuate. Either the Fiji government decided that it was the net loser from the recruitment, or the army may have decided that the exercise cost more than it was worth, although other explanations are possible.

Nothing came of a related proposal Maddocks and Ratu (later Sir) Penaia Ganilau discussed with Worsley–the suggested raising of Fijian battalions to serve, on rotation, in the British Army under similar arrangements to those which employed Gurkhas. At the time Ratu Penaia was Deputy Secretary for Fijian Affairs.

For the new recruits who had been tempted by the prospect of adventure through active service in the Arms Corps of the British Army as much as the attraction of the extra money to support their families, the early sixties were not short of opportunities. In the first years of the '212"s service, the most significant areas of operations for the British Army were in Aden and Borneo.

Radfan/Aden

Aden, capital of what is now known as Yemen at the entrance to the Red Sea, was nominally administered as part of the Ottoman Empire during the nineteenth century. But for all practical purposes, it was governed by the British as part of Bombay province of colonial India. Aden had been a major coaling station for the Royal Navy before the advent of oil fired warships, but Britain's imperial writ withered after WWII.

Aden became a focal point for Arab nationalism in the Middle East in the nineteen fifties, and the last years of British rule were plagued with civil unrest supported from neighbouring South Yemen. Many of the '212' had their first exposure to active service as the British government first committed forces to deal with the uprising in the mountainous Radfan region in October 1963, and eventually withdrew its forces from Aden in November 1967. The early deployments to Radfan included air defence regiments of the RA, as there was a perceived threat from the Egyptian air force in support of the Radfan rebels. Egypt's anti-Imperialist President Gamel Abdel Nasser followed up his nationalisation of the Suez Canal with support for uprisings against the old order throughout South Arabia.

The CO of 17 Training Regiment, Oswestry, where Joe Jang and others allocated to the RA did their basic training, was sympathetic to posting the Fijians to units destined to serve in warmer climates. The options in 1962 were 26 Field Regiment destined for Malaya, and 34 LAD bound for Hong Kong. Joe initially chose the former but was tempted by an offer to take a posting in the UK where he had the chance of representing the corps at rugby. Romano Naceva also elected for 26 Fd Regt, and in 2017 recalled the CO's name was Colonel Broodfox, whose respect for Fijian soldiers derived from his experience during the Malayan Emergency.

Tim Ulaiasi served with 34 LAD in Hong Kong for two years and Malaya /Singapore for four months before deploying to Aden on HMS Ark Royal, where he served on the border of north and south Yemen as crew on an anti-aircraft gun for nine months. Egyptian MIGs were considered a possible air threat at the time.

After completing basic training with R Sigs in 1962, David Lelo was posted to HQ 39 Infantry Brigade in Northern Ireland. In May 1964, the brigade was transferred to Aden to assist with the Radfan Uprising (otherwise known as the Radfan Emergency). The brigade arrived in their winter uniforms, which were suited to Yemen's freezing nights but uncomfortable during the scorching days. The brigade was tasked to build an airstrip at Thumier, and David spent time with Arab soldiers patrolling wadis and manned radio relay posts on high points to which they were moved by Belvedere helicopters with jets in support. Water was scarce and had to be carefully rationed. It was a disagreeable experience.

David Lelo (L) with fellow Sigs in Aden 1964, Don McDonald and John Waring, waiting to be moved to the Radfan. Photo: David Lelo

David was encouraged to re-enlist after six years and was posted to Germany and offered promotion to Sergeant. He was not attracted to Germany because of its Nazi history and declined, preferring to return to Fiji in 1967.

Four of the seven '212' who were eventually successful in passing selection for 22 SAS did so during 1964, and Talaiasi Labalaba followed them in 1965 after a successful tour with 1 RUR in Borneo where his leadership and bravery earned him a BEM. After an initial experience of Borneo's jungles (see below) these men found themselves rotated into undercover operations such as Operation Nina in the souks and alleys of Aden. Many years later the Fijians' dark skins limited their involvement in covert operations in Northern Ireland, but they proved ideal for deployment in 'mufti' (Arab garb) in the counter terrorist operations in Aden. Laba in particular, with his Roman nose, passed easily as an Arab. The biggest risk to these troopers was not the 'adoo' (enemy) so much as the uniformed patrols from other regiments, ever alert to suspicious looking natives. When halted and questioned the troopers' carriage of weapons required some fast-talking explanation. Jim Vakatalai and Laba had this experience when working in an area that was supposed to have been quarantined by MELF HQ for 22 SAS, but the CO of the SCLI took the embargo as an invitation for his soldiers to intensify patrols of the area.

Borneo

The low intensity conflict in Borneo from 1963-66 resulted from Indonesian President Sukarno's antagonism to the way the original Federated Malay States had been formed, including Singapore at the time. Sukarno had led and moulded the modern state of Indonesia since independence from Dutch colonialism in 1949, and eventually wrested what is now West Papua from the Dutch in 1962. Sukarno, or 'Bung Karno' as he was known in Indonesia, was a colourful, charismatic eccentric with a huge ego, multilingual and hugely popular as President for most of his tenure. His anti-colonialism, and notably his hosting of a meeting of 'Non-Aligned' nations in Bandung in 1955, caused severe heartburn to the Eisenhower administration, especially the powerful Dulles brothers. At the peak of the Cold War in the 1950s, Allan Dulles as director of the Central Intelligence Agency fomented secessionism in parts of Indonesia. His brother John Foster Dulles was US Secretary of State at the time. Sukarno was indifferent to some of the basics of economic management and his continued flirtation with the then USSR and 'Communist China' of the day unsettled John Kennedy's early years as US President at the start of the 1960s.

Sukarno objected to the new state as a colonial creation that interfered with his grand dream of a Pan-Malay state he called 'Maphilindo', linking colonial Malaya and Singapore with Indonesia and the Philippines. He was probably encouraged by Subandrio, his leftist foreign minister. Few of his generals shared his enthusiasm for Confrontation or 'Konfrontasi' with the new state, but [26] deployed their special forces to destabilise the border areas with cross border raids against police posts in the east Malaysian states and ill-considered attacks against Peninsular Malaysia.

The newly formed Malaysian state shared a very long common border with Indonesian Kalimantan of more than 1600 km. The British deployment of Commonwealth forces along the border was largely bluff and Malaysia's defences were wafer thin.

1RUR arrived in Malaysia early in 1964 for training at the British Jungle Warfare School at Kota Tinggi in Johore, where their instructors included a platoon of 5 RAR whose immediate past service involved operations against remnants of the Communist Party of Malaya insurgents on the Thai border.

The platoon, commanded by Lieut Pat Beale, included a few British migrants to Australia who delighted in boasting to the Ulsters that, as Australian soldiers, they were paid an extra ten shillings a day as compensation for having to eat British Army rations which Beale noted in his 2003 memoir: '...were decidedly scant in comparison to our ration scale. The contrast was reflected in the difference in physique of our soldiers. The "Paddies' from the Bogside and Derry were weedy little men and this was incongruously emphasised by a smattering of hulking Fijians in the Ulster ranks. Apparently, they recruited periodically in Fiji, primarily to bulk up the Battalion rugby team. I presume their rations were also supplemented. A hungry Fijian warrior could make a worrying roommate.' [27]

Jone Buakula's active service with the SWB in Borneo included an incident when 7 Platoon, C Company 1SWB, part of a company sized patrol of Scots Guards operating from a base at Serudong Laut, was

---

26 Curiously, for all the vehemence of his anti-Malaysia speeches at the time, Sukarno refers only to 'the Malaysian issue' in his autobiography of 1965, with no reference to 'Konfrontasi', a word he coined for the struggle for West Papua. See *Sukarno: an Autobiography by Sukarno as told to Cindy Adams.*

27 *Operation Orders*, p. 16. Beale was later awarded an MC for service in Borneo and a DSO for his subsequent posting to AATTV in Vietnam.

Nadi cousins Asiveni Lutumailagi (L) and Talaiasi Labalaba, 1 RUR, Borneo, 1964/5. Photo: Asiveni Lutumailagi

ambushed by an element of an Indonesian KKO (Marine) battalion based nearby. The incident was resolved with an aggressive counter-ambush drill described at some length by Wayne Protheroe in the October 1986 edition of *Men of Harlech*, the journal of the Royal Regiment of Wales, in which Jone's contribution to putting the enemy to flight is detailed. Jone was one of the larger '212', formidable on the rugby field or enforcing the law in his eventual long career as a police officer and slowing his fixed bayonet charge through the jungle is not something an Indonesian Marine would relish.

Jone would have been a credit to the 24th Foot at Rorke's Drift.

George Chute took a while to adjust to army life and thought initially that he had made a stupid mistake. He lost rank seven times in his first six years and his first time under fire in Borneo was a rude awakening to the reality of active service. 5 RTR replaced the Argyll and Sutherland Highlanders along the 1500 km border between Malaysian Sarawak and Indonesian Kalimantan, inheriting a land Dyak cook with a broad Scots accent. George remembers his first exchange with the man: 'Wots for tea Chappie?' and the reply 'Mince and tatties, Jock'. 5 RTR was deployed to

Borneo with Ferret scout cars and George recalls Lieut Epeli Nailatikau, later the commander of the RFMF, was briefly attached to 5 RTR.

1965 Mankau incident

The incident arose as a result of a cross border attack by Indonesian forces on a police station inside the 2 RGJ border frontage of Malaysian Sarawak. The CO 2 RGJ, (now) Lt Col Bramall decided that the incident required a strong response and reconnaissance patrols were dispatched to identify the base camp used by the Indonesians. A camp was identified several km inside Indonesian Kalimantan alongside a kampung (village) named Mankau on the western side of a small river.

Nine Platoon, commanded by 2nd Lieut Mike Yasa, was chosen for the close engagement of the Indonesian base and covertly assumed an ambush position on the eastern side of the river before last light. The platoon deployed in a linear formation with a GPMG loaded with tracer rounds at either end to define the platoon's left and right arcs of fire, and each soldier linked to those to his left and right with a length of string for communication purposes.

Throughout the night some young soldiers slept badly and made noises that required firm words of reassurance from section commanders.

Mist shrouded the river surface and the Indonesian camp as dawn broke the following morning, and Mike had to wait until he had a clear view of the Indonesian camp before starting the ambush. The Battalion's forward artillery observer and the company commander had a distant view of the camp from a hill behind the ambush site, but Mike's only contact with them before initiating the ambush was via coded clicking of the transmit switch on his VHF radio.

Once the mist lifted and he could see the target, Mike launched the ambush with smoke grenades fired from M79 grenade launchers to give the forward observer and company OC, Major Peter Welsh, reference points for the 105mm howitzers supporting the action to correct predetermined target points of reference.

The ambush was a success with many casualties inflicted on the Indonesians, and 9 Pl was able to withdraw from the ambush site protected by the artillery. *The London Gazette* of 6 May 1966 announced Mike's promotion to Lieutenant, ahead of schedule, probably in recognition of his service in Borneo. But like his involvement in the Mankau ambush, his promotion was not mentioned in his memoirs. In later life Mike explained that his involvement in such hostilities was a matter of regret to him as a clergyman.

Another omission from his memoir is the side effect of prolonged operations in tropical jungles. Mike was hospitalised in Penang for three months with leptospirosis after his tour in Borneo.

Cross border operations of this sort were given the code name 'Claret' and details remained classified for the following twenty years. The deeper penetration 'Claret' operations by 22 SAS and elements of the Australian and New Zealand SAS kept the Indonesian forces from having confidence in their security within their borders.

Bob Dass was one who found himself enlisting by default, through his MBHS schoolmates who were keen. He has happy memories of his posting to Hong Kong where even a L/Cpl was 'somebody' in those days, and the climate was more like home. For Bob his army service in Germany and Hong Kong was 'one huge piss-up'. Bob quickly learned to loathe the class structure and discrimination in UK society but did not encounter these prejudices in the Army. He took his discharge and the return ticket to Fiji.

Operation Crown, Thailand, 1964-67

Operation Crown, the SEATO-sponsored construction of Loeng Nok Tha airfield at Ban Kok Talat, near Ubon north eastern Thailand, was conducted for 'the defence of Thailand' against the menace of communism emanating from what was commonly referred to as 'Red China' at the time. According to David Wicks and Simon Wilson, the airfield was intended as a medium range transport airfield 'as part of the UK's contribution to the SEATO program for improving logistical facilities in Thailand'[28].

---

28 *Destination: Malaya - A History of 2 Field Troop RAE 1963-65.*

The airfield's construction reflected 'Domino theory' fears of the day of a probable expansion of Communist insurrection throughout south east Asia, aided and abetted by 'Red China'. Whilst the airfield construction was not classified as operational service, it involved several of the '212' as sappers, communicators and drivers.

Field Marshall Tun Kittakachorn, PM of Thailand, presided over the airfield's opening ceremony in November 1963, which included a blessing of the huge bulldozers by Buddhist monks. Sappers from the Commonwealth Brigade based in Singapore at the time later completed the airfield and a road to the Lao border. The War Office files on Operation Crown had not been released to the National Archives in July 2014, and the reason for the continued restriction is not known.

'Operation Crown', April, 1964: D8 Caterpillar bulldozer being blessed by a buddhist monk at the opening ceremony for the construction of Loeng Nuk Tha airfield at Ban Kok Talat, near Ubon in north eastern Thailand. Photo: David Whey

In contrast, there are innumerable internet sites dealing with Operation Crown, the construction of the airfield and the road serving it. Harold Wilson's Labour government won power in 1964 and did not share the US government's enthusiasm for the Vietnam conflict. While the USAF's use of nearby Ubon airfield for bombing North Vietnam as well as Laos and Cambodia is well documented, it is harder to find references to USAF use of Loeng Nok Tha. However, it is possible that Air America may have used the airfield in support of covert operations in the region. Whatever use the airfield may have been put to during the Vietnam conflict, it quickly fell into disuse after that. Reporting in *The Royal Engineers Journal* on a visit twenty years after the airfield was completed, John Stevens noted that 'The pavement quality concrete of runway, taxiways and apron appears in excellent condition'—a tribute to those involved in its construction.[29]

David Whey, David Lelo, Fred Maybir and others from Commonwealth units involved in Operation Crown complained bitterly of the difference between the quality of food in their field ration packs and the fresh and frozen foods available at the US base at Ubon. Wicks and Wilson chronicled the value of Cadbury's chocolate as barter for American rations in their book *Destination: Malaya* which included a chapter on Operation Crown. Wicks and Wilson served with 2 Field Troop Royal Australian Engineers as part of 11 Field Squadron. New Zealand Sappers were also involved in building the airfield.

Repatriation and Early Marriages

One of the attractive conditions offered by the recruiting team was return travel to Fiji every five years for single soldiers. The twelve women were not eligible for this benefit, given their three-year period of enlistment. DOMCOL, or Dominion and Colonial Leave, was a remnant colonial benefit for civil servants which was extended to those in the British armed forces recruited in Commonwealth countries and the remaining British colonies. Most of the men took advantage of the first DOMCOL and several weeks leave back in Fiji, when many met or renewed relationships with women they married soon afterwards, including Naibuka Qarau and Seci Drika. A significant number were ineligible, either having married women from Fiji who had followed them to the UK, or women they had met on their early deployments, especially to Singapore/Malaysia. Nic Naico

---

29 Ibid, citing *The Royal Engineers Journal* V104 Number 4.

and Wainikiti Vosabalavu married sisters they met in Singapore, and Pramod Tikaram met Rohani while serving in Kuching. Others married British women in these early years. On return from Malaya with 26 Field Regiment, Kaliova Naivalarua was billeted close to the Ministry of Defence Proof and Experimental (P & E) establishment at Shoeburyness. After a rugby match one afternoon Kaliova was introduced to Janice, 'the most beautiful woman I had ever seen', a WRAC then serving with the P&E establishment. Kaliova and Janice married a year or so later.

Mahendra Vijaynand was slow to take advantage of DOMCOL or other opportunities for finding a wife, but did so on his third DOMCOL in 1976, marrying Sheila who was the daughter of a family friend of his father.

Wainikiti Vosabalavu with his first wife, Shelley Gopal, married in Singapore around 1966/67. Photo: Cyril Browne

Prior to their deployment to Borneo, 1RUR was sent to Australia for an eight-week exercise with Australian forces west of Sydney. Watisoni Rogose recalls that the CO, Lt Col Corran Purdon, appeared to have an affection for Fijians, having served in the Malayan Emergency with the Fiji Battalion. Lt Col Purdon decided that his Fijian soldiers were unlikely to get so close to home again for a long time in their projected service and gave the seven men six weeks leave. Purdon had a remarkable career before and after his posting as CO, 1RUR, and later served as Commander of the Sultan's Armed Forces in Oman.

One aspect of repatriation that had not been considered by the MOD was the need for consideration of compassionate leave arrangements for the '212' to attend the funerals of their aging parents. Empathetic COs and their staff who knew how to maximise the flexibility British forces enjoyed with allies at the time coped with the first couple of instances of Fijians wishing to attend the funeral of a parent before the issue was addressed. Mike Thoman had no regrets about his army service, apart from the War Office's refusal to endorse his regiment's approval of leave to attend his mother's funeral in Fiji in January 1970. Bereavement leave was limited to 3 days.

The RFMF had to address the same problem when it first deployed to peace keeping operations in Lebanon and Syria.

David Lelo's return to Fiji was not as simple as expected, because his wife Wendy did not have the appropriate visa for entering colonial Fiji as a resident. David found work with the Peace Corps, but it did not pay well and after six months he decided to join two brothers and a sister who had moved to New Zealand. To get approval for the move, David had to have a job offer and a brother found a position for him on a farm processing poultry at Waitoa.

It was a grubby job and he soon moved his family to Masterton where he worked on the factory floor of a white goods factory and later became the foreman in the service department. He later worked for a printing firm before starting his own floor sanding business in 1972-73, and subsequently earned his living this way for thirty-five years in both New Zealand and the

UK. During this period, he was appointed a bishop in the Church of LDS and ministered to a Mormon community of about five thousand.

The Union Jack Club in London served as a base for most '212' when on leave or immediately after discharge. Mat Vatu gravitated to the Union Jack Club after his discharge, but because accommodation was scarce he was assisted when his German girlfriend visited him, and they could pose as a married couple to rent a flat.

At the time many Londoners were openly hostile to foreigners living and seeking work in the UK. Mat's first job was with the Post Office, working with West Indians, Africans, other 'Colonials' and migrants from throughout the UK. Mat has fond memories of 'Kangaroo Valley', as Earl's Court became known, and especially the King's Head pub. He remembers Martin Luther King's assassin, James Earl Ray, also lived in the area in June, 1968, before Ray's arrest at Heathrow airport, travelling on a false Canadian passport.

On leave in Singapore from Borneo during the monsoon (note the wet 'brothel creepers'); L to R Jim Vakatalai, Watisoni Rogose, Dave Rosa and Sek Takavesi. Photo: Ann Rosa

Kim Yabaki operating a ferry from Labuan to Borneo, circa 1964.
Photo: David Whey

CHAPTER 4:
MIDDLE YEARS, 1967-77

Regardless of whether the men who served only six years returned to Fiji or not, they tended, with notable exceptions, to drift back to their village or itinerant lifestyles and not keep in touch with those with whom they enlisted. Those of Girmitya extraction in particular were a case in point. Very few returned to Fiji, or chose not to stay long, and became part of the Indian diaspora, which had predominantly scattered to the UK, Australia and Canada. Sam Pillay, who returned to eventually follow his father into politics and was elected to parliament in 1987, corresponded with those who served with him in R Signals for many years but stopped when he lost his address book. The Fijians present as more cohesive, if not better correspondents, either because of family, island or old school links. Many returned to their rural villages on the three main islands and were rarely heard of again by their cohort in Suva or elsewhere.

Levani Naucusou Damuni's life after the army, however, is worth noting. Levani enlisted under his second name but chose to be known as Levani Damuni in later life. Several of his former colleagues in Suva recalled him under his enlisted name in 1992 and advised their biographer that Levani had served twelve years with the Royal Hussars and said he was 'driving a taxi in Hawaii' at that time. Joe Tuwai, who served with another armoured regiment, recalled in 2014 that Levani served only six years before returning to Fiji. Levani's widow Donna was later located through US telephone directories and explained Levani's attraction to Hawaii. An older brother had been involved in building a Fijian village in the Polynesian Cultural Centre established by the Church of Latter Day Saints in Hawaii, and a cousin had told him of employment opportunities with the Peace Corps. Levani joined the Peace Corps program as a Fijian language instructor where he met Donna from Worcester, Massachusetts. Levani and Donna married in 1969 and the first of their three sons and two daughters was born in Hawaii in 1971. Levani completed a course in hotel management and returned to Fiji with his young family but decided to return to the US when he found an Australian secretary was paid much more than his salary as a hotel manager. His second son was born in Fiji, but the family eventually settled in Worcester, where Levani worked for a company owned by Donna's father. Donna advised that Levani had never driven taxis but visiting nephews had done so, leading to erroneous advice recorded in 1992.

Perhaps not 'England's first black shepherd' but quite possibly England's first Fijian shepherd. Ben Temo at the Wilton sheep fair, late sixties.
Photo: Ben Temo

Jake Tulele returned to Fiji in 1976 and 'felt like an expatriate... a black expatriate' in his own country. He was appointed as a marketing officer for the Business Opportunity and Management Advisory Service (BOMAS) on a five-year contract from 1977 during which he was twice 'carpeted' by the then Minister for Fijian Affairs, Ratu Penaia Ganilau, for writing letters to newspaper editors. During this time, he attended two technology transfer courses in PNG and India. His contact was not renewed. Jake later established a successful small business and remained in Suva.

————†————

In the early seventies the absence of minor conflicts for the British Army, aside from the 'troubles' in Northern Ireland, inclined some of the '212' to look elsewhere for action. Two of those who had served or were still serving with 22 SAS thought New Zealand's involvement in the Vietnam conflict offered opportunities. Both **Labalaba** and **Sotia Ponijase** were single at the time and Ponijase was successful in transferring to the NZ SAS squadron around the time that the newly elected NZ government withdrew its forces from Vietnam. Laba was on his way to NZ with a similar ambition when a chance meeting with the 22 SAS squadron en route to Dhofar persuaded him that HMG could still find conflicts for elements of her armed forces. Laba's decision proved fateful (Appendix F).

————†————

Leaving the army after nine years, **Felix Lockington** elected to stay in England, initially working on building sites, spending too much time operating jack hammers without ear protection which affected his hearing. He eventually returned to his original trade and in 2015 was still working as a maintenance officer in an historic hotel on the Thames, completing a rewiring of the building under the direction of a qualified electrician. Felix survived some difficult times in his early years out of the army, losing his passport and most other important documents in the early seventies, and has never replaced the passport.

Felix never married, volunteering that he was 'unlucky with women,' but was lucky enough to father two daughters in 1970 and 1984, both of whom eventually tracked him down to establish contact. Felix had occasional contact with former comrades through the King's Head hotel in Earl's Court in his first years out of the army and was a tenant of Jack Shepherd's for a period. In retrospect, Felix regrets that he did not make more of the opportunities his army service opened to him. He enjoys his part time work in the hotel, but a hearing impediment and arthritis hampers his guitar-playing.

———†———

When **Fred Dewa** first enquired about entering the Open University through army channels, he was advised that the Open University was 'only for officers' but a WRAC clerk gave him an application form. Other British Universities wanted passes at 'A' level for admission and did not accept his qualification for university entrance in New Zealand. In 1975/76 Fred completed his last assignment for his Open University B. Sc degree after sitting through innumerable lectures on TV at six o'clock in the morning.

Those who enlisted for nine years or more were paid slightly more than those who enlisted for the minimum of six years. When interviewed about their army service 20-50 years after the event, very few had regrets of any sort about their decision to enlist, regardless of the consequences. A small number regretted not having maximised the opportunities it offered. Inevitably perhaps, the UK's withdrawal from 'east of Suez', changes of government and fewer opportunities for active service in 'the Far East' and elsewhere made the army less attractive than it had been in Fiji in 1961. From August 1969 onwards, the repetitive demands of Operation Banner, attempting to contain the 'troubles' in Northern Ireland, kept the incentive to remain in the army under scrutiny.

———†———

In tandem with this introspection came opportunities for examining alternative career progression. In his last years of service **Sam Tamata** became involved with the Soldiers & Airmens' Scripture Readers Association (SASRA) and on 13 April 1970, he realised that his true vocation lay with the Church. In his own words:

> Before I left the Army I was 'converted', what is generally called 'born again.' My desire then was to have some kind of Biblical Training and then to return to Fiji.

Sam's SASRA membership card refers to Matthew 24.44:

> Therefore you also be ready, for the Son of Man is coming at an hour you do not expect.

SASRA is a non-denominational organisation and Sam had drifted a little from his Methodist upbringing. He was attracted to the interdenominational Bible Training Institute at Glasgow, beginning a two-year course in 1970 while utilising the last of his accumulated army leave. The BTI was run by the Overseas Missionary Fellowship (OMF). Sam met his wife Muriel on the course and they married on the final day of the last term.

Sam and Muriel worked in St George's Crypt for women and children in Leeds from 1972-74 before moving to Glasgow to manage a facility for homeless women and children run by the Strathclyde local authority. They began attending a local congregation of the Free Church of Scotland (FCS) at this time.

Free Church College, Edinburgh, 1979-80. Sam Tamata fourth from left in second row.
Photo: Sam Tamata

The Presbyterian Church of Eastern Australia (PCE) is a 'sister church' of the FCS, sharing the same doctrine, principles and practice of the FCS established by Rev. Thomas Chalmers in 1843.

Sam told his local FCS minister of his wish to return to Fiji for mission work and the minister contacted Rev Allan Harman, an Australian who had been professor of Hebrew at the FCS college in Edinburgh but had returned to work in Melbourne. Through this connection Sam was interviewed for admission to the FCS college on behalf of the PCE. He then spent three years with the Free Church of Scotland College.

———†———

After nine years in the RE **Isoa Rabola** returned to marry and settle in his wife's village of Dreketi on Vanua Levu and became a farmer. He became a pastor for the Lutukina Assemblies of God congregation on Vanua Levu from 1976-2003 and for the Batiri community from 2004-2014.

———†———

The RASC was a natural fit for **Laurence Billings**, who was an apprentice motor mechanic when he enlisted. He served for nine years in the UK, Wuppertal, Dortmund and Bunde where he was discharged as a corporal and remained a total of twenty-two years. He met Heidemarie while in Wuppetal on an exercise in 1963. He returned to Fiji on DOMCOL in 1966 but married Heidemarie in 1967 and eventually settled in the house where she was born in Esens. He visited Fiji a second time, with Heidemarie, in 1981 and together they attended the farewell parade in Dortmund in 1983. They had no children.

Laurence worked as a civilian storeman on an army base at Bunde until moving to Esens in 1989 where he found work as a groundsman in the city's parks and gardens until he retired. Laurence has occasionally had pangs of homesickness for his village of Dogotuki but has enjoyed a life in Germany that he could not have had back on Vanua Levu. He has often been mistaken for a Turk over the years but never experienced racial prejudice in Germany.

———†———

Mike Vuli recalls that there were plenty of jobs for those who wanted them when he left the army in the seventies, and he spent his first four years working as a security guard before being attracted to coal mining for several pounds a week more (Appendix H).

———†———

Regardless of their length of service, those '212' who returned to Fiji with foreign wives frequently encountered difficulty acclimatising or acculturating their wives to life in Fiji in the nineteen seventies and eighties. One who might have been a role model for dealing with this issue was **Dave Rosa**, who never doubted that the 22 years of his army service was intended as preparation for his eventual return to Fiji and contribution to national development through his role as head of his *mataqali* on Kabara in the Lau group. Dave met his wife Ann on a skiing holiday in Scotland in 1970 and had always made it clear that he wanted to return to Fiji after completing his twenty-two years. They married in 1974 and Ann's preparation for settling in Fiji included supplementing her degree in physical education with an honours degree in geography and history from the Open University. A couple of visits to Fiji, including Kabara, ahead of their eventual settlement in Suva helped Ann's appreciation of Fijian village life and the future importance of Dave's role. There were thus no surprises when they returned in 1984.

———†———

In 1974 the then **Cpl Joe Tuwai** and **L/Cpl Naibuka Qarau** volunteered for one of the more unusual assignments experienced by any of the '212' during their army service. The two Fijians added to the multi-national composition of an exploration of the River Congo in Zaire, now known as the Democratic Republic of the Congo. The expedition was led by the rather eccentric Colonel John Blashford-Snell RE, with the primary aims of exploring the Congo river and investigating onchocerciasis, or river blindness, one of the world's 'neglected tropical diseases' that affects about 1.5 billion people in around 150 countries. The expedition included doctors and assorted scientists of varied disciplines, and many army personnel that were given leave or secondment to assist. Its secondary aims included searches for the rare Johnston's Okapi and the otter shrew!

Joe and Naibuka provided the communications link between the forward land party and the river party over distances of more than 1600 kilometres. One of Naibuka's more vivid memories is living with a tribe of pigmies in the Uturi rain forest for more than a week. The expedition took place a century after American journalist Henry Morton Stanley located the renowned Scottish explorer and missionary Dr David Livingstone in the same area. Blashford-Snell's rather uninformative account of the expedition, *In the Steps of Stanley*, in the form of a cryptic log, is dedicated to the US Ambassador to the Court of St James appointed by Richard Nixon, publisher and philanthropist Walter Annenberg, who is credited with much of the support needed to launch the expedition.

———————†———————

After finishing the six years of his short service commission **Mike Yasa** elected to return to Fiji and serve in the RFMF in the first instance. This proved a major disappointment after his service with RGJ—it was 'not real soldiering' and the pay was poor. The RFMF of the time bore little resemblance to the force it has evolved into, particularly post-1987. In the late sixties it had a regular cadre of thirty of so officers supported by administrative staff, and in the first years of independence from 1970, the RFMF had just one Territorial battalion.

From 1967-69 the RFMF was commanded by Colonel Frank Rennie, a career New Zealand army officer and founder of the New Zealand SAS squadron which he had commanded in Malaya. Mike found the RFMF environment 'stifling' and was disturbed to find that officer promotions were influenced by senior chiefs.

Mike married another Lauan, Dr Jiko Luveni, who was the first Fijian woman to graduate as a dentist from USP. The couple had three children. Two Colonial Civil Servants of the day offered Mike advice and encouragement to re-join the civil service. Peter Lloyd had served with the 60th Rifles and John Deverell had served with the King's African Rifles (where the CSM in his company was WO2 Idi Amin, later the notorious third President of Uganda). Deverell followed his distinguished father, British colonial administrator Sir Colville Deverell, into the Colonial Civil Service and had served as District Officer, Nausori. He had also been a mentor to Rabuka as a young officer, but returned to the UK after Fiji's Independence in 1970, and joined the security service (MI5) where he prospered. Deverell was a bluff but persuasive negotiator, credited in later years with convincing his government to enter into secret negotiations with the IRA in Northern Ireland. But in May 1987, he failed to persuade the FCO to let him return to Fiji and 'sort out' the upstart Colonel[30]. In June 1994, Deverell was a director of MI5 in charge of their Northern Ireland operations when he was killed in a helicopter crash while travelling to a conference in Inverness.

Mike resumed his civil service career initially as District Officer Lautoka. Many who encountered Mike in subsequent years were impressed with how effectively he communicated with villagers. He did not sever his connection to the RFMF and served two tours as a peace-keeper in the Lebanon and Sinai as a Territorial officer.

In 1968 Ratu Mara was the Secretary for Fijian Affairs in the colonial administration and a New Zealander named Thomas was general manager of the NLTB which Mike had left in 1961. Mike worked in the NLTB archives before a succession of DO appointments in Lautoka, Nadi, Nadroga, Nausori and Labasa in the years that followed.

Mike remained in the RFMF as a Territorial officer and in 1979-80 served with RFMF's first peace keeping force in Lebanon. Ratu Epeli Nailatikau commanded the battalion with Jim Sanday as his 2IC and Ratu Epeli Ganilau was Mike's company Commander. Nailatikau and Sanday eventually became the RFMF Commander and Deputy Commander respectively, usurped by Sitiveni Rabuka in 1987. Ganilau also eventually commanded the RFMF and his father, Ratu Sir Penaia Ganilau became Fiji's second indigenous Governor General and, when Rabuka declared Fiji a Republic, its first President.

---

30 Personal communication with one of Deverell's former staff.

In May 1972, Fiji hosted the first Festival of South Pacific Culture which has evolved into the Festival of Pacific Arts at four yearly intervals in subsequent years. Mike won a competition sponsored by the festival for an original play in the Fijian language. His *Na Tawa Vanua* about Fijian occupation of the land, based on the legend of the ancestral spirit god *Degei*, has since been adopted by the Fiji Education Department as a text for study in Fijian schools and reprinted four times in the decades that have followed.

In 1982-83 Mike served again as a peace keeper in Sinai commanding a company in Lt Col Inosi Tawakedrau's battalion. During these peace-keeping deployments Mike had two significant experiences which profoundly changed or enhanced his Christian beliefs and were to determine his vocation in later years.

On returning to duty with the civil service in 1983, Mike was posted to the PM's office as secretary to the Africa Caribbean Pacific-European Economic Community (ACP-EEC) Conference to be held in Suva the

Anare Ravai (L) and Nat Ledua with Captain Philip Browne (R) at an army base in Northern Ireland, probably mid-late seventies. Browne followed the '212' to the UK several years later, graduated from Sandhurst, served with the Cheshires and eventually settled in Spain. Ravai, like Ledua served twenty two years in the infantry. Photo: Kit Uluinayau

following year. This was the largest international conference held in Fiji since Independence, with representatives from more than 200 countries, and he was able to demonstrate his considerable administrative and organisational skills and experience to good effect. Mike met his future wife Sereana during this conference and they married in 1984.

CHAPTER 5:
EXERCISE 'FIJIAN FAREWELL'
PARADE AT DORTMUND

'Fijian Farewell' was the name given to the British Army's farewell parade at the Dortmund Garrison on 24 September 1983, to thank those '212' still serving for their service. Sixty-four of the original 200 men were with the British Army, scattered around the globe. As a gesture to a single group of long-serving recruits, it was probably unprecedented. WO2 Romano Naceva, serving with 26 Field Regiment at Dortmund at the time, credits 'an old rugby pal', Brigadier Mike Jones, then Commander Royal Artillery for 3 Division BAOR, as the originator of the idea for a special farewell parade. Romano was given responsibility for coordinating the administrative details required, and made full use of the army communications system to ensure that as many serving '212' as possible could attend.

The '212' were accustomed to celebrating their national day, the tenth of October, since their country's Independence in 1970. Fiji's 'double tenth' (as the Taiwanese call their national day with the same date) also commemorates Fiji's Cession to the British Crown in 1874. During the decade or so after Independence, many of the '212' gathered in Dortmund to sing, dance, drink much kava and other stimulants and roast the odd pig or two in a *lovo* (earth oven). Fiji's High Commissioners in London, also accredited to the EEC, usually attended these functions. Romano Naceva had been associated with these celebrations over the years he had been stationed in Dortmund with 26 Field Regiment.

In 1981 the celebrations attracted a cohort of younger Fijians serving with the RFMF in Lebanon on UN peace-keeping duties. On that occasion, the celebrations interfered with the scheduled departure of the visitors who missed their return flight from Frankfurt. Romano was given a free hand by the Brigadier after assuring him that at least thirty of the remaining serving '212' would be on parade. A MOD memorandum of 24 February 1983, entitled *Repatriation of Fijian Soldiers* and addressed to forty-four regiments scattered around the globe, referred to a total of fifty-five men due to be discharged later in the year. The list did not refer to about ten other individuals such as WO2 Tom Morell, serving in Germany at the time, and Sgt Joe Tuwai, both of whom had elected to serve for a couple more years for the sake of children finishing their education. Joe later stretched his extension until 1996, becoming the longest serving '212'.

WO1 Conductor (later Captain) Ratu Manasa Talakuli, serving with the Royal Brunei Regiment in 1983, was deemed too far away to justify the cost of bringing him to Germany for the final parade. WO1 Sam Basu, RSM of 1DWR, was however brought back from Gibraltar where he was serving at the time to be the parade RSM. WO2 Keith Zoing was serving as a Foreman of Signals in Cyprus and was brought back for the occasion. Romano recalls that Keith was the right marker for the '212' on parade—hardly surprising, given Keith's height.

Jone Tunidau was busy Sappering for the Queen in Sierra Leone at the time but his brother Tomasi was at Dortmund.

Chelsea Barracks in London was the designated pickup point for a bus provided to bring those serving in the UK, and other '212' who had served shorter terms, to Dortmund. Mrs Thelma Lalabalavu, mother of Sergeant Ralph Lalabalavu who was 100 Field Regiment, travelled from Fiji for the occasion. Naibuka Qarau and Jim Masuwale, who each served sixteen years with DERR and R Signals respectively, had joined the RFMF on return to Fiji and travelled to Dortmund under controversial circumstances from Sinai where they were serving at the time.

Regiments in which the '212' had served, or their amalgamated descendants which had survived the downsizing of the army over the previous two decades, were represented at the parade and sent representatives to the preparatory planning meetings chaired by Brigadier Jones, with Romano as secretary.

At one of these meetings the representative of 1RHA (the Royal Horse Artillery) suggested his regiment should fire an eighteen-gun salute for the parade; when on parade with its guns, the Royal Horse Artillery takes precedence over other regiments. Romano had no difficulty, however, in securing that honour for his own battery of 26 Field Regiment, 17 (Corunna) Battery. The Corunna battery is the most senior in the Regiment and traces its history from 1757.

Jones was the formal host for the parade, and as President of the Royal Artillery and Dortmund Garrison Golf Club he had expanded the course from nine to eighteen holes and was credited with designing much of the expanded layout. Not surprisingly, golf eventually featured in the farewell celebrations as a safe alternative to Jones' initial suggestion of a rugby match for men in their forties.

Romano coordinated his efforts with those of the Fiji High Commissioner in London, Ratu Josaia Toganivalu, and his staff who in late 1982 hosted a function in the Westminster Cathedral Hall to brief those '212' who were due to be discharged, on life and opportunities in contemporary Fiji. The Fiji government was concerned to avoid 'reverse culture shock', particularly for those returning '212' who had made few, if any, visits to their homeland during their service. Many of the '212', but particularly those who had non-Fijian wives and/or children born in the UK, Germany or elsewhere who did not speak Fijian, had serious concerns, not least for the education and other opportunities for their children.

Ratu Josaia accompanied the Prime Minister of Fiji Ratu Sir Kamisese Mara to the parade, at which Romano was presented with his MBE by the British Ambassador to Bonn, Sir Jock Taylor. Brigadier Jones was the parade

Commander and the CO, 26 Field Regiment, Lt Col David Gay was the parade Adjutant. The Commander in Chief, BAOR, General Sir Nigel Bagnall and Commander, 1 British Corps, Lieut General Sir Martin Farndale took the salute with Ratu Mara and the Ambassador.

Ratu Meli Vesikula, MBE, as RSM Sam Basu of 1DWR, on parade at Dortmund for Exercise Fijian Farewell, September, 1983. Photo: Romano Naceva

A good account of the 'Fijian Farewell' was written by the late Rodney Tyler, confidant of Margaret Thatcher and Joan Collins, and apparently freelancing again after working for *The Daily Mail* and *News of the World*. Tyler's article, headlined 'The Last Farewell' was reproduced in a Fiji newspaper.

A concise summary of the '212's' service for their Queen, the article was written with Tyler's usual attention to detail but for one lapse into hyperbole referring to 'dozens of awards for gallantry.' A couple of Tyler's observations, however, are especially worth noting:

> Were it not for accidents and compulsory redundancies in the past few years, 70 per cent of the original 200 (men) would still be serving—against an average of only 25 per cent for a normal army intake...

Between them, the Fijians represented the army at almost every sport possible.

The Guardian's Will Bennett was more cryptic and less effusive, recording more accurately several gallantry awards but noting archly that the Fijians 'did less well at qualifying for good conduct medals.'

On the parade ground, two flank guards of honour were provided by 26 Field Regiment and the First Battalion of the Gordon Highlanders. Representative detachments of ten men from the following units symbolised the spread of '212' service in the army: 1RHA, 5 Heavy Regiment, 16 Air Defence Regiment, 28 Amphibious Engineer Regiment, Royal Signals, 1 Light Infantry, 2 Royal Irish Rangers and 3rd Armoured Division Transport Regiment. The RA Alanbrooke Band provided a blend of traditional Fijian and British melodies, concluding with *Will Ye No Come Back Again* and *Auld Land Syne*.

Led by RSM Basu (aka Meli Vesikula) the Fijians slow-marched through the open ordered ranks of the guards in their honour before passing the saluting base and receiving an eighteen-gun salute from eight M109A2 self-propelled 155mm howitzers. As the smoke from the guns cleared the guests heard the Fijians singing *Isa Lei*, a traditional Fijian song of farewell and *Now Is The Hour* in both English and Fijian. There were few dry eyes among the onlookers.

Romano asserts that this parade represented a singular honour to those concerned, and that it was the first time a group of serving soldiers had been so honoured. Substantiating that claim is not easy, but 'Fijian Farewell' was clearly a singular honour to those on parade and the others who had enlisted with them. A commemorative medallion was struck to present to all those who completed their twenty-two-year indenture.

Ratu Mara's Speech

Prime Minister Mara's speech received a mixed response. There were many on parade who were very receptive to his exhortation to all present to return to Fiji, where their skills and experience could be put to good use in a variety of ways to help build the young nation. Sgt Emani Tabalili, for example, who was impressed by Mara's speech, when asked a decade later why

The '212' who were on parade at Dortmund assembled on the steps of the Officers' Mess.
Front Row
WO1 (RSM) M.Basu, LCol D.S.Gray RA CO, 26 Fd Regt, RA, Brigadier J.M.Jones,
Commander Royal Artillery, 3rd Armoured Division, WO1 (RSM) D.E.Naylor, RSM
26 Fd Regt, RA. Photo: Romano Naceva

he had returned, replied 'to help my people'. Emani had enlisted to learn a trade and had acquired considerable experience in the RE throughout his army service. WO2 Dave Rosa was another Sapper with no doubt that he had skills and experience he could put to good use for Fiji and his family.

Some of those on parade believe they heard Ratu Maru not only encourage them to return to Fiji with their skills and expertise but thought he had promised them jobs that would utilise their experience. Others swear he made no such promise. Every effort to locate a copy of the speech has been unsuccessful.

Kalioni Ratunabuabua, one who was unimpressed by the PM's exhortations, had not visited Fiji during his years of service and had no intention of returning. Over thirty years later Kalioni's eldest daughter, Mere, recalled her father frequently complaining that 'unless you are from Lau or

Bau (the tiny island home to Fiji's highest chief, the *Vunivalu*, or Paramount Chief of the Kubuna Confederacy) forget about advancement in Fiji.' This latter view of Mara and the role of the chiefs was by no means restricted to odd individuals like Ratunabuabua. Many others present would have been aware from relatives in Fiji that some of the worst aspects of the Fiji they had left in 1961 had not changed, not least the belief that what was most important was 'not *what* you know but *who* you know'.

In September 1983, Naibuka Qarau and Jim Masuwale, serving with the RFMF on peace-keeping duties in Sinai, decided to accept the invitations they had received from the British Army to attend the farewell parade. These two scallywags and notorious leg pullers maintain that they had valid leave passes for their projected absence. Their CO at the time, Commander Sekove Cama, disagreed after their departure and declared both men AWOL, despatching his designated successor Sitiveni Rabuka to London to bring Naibuka back to duty. Rabuka was easily distracted by the Fiji High Commission in London and took two weeks to locate Naibuka and take him back to Sinai to face a court martial. Naibuka claims he had written to PM Mara and the then Defence Minister Ratu Viliame Toganivalu to resign his Commission before leaving Sinai. He returned to the UK on the bus that brought those from the UK to Dortmund and arranged for Makareta and his three daughters to join him in London where the family remained until he lost Makareta to breast cancer in 2010.

Naibuka recalls:

> I came from Sinai on leave to attend the parade and told most of the boys not to believe him (Mara) for there are no jobs back home.
>
> I was then making my move to come back to the UK for the family's sake,'

adding:

> Ratu Mara was an orator who only says (sic) what you wanted to hear and to me personally, after being in Fiji for that time, I know that (his) speech and promises without actions is useless.

WO2 Romano Naceva and his wife Bulou Wainikiti Naceva (standing, left) with, Bulou Elenoa Vuiyasawa (standing, middle), Mua Ratuloaloa and Mereani Baleitilagica (Raboro) kneeling, after the 'Fijian Farewell' parade coordinated by Romano at Dortmund, 23 September, 1983. Photo; Romano Naceva

Naibuka was bitter about the circumstances of a bank's refusal of a loan for expansion of his piggery, when the bank's approving officer later approved an identical proposal for his brother in law, a ranking chief, presented in more detail in Appendix E.

Ratu Mara, however, had a good day. Partnered by Colour Sergeant Bill Vodo, the PM beat his host Jones and his partner the General at golf. Bill still had a single digit handicap despite a spinal cast which prevented him fitting into his uniform and being on parade! Parade RSM Basu's view of that situation can only be imagined.

Speeches aside, 'Fijian Farewell' was a remarkable tribute from a grateful nation, and the less formal celebrations were enjoyed by all.

Ten years after the farewell parade, Mo Beg recorded another role played by RSM Basu/Vesikula on the day: Vesikula 'acting as spokesman[31] for the 212s and in the traditional Fijian custom, on his knees, presenting a *tabua* (*sevu sevu*) to Ratu Mara, Tui Lakeba and High Chief of Fiji. In my mind's eye this cameo seems moving in view of what happened in Fiji in 1987 and later.' Beg's observation will be clear at the end of Chapter 7.

'212' senior NCOs and warrant officers on the occasion of the Royal Tournament for the Queen Mother, Earl's Court, 19 July 1983. Photo: Pramod Tikaram
Back row, L to R:
WO2 Isireli Buadromo, Sgt Solomone Tarogi, Cpl Tomasi Tunidau, S/Sgt Nakaleto Vakavodokinaivalu, known as Bill Vodo, Sgt Nacanieli Ledua, S/Sgt Josaia Tuwai, Sgt Noa Larua, Sgt Lasarusa Turaga, S/Sgt Tomasi Matakitoga
Middle row, L to R:
Sgt Emani Tabalili, WO1 Fred Marafono, Sgt Soro Vuniwaqa, Sgt Samuela Seruidakuwaqa/Rogers, Sgt Levani Tamanikairukurukuiovalau, WO1 Pramod Tikaram, S/Sgt Charlie Giblin, WO2 Anare Ravai, WO2 Jonasa Jang
Front row, L to R:
S/Sgt Sikeli Vakalala, S/Sgt Saiasi Baleimatuku, Sgt Asesela Waqairoba, S/Sgt Joe Ravu, Fiji's High Commissioner to London Ratu Josua Toganivalu, WO1 Sunia Mataikitoga, S/Sgt Bill Parrott, S/Sgt John Riley, WO2 Tevita Rosa.

---

31 Or *mata ni vanua*, literally 'spokesman for the people', a traditional Fijian formality welcoming any senior visitor, but especially those who were in a position to help the *vanua*.

CHAPTER 6:
FIJI, 1984-87

While this brief interval was not a primary focus of this study, it is worthwhile to collate the experiences of many of the longest serving '212', the men who were discharged after 22 years of dedicated service to their Queen and the army and returned to Fiji soon afterwards. Some, such as Dave Rosa, had never doubted that they would return and put the skills and experience they had gained during their army service to good use at 'home'. Most had returned on leave at least two or three times during their army service and had a good idea of the challenges they would face back in Suva, or in the larger towns or their villages. None would have been surprised by the expectations of relatives for traditional *kerekere*[32] largesse from the returning prodigal sons. At least one of these men deliberately avoided the expectations of his *mataqali*, by taking his family to New Zealand and maintaining an unlisted telephone number for the decades that followed.

Jone Oba returned to Fiji after seventeen years' service in armoured regiments and secured the position of Officer in Charge of the Prime Minister's transport pool, a much-coveted position to which his appointment

---

32 The custom of making demands on relatives, friends or employers which Fijians find difficult to refuse. It can be abused and in 1959 was highlighted by Oskar Spate as a limiting factor to the advancement of Fijians. In 2009 Ronald Gatty noted that the problem remained.

was resented. Other long serving '212' found that they were resented for having had the advantage of gaining experience in other countries with the British Army and then returning to usurp positions to which those who had remained in Fiji aspired.

Peni (Ben) Waqa and his family returned to Fiji after his twenty-two years of service to introduce his family to his country of birth. At an initial temporary residence in Suva's then-named Travelodge Hotel (now the Holiday Inn), Ben recognised a Leeds accent at the next table and was offered a job in the security department of Carpenters Shipping. 'Carpenters' was experiencing problems with staff pilfering of imports, particularly in Labasa. Ben's success in solving this problem led to his rapid promotion in the security department but caused resentment and he found himself being undermined by subordinates and other work-mates. He stayed for nine months and his older children, then aged 11 and 10, attended Suva Grammar school. During this period Ben was invited to join the RFMF but declined. Eventually he accepted advice from his mother that it would be best if he returned to the UK.

Some marriages failed in these early years, as many European wives could not come to terms with the circumstances in which they found themselves and the lack of education or future employment opportunities for their teenage children.

Joe Jang met his wife Peg in 1964 and they married the following year, making him ineligible for DOMCOL. He did not return to Fiji for seventeen years, by which time he decided the family 'could never bridge the gap' between the lifestyles of the UK and Fiji. Their four children all live in the UK and Joe has made two subsequent visits to his homeland. A brother lives in Sydney.

Nic Naico met his second wife, Anna, in Germany late in his service. He returned to Fiji with Anna in 1984 for only his second visit since his DOMCOL in 1966, not because of Ratu Mara's exhortations, but primarily to visit his mother and to assess the opportunities for future employment and his son's education. In 1984 his village of Namuana on Kadavu still had no electricity. Nic and Anna decided to return to Germany where the opportunities were clearly better, and never regretted their choice.

John Riley had three months' accumulated leave at the end of his service and used his return air fare to Fiji to assess whether the family might like to settle there. The children loved it, but his German born wife Mada thought Fiji 'a nice place for a holiday' but with too many negatives for the family. John returned to Catterick and spent the rest of his working life with the UK Government's Directorate of Telecommunications and NTL, retiring when he turned 60. His son spent 13 years in the RE and later joined the Police Service.

Tim Ulaiasi returned to Fiji to 'return to the Bible'. He had married Ursula, a West German Roman Catholic who attended a dance where Tim was playing in a band. He returned to Fiji with his family in late 1984. After finishing school, their sons returned to Germany with their mother. In 2013 Tim still kept a portrait of Ursula on the wall of his house in the village of Levuka outside Savusavu.

By October 1995, Tim felt his missionary work for the church was compromised by his agreement to requests from his parishioners to bring supplies of kava which he enjoyed drinking with them. His concern manifested itself in a recurring dream he had of swimming in a lake of stagnant water.

He concluded that he could not continue preaching against the evils of alcohol and kava if he continued to agree to the requests of villagers on his circuit to bring a kilo of kava to each village. Tim recalls that the Lord appeared before him in one of these dreams and said: 'this is not the way,' and Tim asked to be shown the way.

Tim became a proselytiser for the AOG church, handing out messages from the Bible outside the hot bread shop and ANZ Bank in Savusavu on Saturday mornings, but also outside Hindu temples and mosques in Labasa, where he sometimes provokes arguments with worshippers. Tim sees his mission as one of conversion of Hindu and Muslim Fijians to Christianity.

His metamorphosis from a Methodist to the AOG occurred over ten years and finished in October/November 2006. Tim says he sleeps much better now and dreams of swimming in crystal clear water. He has built a chapel next to his home in the village of Levuka outside Savusavu.

Lasarusa Turaga was influenced by Ratu Mara's speech at Dortmund. He recalls the PM exhorting those on parade: 'Fiji needs your expertise' and 'my office will ensure that you are slotted in to Government at an appropriate level'. Efforts to locate the text of this speech from Fiji's National Archives and former senior staff for the late Prime Minister have been unsuccessful. Even stranger was the lack of any reference to the PM's absence from Fiji or attendance at the parade, let alone a copy of his speech, in the *Fiji Times* in the weeks following the parade. In 1992 Lasarusa argued that he would not have come back to Fiji without this encouragement—'If you can't trust the PM who can you trust?' Some of the returnees, including Lasarusa, may have had unrealistic expectations that they would get the same sort of well-paid employment in Fiji that they could expect in the UK. Several of the '212' were appointed to middle ranking civil service positions shortly after returning.

In 1984 Lasarusa was appointed to a position in the Ministry of Rural Development, but in late 1986 he accepted an appointment as Personnel Manager at The Fijian hotel near Nadi. In this capacity he often found himself partnering coup leader Sitiveni Rabuka on the nearby golf course, as the modern Major General was a frequent guest at the hotel. In the late eighties, however, Lasarusa and his English wife Debra became disillusioned and sold everything, preparing to go back to the UK. They were within seven days of Debra returning to the UK for six months when Lasarusa was appointed CEO of the Family Planning Association of Fiji.

Several of the returning senior NCOs were offered appointments as assistants to the *Roko Tui* in many districts. This suited **Sikeli Vakalala** who returned to Fiji in 1984, was appointed an assistant *Roko Tui* with the Fijian Affairs Department and was promoted to *Roko Tui* of the Ra provincial administration in 1993.

Certainly, some men had initial difficulty finding jobs. There was none of the UK infrastructure where a Resettlement Board and other organisations assisted ex-Servicemen. A delegation of concerned returnees, with Mike Yasa as spokesman, made a traditional representation to Ratu Mara, recognising his status as a high chief, at the PM's Veiuto residence. This also produced no apparent action and it would have been impolite in Fijian cultural terms to repeat the appeal.

Ratu Meli Vesikula had a strong interest in Fiji's provincial administration, and on his return was one of several '212' to accept Ratu Mara's Dortmund challenge. He was appointed *Roko Tui*, or District Officer, for Naitasiri Province, responsible to the Ministry of Fijian Affairs (MFA). His concern for the sad state of affairs rural Fijians were experiencing prompted him to write a twenty page-long memorandum to Ratu Mara with recommendations for redressing the worst faults. The PM never directly acknowledged the memo, but directed the then Permanent Head of the MFA to reply on his behalf.

While Meli never received a formal response, he took some satisfaction from the fact that Mara ordered his memo copied to various ministries.

Ratu Meli became frustrated with the MFA bureaucracy, and eventually left to concentrate on business activities, including a restaurant. He became increasingly involved in politics ahead of the 1987 election and its aftermath, serving briefly as Minister for Fijian Affairs in Colonel Rabuka's first military government, as outlined in the following chapter.

A decade after their return to Fiji, **Dave Rosa's** wife Ann recalled that Dave was very unsettled for the first few years. He was offered an assistant *Roko Tui* (District Officer) position with the MFA, at Vunidawa, Naitasiri, but it was not what he was seeking. His younger brother, Sefanaia Koroi, had represented Fiji in swimming, studied physical education at Otago University and suggested investing in a sports centre with Dave after his return to Fiji. **Nat Ledua**, who left the Cheshire Regiment as a physical training instructor was back in Fiji at the time, was interested in joining such a venture but Dave was sceptical.

Dave later worked as berthing master for Carpenters Shipping in Suva before working with a Taiwanese *beche de mer* project. When diagnosed with leukaemia in 1993, Dave was Operations Manager for the *Tai Kabara* inter-island trading vessel, which served the Lau Island group for two decades from the mid-1980s to the mid-2000s.

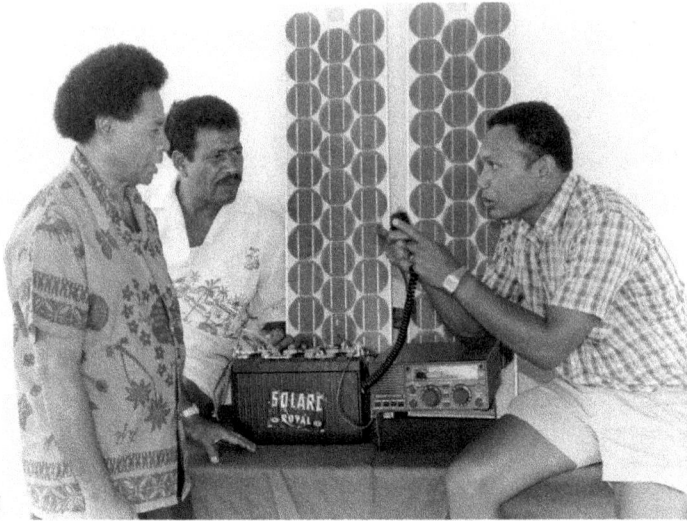

Transferring skills acquired in the army, Dave Rosa obtained a radio telephone for his village, Udu on Kabara, and instructed his mataqali in its operation in 1984, shortly after his return to Fiji. Photo: Ann Rosa

Nat Ledua was another who was influenced by Ratu Mara's speech at Dortmund and nourished an ambition to return to Fiji to start a business. He was thwarted in this but found subsequent employment with Carpenters Shipping, the Ports Authority of Fiji and Tai Kabara Shipping Co.

Alex Kubu attended a ten-week resettlement course in business management at Plymouth University, using as his business model a plan he had devised with several other '212' to develop a Volkswagen (VW) car sales and servicing agency in Suva. The business was registered as Bolatagane (literally 'Great Britain') Motors Ltd. Alex put the proposal to Volkswagen management in Wolfsburg, who agreed to supply the new business from Australia. If this was successful, VW would consider investing in a full dealership and showroom.

Alex recalled that the original directors/shareholders of Bolatagane Motors included himself, Ratu Meli Vesikula, Akuila Vaniqi, Lepani Tamani, Sikeli Vakalala and Semi Degei. Nic Naico was also listed as a director of the company when it was first registered in July 1985. Each contributed £5,000 to the working capital of the company, held initially in a Jersey bank account. Alex fell out with Ratu Meli over the latter's management style and considered himself lucky to have recovered his investment. From then on, he had nothing further to do with the company or the other directors. He is quite pessimistic about such business enterprises in Fiji, claiming: 'Fijians are their own worst enemy—they are like crabs in a pot with some trying to climb out and others pulling them down'.

Alex returned to England, settling in Harrogate and putting his army experience and well-developed salesmanship skills to good use as manager of a government-funded company running training programs. The company foundered but Alex took it over, renamed it 'Kutronic Training' and ran it as a very profitable enterprise for six years. He later spent six years as the security manager for a police convalescent home.

Bill Pareti was persuaded by Ratu Mara's speech at Dortmund to return to Fiji in December 1984, declining an attractive job offer in Germany. He elected to take a course as a refrigeration technician prior to his discharge, thinking such a qualification would be useful back in Fiji. In the UK refrigeration technicians earned fourteen pounds an hour but in Fiji he was paid only FD2.50 an hour as a maintenance supervisor with Rewa Dairy, packaging UHT milk. He did not stay long and later worked as a civilian at QEB during Rabuka's time as Commander. In later life he managed the Fiji Golf Club in Suva.

Iliesa Saqusaqu returned to Fiji and was briefly a director of the ill-fated Bolatagane Motors project. He later found a position at the Centre for Appropriate Technology and Development (CATD), established at Nadave, Tailevu, in the mid-1980s to teach technical and leadership skills with a focus on community development. He taught engineering skills which helped young rural people to carry out household repairs on electricity, plumbing, gas cylinders, generators and outboard motors. After Iliesa's death, Ratu Meli Vesikula recalled that Iliesa was 'well content with that line of work' and spent over twenty-five years at CATD.

Emani Tabalili had always wanted to return to Fiji 'to help my people' and did so with his English wife and two daughters, who had difficulty adjusting to life in Fiji. They returned to the UK, but he stayed to buy land on Viti Levu for his brothers as there was no land available on his home island of Kadavu. He found it very difficult attempting to assist Fijians in business. His interest in a stall in the Ba market amounted to nothing when a relative spent all his money. At about the same time his wife filed for divorce.

Emani later invested in a fishing venture, which continued to preoccupy him in 1992, by which time he had settled in his second wife Makareta's village of Nawaka outside Nadi. At the time of his initial interest the local fishing industry was dominated by Indo-Fijians whom he found 'not helpful'. He persisted, however, was eventually moderately successful, and encouraged other Fijians to follow his example. He felt this was one way in which he could usefully apply his army experience. In early 1992, however, he said there were only five Fijians in his immediate area engaged in fishing as a livelihood. He was very critical of the lack of follow up support for his efforts from the Fiji Government.

Jake Tulele's frustration with Fiji's racial divide eventually drew him to politics, and he was an unsuccessful candidate for the Fiji Nationalist Party in the 1982 election. He had become convinced that the key to peaceful development in Fiji was 'Fijians must hold their own in business...the only solution to Fiji's problems'. Jake abhors racism, and in the mid-eighties he became convinced that the new Fiji Labour Party was the key to bridging Fiji's racial divide. He stood unsuccessfully as a candidate for the FLP in 1987.

When not consumed by his official duties, **Mike Yasa** found time to write *Na Tawa Vanua*, a play to illustrate the origins of the Fijian people as he imagined them, responding to a national drama writing competition.

Several other plays followed, including a couple for children, but it was by accident over thirty years later that Mike learned from a cousin that *Na Tawa Vanua* was on the curriculum for study throughout government schools in Fiji. In 1985 Mike was appointed Fiji's Consul General in Auckland, representing Fiji's diplomatic and trade interests, unaware that his biggest challenges lay ahead of him.

The Methodist Church was a consistent thread throughout Mike's life, and he was fortunate with the Christian family he boarded with as a student in Poona. Mike developed his connection to the church as a lay preacher on his return to Fiji and was particularly moved by the experience of climbing and spending a night on the summit of Mt Sinai whilst on leave from one of his peace-keeping tours with the RFMF in the Middle East.

Delighted as he was to be appointed Fiji's Consul General in Auckland in December1985, he recorded in his autobiography that 'my first[33] priority in life was serving Almighty God. So, the first thing I did when we arrived in Auckland was to present my Lay Preacher's Certificate to our Methodist Church Minister, Reverend Elia Samusamuvodre.'

---

33 *Of Baluka and Nibong Palm*, p. 29.

CHAPTER 7:
'OPERATION KIDACALA'
MAY 1987

The events of 1987' was a euphemism widely used throughout Fiji for years after the election in early April of that year, to refer to the civil unrest and subsequent military coups following the election. *Kidacala*, or '(pleasant) surprise', was the code word chosen by the coup leader, Lt Col Sitiveni Rabuka, for planning and briefing purposes with those involved in 'the neutralisation of the coalition government of Fiji' (his term). Several returned '212' were[34] ardent supporters of Rabuka's coups, and several others were equally strong objectors. The divide remains.

The circumstances that led to the first coup have been well chronicled by others, not least by Professor Brij Lal in an excellent chapter of his book *Broken Waves*, including a description of Rabuka's announcement of the first (May 1987) coup to the parliament.[35] We are concerned here only with the involvement of several of the returned '212' in the weeks before and months after Rabuka's coups. The first coup was intended to end violent disturbances by indigenous Fijians who objected to the election result, in which the Alliance Party, which had governed the country since Independence, lost to a coalition of parties dominated by Fiji Indians.

---

34 *Rabuka - No Other Way* 1988, p. 163.

35 'Things Fall Apart' in his 1992 book *Broken Waves*, a history of Fiji in the twentieth century.

Rabuka was a talented, experienced and decorated officer, respected by his colleagues and no stranger to the idea of military intervention in the affairs of a nation. He attended the Indian Armed Forces Staff College at Wellington, Tamil Nadu, in 1979. His thesis for his Masters' degree in Defence Studies from the associated University of Tamil Nadu was written on the subject of military coups. One of Rabuka's biographers has claimed that the focus of Rabuka's thesis was the importance of the post-coup role of armies in the African and Latin American countries he had studied.[36] In 1982, Rabuka attended Australia's Joint Services Staff College (JSSC) where one of his class mates was Australia's Colonel Andy Mattay. Rabuka remained close to Mattay and after his 1987 coups he sent his friend a copy of the first of his two authorised biographies inscribed 'To my good friend Andy Mattay—I told you I would do something like this one day.'[37]

Young officers of Rabuka's generation were influenced by their Honorary Colonel, George Serevaki Mate, OBE, MC, MM who had distinguished himself on operational service in the ranks of the FDF in the Solomons in WWII, and as an officer in Malaya in the early fifties. Colonel Mate was fond of reminding the officers' mess: 'Always remember, Gentlemen, that we are the alternative government'.

A nephew, Jioji (George) Lesi Mate, and another '212' died in a car accident in Germany in August 1967, and Colonel Mate attended the funeral in Hanover.

The 1987 election was won by a coalition of the newly-formed Fiji Labour Party (FLP) and the established National Federation Party (NFP) with a couple of lesser parties, led by Dr Timoci Bavadra, a medical practitioner from western Viti Levu. Only seven of the Coalition's twenty-eight elected parliamentarians were ethnic Fijians, and the coalition was seen by those who did not vote for them as dominated by the interests of Indo-Fijian trade unionists, cane farmers and small businessmen.

---

36 John Sharpham: *Rabuka of Fiji*, p. 66.

37 The late Andy Mattay showed the author his copy of the book in 1995.

Rabuka's justification for his first coup, on 14 May 1987, was to settle unrest among indigenous Fijians (or *iTaukei*) outraged by the election result, who expressed their dissatisfaction by rioting and attacking Indian businesses. The *taukei* movement, as it came to be known, represented the interests of the Fijian chiefs but drew wider Fijian support. The movement was led by several established hard-line nationalist politicians, including Apisai Tora and Sakeasi Butadroka, supported by a few Fijian trade union leaders such as Taniela Veitata, known as Big Dan, the general secretary of the Fiji Portside Workers Union. Veitata had a record of militancy and was a key figure in encouraging violence by dockworkers, unemployed youth and criminal elements throughout 1987. He was a colourful figure and prominent speaker at *taukei* gatherings, arguing that Fijians had to avoid the fates of Australia's Aborigines and New Zealand's Maori. He once labelled New Zealand the 'land of the wrong white crowd'.[38]

Australia's *Bulletin* magazine of 13 October 1987 referred to the 'Taukei Movement' as an 'extreme right-wing Fijian nationalist group which stands squarely behind the military coup of Colonel Rabuka' and referred to the 'Taukei belief in Fijian racial superiority as God's truth.'

Another prominent *taukei* activist was Ratu Meli Vesikula, the former RSM 'Sam Basu' of 1DWR, from a chiefly clan of Verata, in Tailevu. Ratu Meli was seen by some to be propelled by chiefly dynastic ambition and shared with Dr Bavadra the objective of overthrowing PM Mara whose personal dynastic ambitions Ratu Meli despised. Bavadra and Ratu Meli, however, differed in their wider social agendas in April-May1987.

Ratu Inoke Kubuabola was yet another chief and aggressive nationalist whose traditional status was useful to the *taukei* movement. Ratu Inoke was the nephew of then Governor General (and subsequent President) Ratu Sir Penaia Ganilau, and in the aftermath of the coup was well-positioned to exert pressure on his uncle. Ratu Penaia's leadership was criticised by many at the time, and he had yet to be confirmed as the *Tui Cakau*, or High Chief,

---

38 Veitata's description was not original and was borrowed from Maori activists.

of Cakaudrove Province. Ratu Inoke was a convert to the Baptist Church, a born-again Christian, and President of the Fiji Council of Churches.

The church was not a common career path for Fijian chiefs aspiring to politics, but Ratu Inoke has enjoyed a successful career in several of Fiji's post-coup governments and is currently the Defence Minister. Kubuabola and Vesikula may have shared common interests in early 1987, but by early 1989 they were poles apart when Vesikula considered the then Information Minister 'the most dangerous man in Fiji,' more so than the likes of other hard-line nationalists such as Apisai Tora or Taniela Veitata.

Throughout his twenty years in the Duke of Wellington's regiment, Ratu Meli was known as Sam Basu. As the senior NCO of the remaining '212' soldiers and NCOs still serving in September 1983, WO1 Basu had led the farewell parade at Dortmund.

Ratu Meli's army career included several tours in Northern Ireland with DWR, and the experience of violence between dysfunctional communities raised his concerns for the future of Fiji and the need to protect indigenous Fijian interests. In 1989 he recalled that he first became worried about developments in Fiji on his first home leave in 1972. Subsequent exchanges with expatriates returning from visits or postings to Fiji fuelled his concerns.

Brij Lal described Ratu Meli as 'combat-hardened, Ireland-experienced' in the context of his perception of Meli's perceived preference for a surgical military solution to the unrest in 1987. In one sense this description may have gilded the lily somewhat, as Ratu Meli's extensive service included very little conventional combat and he did not, as reported by some newspapers at the time, ever serve in, or seek selection for, 22 SAS. That said, DWR lost three men killed on one of their tours in Northern Ireland and James Naughtie described Northern Ireland as 'the most testing active service' most British Army personnel were exposed to at that time. Ratu Meli's CO in Northern Ireland, Lt Col (later Brigadier) Dick Mundell, who appointed Meli as RSM, has described the modus operandi of the 'Ballymurphy gun team' who ambushed his soldiers by taking over suitably located houses and firing through closed windows. Dealing with IRA tactics of that sort, and terrorists[39] dressed as hospital staff in the Royal Victoria Hospital in Belfast, certainly justified Brij Lal's description of Meli.

Ratu Meli had a bent for colourful, though not profane, language and was often quoted by journalists in 1987. He does not deny that he threatened on one occasion to 'throw into the *lovo*'[40] Dr Bavadra or one of his staff, reminding his audiences then and since of Fiji's past cannibal practices. Ratu Meli's views of contemporary Fiji reflected his intense interest in Fijian history, which he said he inherited from his father.

He shared his late father's conviction that the Fijians are remnants of one of the lost tribes of Israel, and still held that belief in 2013.

It was hardly surprising that the *taukei* movement attracted support from other members of the '212' who had returned home in 1983-84 or earlier. Nat Ledua returned to work in the shipping industry and became a manager with the Ports Authority of Fiji. Semi Degei, who had been a director of the failed Bolatagane Motors enterprise with Ratu Meli and later established a successful office cleaning business, was another supporter.

In 1987 Vaciseva Tabua was also employed by the Ports Authority of Fiji and became active in the *taukei* movement. On the evening of 13 May, she attended a meeting at the PAF to discuss a proposal for the 'burning of Suva' which was dropped after one of the organisers of the meeting received a telephone call from Rabuka advising 'don't take any action, leave it to me.' A current expatriate '212' claims that another Bolatagane director, the late Sikeli Vakalala (the Roko Tui for Namosi province at the time), hosted a meeting with Rabuka and several *taukei* movement leaders at his home on the evening of 13 May.

The question most frequently asked at the time, and a subject for speculation over *tanoas* of *yaqona* or cartons of Fiji Bitter for years after 1987, was: 'Just who

---

39 *Recollections of Brigadier Dick Mundell: CO 1 DWR: 1979-82*, November 2005, entry on the website of the DWR Regimental Association.

40 A *lovo* is an earth oven, essential to Fijian cuisine, favoured by anthropophagic Fijians in past centuries.

were the key players who helped Rabuka in preparing and executing his coup'? Who took care of the essential details in the planning, training and execution of the coup? Whose identity was protected by the balaclava masks worn by those with automatic rifles who accompanied Rabuka into the chamber of the Parliament? The most commonly accepted villain of the piece was (then) Captain Isireli Dugu, an officer who had risen from the ranks of the RFMF but whose service outside Fiji at the time was limited to peace-keeping tours with UN forces in the Middle East. Ilisoni Ligairi understands that Rabuka was the primary planner and describes Dugu as 'a doer, not a thinker'[41].

Dugu kept (or was kept in) a low profile in the years immediately after the 1987 coups, but Ligairi assumed a higher profile, mainly through his close association with Rabuka as his personal protection officer or bodyguard. Ligairi shared Rabuka and Ratu Inoke's Cakaudrove origins. Most observers assumed that Ligairi was an active party to the coup, including some of his former comrades in 22 SAS. Much of the speculation about Ligairi's involvement derived from his known service with 22 SAS, and the publicity surrounding his arrest in Ireland in 1976 (appendix F). Ligairi insists that he had nothing to do with the May 1987 coup but responded to Rabuka's call for assistance afterwards. Ligairi served with the RFMF for thirteen years, retiring to his village again in 2000, before George Speight and others with Fijian nationalist sympathies attempted to overthrow a second elected FLP government led by Mahendra Chaudhry. Ligairi is not closely related to Rabuka but recalls that their fathers were close—his father was a Methodist minister and Rabuka's father was a teacher and lay preacher in Drekeniwai village on the other side of Savusavu.

In the immediate aftermath of the first coup, Rabuka became concerned about possible internal and external threats to Fiji and believed the RFMF needed to develop new defensive capabilities. He asked Ligairi to select and train suitable soldiers for a Close Personal Protection detachment. This eventually evolved into the Counter Revolutionary Warfare (CRW)

---

41 On 12 July 1987, Britain's *Times on Sunday* named the then Captain Dugu as having trained and led the soldiers who supported Rabuka in Parliament.

unit, with a counter terrorism capability, embracing the terminology developed by Tony Jeapes and others at Hereford. Ligairi was gazetted as a temporary captain in the first instance but later promoted to Major during his RFMF service. The 'fourth estate' frequently referred to him as a Colonel, particularly around the time of the Speight coup attempt in 2000.

In the year or so following the coup, Ligairi's close association with Rabuka, some of it in a bodyguarding capacity, led many to assume their close working relationship had preceded the coup. Several of the Fijians who had stayed at Hereford to develop second careers were concerned that Ligairi was actively assisting Rabuka. Tom Morell recalls Jim Vakatalai calling Ligairi to register his concern, if not disapproval. Twenty years after the event, Ligairi recalls 'someone' ringing him and expressing concern but he has forgotten who it was. Many also believed Ligairi and Rabuka to be close relatives.

Another of Rabuka's concerns was the lack of a dedicated intelligence unit in the RFMF, which, combined with his lack of confidence in the Special Branch of the Fiji Police Force, led him to create a Joint Intelligence Centre staffed by the RFMF and selected Fijian police officers. Lt Col Metuisela Mua, a Lauan from Moala, headed this unit which evolved into the Fiji Intelligence Service. Mua reported directly to Rabuka as the Commander RFMF, and eventually to President Penaia Ganilau and the interim Prime Minister, Ratu Sir Kamisese Mara.

Following the first of Rabuka's coups, the New Zealand and Australian governments considered their options for some sort of military intervention, if only for the secure evacuation of their citizens in the event of the RFMF failing to keep order. WO2 Sotia Ponijasi, serving in New Zealand's SAS Squadron at the time, found his loyalties being evaluated by both sides. In 1992 his wife Mere recalled that 'someone from the RFMF' contacted Poni, either to assess his willingness to join the RFMF or to gauge New Zealand intentions. He was also paraded before his commanding officer to assess his willingness to participate in any expedition to Fiji and Poni made it clear he was not prepared to risk hostile engagement with the RFMF and applied for a discharge. The family returned to Fiji in a freighter at Christmas, 1987.

Poni was initially treated with suspicion and became aware of surveillance. According to Mere there were suggestions that he should be deported. It appears that his loyalty was questioned but by whom, exactly, is unclear. He was eventually accepted into the RFMF as a Warrant Officer based on his his experience in the British and New Zealand armies. The *Fiji Republic Gazette* of 6 April 1990 announced that WO1 S. Ponijasi 'is granted a Short Service Regular Commission in the rank of Temporary Captain in the Fiji Army Infantry Corps with effect from 1st November 1989'. He was later put in charge of a 30-man 'Special Operations Security Unit' for corruption investigations.

On the night of 24 October 1990 however, masked men in an old car kidnapped a University of the South Pacific academic who had featured prominently in a public burning of Fiji's new draft Constitution a week earlier and drove him to Colo-i-Suva on the city's outskirts. Dr Anirudh Singh was bound, blindfolded and beaten in a prolonged interrogation of his activities and associates in the Group Against Racial Discrimination (GARD) movement. Dr Singh survived his ordeal but required treatment in Australia. His attackers proved to be quite inept at covert activities, because a witness noted the number of one of the cars used in the abduction and the Fiji police found it was last registered to an FMF soldier. Five serving soldiers, the most senior of which was Ponijasi, were later convicted of the abduction and assault. Ponijasi was apparently not involved in the actual kidnapping but as the OIC of the soldiers' unit he accepted responsibility for the actions of his men.

In November 2006, a court in Fiji belatedly awarded significant damages to Dr Singh, but the following month Commodore Bainimarama seized power in Fiji and in a 2013 posting on the internet Dr Singh claimed he had yet to receive any of the compensation.

Mere claimed in 1992 that Ponijasi was ordered to take responsibility for the kidnapping, and the issue of who was ultimately responsible remains an open question. Like Isireli Dugu and others loyal to Rabuka, Ponijasi was posted to a highly sought-after appointment with the United Nations, in his instance UNIKOM, the UN Iraq Kuwait Observer Mission. Former ministers in the deposed FLP government and officials in the Fiji Trades Union Congress successfully protested the suitability of this appointment to the UN and Ponijasi was recalled in May 1991.

Four of the '212' who had returned to Fiji were Coalition candidates in the election. Jioji Areki fared poorly for the FLP in opposition to Filipe Bole, the sitting Alliance Party member for the Fijian Communal seat of Lau/Rotuma. Sam Pillay, however was elected MP for the Tavua/Vaileka Indian communal seat previously held by his father, R.S. Gounder, for the NFP for two terms.

After seventeen years in the army, George Chute returned to Fiji and began a second career with Fiji Forest Industries (FFI) on Vanua Levu. In England he had been attracted to the social welfare and other policies of Britain's Labour Party, and was an early recruit to the FLP. He won a Northern Division seat on Vanua Levu for the party. George's service with FFI led to appointments as a board member of the Lololo Pine Forest station and as a member of the Forestry Academic committee. Dr Timoci Bavadra invited George to join his Cabinet as Minister for Forests. George declined after receiving telephone calls from other '212' returnees, whom he chose not to name, who suggested he might strike similar difficulties to those other Bavadra supporters had experienced. He was concerned that his home might be fire-bombed.

A frustrated Fijian small businessman, Jake Tulele Mateyawa, who served fifteen years with 216 Parachute Signals Squadron, was another failed FLP candidate.

Sam Pillay recalls the moment on 14 May 1987 when he was sitting in the Parliament and Rabuka entered the chamber in civilian clothes, accompanied by balaclava-clad soldiers brandishing automatic weapons. He briefly considered trying to disarm the soldier standing close behind him but quickly realised the foolishness of such thoughts. Rabuka was sitting in the public gallery and the manner of his introduction of the coup is well described by Brij Lal.

Sam Pillay (R) with Mahendra Chaudhry, 03 Dec 61. Their paths crossed again in 1987 when Lt Col Rabuka terminated their Fiji Labour Party coalition government. Chaudhry was elected Prime Minister in 2000 but his government was truncated by the attempted coup of George Speight. Pillay was disinclined to pursue a career in politics.
Photo: Sam Pillay

Jioji Areki, whose views of excessive government support for *i-taukei* won him few votes in his Lauan home electorate, was so disappointed by Rabuka's actions that he took his second family and his skills to Australia for the next seven years. His second son recalled in 2015:

> He became disillusioned with Fijian (*i-Taukei*) leadership. He felt that it had let the future generations of Fijians down by lending its support to the overthrow of the Bavadra Government.

Jioji returned to Fiji in 1995 to spend the next ten years of his life working as a maintenance officer on the Lacaula and Turtle Island resorts and as a self-employed contractor.

Regional reaction to Rabuka's coup varied considerably. Criticism from neighbouring Melanesian countries was muted, but Australia and New Zealand's Prime and Foreign Ministers fulminated, reflecting what Ratu Penaia's Private Secretary, Peter Thomson, described years later as an 'endemic Australian ability to thoroughly peeve its neighbours from time to time.'[42] Whitehall already had much experience of military coups in former colonies, but not until then in the placid Pacific. In 1985 and 1986, Western leaders had been alerted to unwelcome developments in Pacific Island Countries by Soviet fishing agreements with Vanuatu and the Solomon Islands, and by Vanuatu's diplomatic flirtation with Colonel Ghaddafi's Libya. A few years earlier, Denis Warner, one of Australia's more hawkish foreign correspondents, speculated about the possibility of Cuban intervention in the New Hebrides under the headline 'Gurkhas of the Russian empire.' [43]

A little over 2000 km away from Fiji in Auckland, Mike Yasa was initially baffled but later outraged by the announcement of a coup in Fiji. After his first marriage failed, Mike met his second wife Sereana whilst organising the first meeting of the Africa Caribbean Pacific states with European Economic Community representatives in Fiji in April 1984. In 1985 Ratu Mara appointed Mike as Fiji's Consul General in Auckland. Mike enjoyed the work in Auckland and was kept busy with trade and investment and tourism promotions in New Zealand.

The news blackout in Fiji after the first coup, and lack of formal advice of developments to Fiji's missions abroad, left representatives like Mike in an invidious position when local media asked him for comment. At first Mike assumed that any military coup in Fiji must have been initiated by foreigners. But when it became clear that the RFMF were behind the coup he told one interviewer 'I am not supporting that kind of nonsense' and cited his experience in the Green Jackets controlling riotous assemblies in British Guiana in 1962 (Appendix E).

It seems doubtful that Rabuka or others in authority in Fiji at the time had any recent experience of such serious crowd control, and equally doubtful that RFMF officers would have been capable of threatening to shoot their own kind to preserve law and order. That doubt remains nearly thirty years later, despite the RFMF's assumed mantle of protector of all the people of Fiji.

---

42 Thomson, *Kava in the Blood*, p 95.

43 *The Herald* 13 March 1978.

Mike's sense of right and wrong, developed by his parents and the Church and enhanced by his years as an officer in the British Army and the RFMF, was outraged by Lt Col Sitiveni Rabuka's coup. In his view, an officer responsible for a military coup against an elected government was guilty of mutiny against his superiors and of treason against the State and the Queen. He resigned from the civil service and the RFMF in protest shortly afterwards. He received no pension from the Fiji Government and life was very difficult for the Yasa family in the immediate years that followed. Recalling these developments nearly thirty years later, Mike gives no indication of bitterness and refers to Fiji's first coup leader as 'Steve'.

Ratu Meli Vesikula is a devout Christian who eventually distanced himself from the *taukei*/nationalist agenda, much to the concern of some of his former '212' colleagues with *taukei* sympathies. Many observers of the time saw this as an opportunistic move, particularly his recognition that Dr Bavadra and the FLP/NFP coalition had the right policies for Fiji. In 2013 Ratu Meli explained that his conversion began with a phone call from a man he had never met, who later explained that he had been watching Meli's public performances for some time and considered him to be 'on the right path but using the wrong methods'.

The late Rev Josefata Davui from Rakiraki was an Assemblies of God pastor who convinced Meli that nothing good would come from violence and showed him the error of his *taukei* approach to protecting Fijian interests. By the early nineties Ratu Meli had embraced the Moral Re-Armament movement and made frequent use of letters to the editors of Fiji's newspapers to share his changed points of view.

Peter Thomson, who was a target of Ratu Meli's *taukei* ire while serving as secretary to Governor General Ratu Sir Penaia Ganilau in 1987, has recorded in a memoir a moving description of Ratu Meli's apology to him a decade later.[44]

As WO1 'Sam Basu,' Ratu Meli served as RSM of the 'Dukes' under Lt Col Charles Cumberland and was awarded an MBE for his service in 1984.

---

44 *Kava in the Blood*, pps. 340-341.

Several years later, Ratu Meli was remembered at Buckingham Palace when Cumberland's successor, Lt Col Johnny Walker, was presented with an OBE and the Monarch enquired 'What do you think of RSM Basu and Fiji'? Queen Elizabeth took a close interest in developments in Fiji throughout this turbulent period and its aftermath, with the FCO's Royal Matters Section receiving acknowledgement of the Palace's appreciation of reporting on the subsequent evolution of a new Fiji Constitution. The Queen had independent updates of developments in Fiji from Sir Len Usher, KBE, whom she had met many times over the years since her first visit to the country in 1954. Sir Len, a prominent and respected public figure, newspaper editor and businessman in Fiji, had developed a close friendship with Sir William Heseltine in the intervening years. The pair maintained a regular correspondence as Sir William's varied career progressed to appointment as Queen Elizabeth's Private Secretary in 1986. Sir Len kept the Queen informed of developments in Fiji prior to the election in 1987, and after Rabuka's coup Sir William asked for more frequent reports.[45] Protocol dictated that neither the Queen nor her Private Secretary would ever acknowledge these letters but in his Christmas-New Year letter of 1992-93 to his old friend Stuart Inder, Sir Len referred to the recent publication of his book of these letters, adding 'When I saw the Queen in London she commented 'I read you frequently'.[46] 'Deryck Scarr noted in his 1988 book on the military coups in Fiji that the Queen had been heard to comment 'Poor Fiji' at a recent investiture.[47] Sir Len confided to close friends his understanding that when former PM Ratu Sir Kamisese Mara sought an appointment with Queen Elizabeth after May 1987, he was advised by Sir William that a formal appointment would be inappropriate, and suggested that Mara wait in the Buckingham Palace library while Sir

---

45 *Letters From Fiji 1987-1990*, p. 9.

46 The author acquired the original letter by serendipity, when he purchased Stuart Inder's copy of Usher's book from a second-hand bookshop in Canberra in 2016. The letter was tucked between the book's pages.

47 *Fiji: The Politics of Illusion* p. 123.

William recorded their exchange in his diary. When Mara entered the library, he found the Queen browsing and was able informally to put his view of recent developments to an interested monarch.

Regardless of whether a military coup was necessary, and whether Rabuka and other Fijian leaders had considered other means of resolving a difficult and dangerous situation, once the coup had been staged there was no turning back. The consequences of Rabuka's actions will be analysed in the subsequent chapters, but the reality was that the RFMF was the only credible force with the resources to maintain law and order. The Fiji Police Force of the day had been neglected, lacked essential equipment and was poorly led. Rabuka dismissed the Indo-Fijian Commissioner and promoted indigenous Fijians he trusted to key positions. The stolid but effective Director of the Police Special Branch was bypassed with the creation of a Joint Intelligence Centre (JIC), staffed by carefully selected RFMF and Fiji Police officers, and almost exclusively Fijian. The JIC evolved into the Fiji Intelligence Service in 1988.

Under pressure from Ratu Penaia and Ratu Maru to decide whether he wanted to remain in the RFMF or become a politician, Rabuka decided on the latter. At short notice he called a parade at QEB to announce his decision on his future and his successor. In doing so he had several messages for the assembled officers and men. The first was to emphasise that 'our work, our responsibilities are still there'. Colonel Mate would have approved! Rabuka also expressed the hope that future 'leaders and commanders will have the interests of the nation at heart'. He then noted that it was 'more important to be loyal to the institution, the ideology, than to the leaders or commanders of the society we live in.'[48] He concluded by noting the 'very important role the RFMF will be required to perform from time to time'. Like Brigadier Ian Thorpe before him, Rabuka's first choice of a successor was over-ruled by the two High Chiefs. He announced that his successor would be Ratu Epeli Ganilau, Ratu Penaia's son and Ratu Mara's son-in-law.

---

48 The Information section of the Australian Embassy of the time obtained a recording of the speech. The author has a copy.

In common with coup leaders elsewhere, Rabuka eventually used a compliant judiciary to endorse decrees absolving him and others involved in his coups from any future accountability for their mutiny and treason. Rabuka successfully morphed into a politician without a uniform, making the most of his eventual military rank of Major General. He may not have had the high chiefly rank of Fijian leaders of the previous century, but he had the other requisite qualities. He was a *batu* (warrior), a Methodist lay preacher, and a talented sportsman, representing his country in test rugby union from 1970-77. In the years immediately following Rabuka's 1987 coups, Australia's diplomats maintained their government's disdain for his administration, but a senior officer of the Office of National Assessments advised one departing diplomat to always remember that 'Rabuka is the one in the white hat'.

Mike Thoman and his wife successfully applied to emigrate to Australia in 1983 and sent their children to Melbourne for the final years of their schooling and university education. After the first RFMF coup in 1987, the children insisted that Mike and his wife take up residence in Australia.

Mike initially worked as a storeman at Monash Medical Centre until he attended an assessment with Telecom at Moorabin in August 1989. He impressed with his answers on testing receivers and transmitters and was employed in a paging centre. His first grandchild was born in 1988. His wife was employed at St Vincent's and other hospitals and later in private practice. She was still working part time in 2014, while Mike looked after his grandchildren and supplemented his pension with a gardening business.

In 1993 Ratu Meli and his family returned to the UK. For some years afterwards, he was the chief security officer at Marthyr College in South Wales. In 2000 Meli and his wife Elizabeth returned to Fiji, where Meli became a social worker. Elizabeth died in 2005 and Meli has since devoted his energies to assisting Suva's urban poor and to the work of the Royal British Legion in Fiji, helping veterans in trouble and younger men who wish to follow the '212' into the British Army.

CHAPTER 8:
AFTERMATH

So, what did the recruitment of the '212' amount to and why was the exercise not repeated? What was the sum of the gains and losses in the emerging nation's balance sheet in the decades that followed? And what were the issues surviving '212' or their children in Fiji have had to address as a result of successive RFMF interventions in Fiji's politics?

The easiest group to analyse is the '212' women. Three of the women discharged to marry or return to Fiji within a year. The remainder appear to have all served the full period of their enlistment. Only Munivai Aisake remained in the UK and never returned permanently to live in her homeland, but her two British born daughters still identify with her birthplace through Rotuman websites.

Only four of the twelve women returned to spend all or most of their lives back in Fiji, with Fane Sivoki/Morell spending twenty years in Aldershot and Hereford with first husband Tom, raising their sons. Doreen Petersen and Emma Heffernan appear to have returned briefly to Fiji before moving to Australia. Emma returned to Fiji a second time for a few years after her marriage, but eventually settled in Sydney. The remainder of the women appear to have been restless, and spent between five and fifteen years back in Fiji before emigrating to either New Zealand or Australia.

Vaciseva Tabua/Seruitanoa with two of her forty grand children, Earlyne and Darren Whippy at Kasavu settlement, near Nakobo village on Vanua Levu, 2013. Photo: Author

All these young adventurers, however, were excellent role models for other young women in Fiji, but as Teresia Teaiwa has shown,[49] it took another generation before Fiji's young women were encouraged to join the Fiji or other military forces, an opportunity generated in Fiji by Rabuka's coups. Several of the daughters of the '212' men, however, took advantage of their birthplaces to follow their fathers into the British Army.

It was inevitable that there would be a significant loss of talent and experience from Fiji over the period following the 1961 enlistment of the men in particular, in the manner of the song sung by US troops in WWI:

'How ya gonna keep em down on the farm once they have seen Paree'?

As they left Nadi in 1961 most of the young men probably thought that they would return to their home towns and villages on completion of their enlistment periods. They were ill prepared for what lay ahead, the opportunities they would have and the obligations that marriage and children born and raised abroad would place on them.

That said, most coped very well in the first year or two, apart from one who could not stand the cold and a couple of others were discharged

---

49 Teaiwa, Teresia: *What Makes Fiji Women Soldiers? Context, Context, Context. Intersections: Gender and Sexuality in Asia and the Pacific,* Issue 37, March 2015.

for previously undiagnosed deafness or epilepsy. Kit Lalakomacoi, a fine sportsman, died in 1965 of deep vein thrombosis. A couple of others could not cope with their introduction to heavy social drinking and were eased out with dishonourable discharges for serial offences. Several more admitted in the autumn of their lives that they regretted not making more of the opportunity the army provided, whether they returned to Fiji or not. The statistics on these losses are largely anecdotal, but it appears that eighteen or nineteen of the men were lost for these reasons or because of accidental death (three of the latter on duty) inside the first six years. A total of fifty-seven men served for the minimum six years or less.

A British tabloid newspaper enquired into the cost of recruiting the '212' at the time of their arrival and was told it was 'secret'. It appears to remain so, or the arithmetic is lost in the War Office files of the time, and while Major Worsley's report on the recruitment activities in Fiji does not address this aspect, it was clearly not a cheap exercise and certainly much more expensive than recruiting in Britain.

Many of the COs who had initial responsibility for the basic training of the Fijians, or were the commanders of their first regiments, probably read Major Worsley's recommendations for care in the initial handling of these recruits. Worsley advised that the newly-arrived '212' would benefit from consideration of their very different backgrounds, compared to those of the army's usual recruits and those from other colonies. Appendix K refers.

With the passage of time it has not been possible to determine exactly how many of the '212' men, like Mike Yasa and David Lelo, were happy to have served the minimal enlistment of six years and return to Fiji. But one such who shared that intention was Watisoni Rogose, who killed time at the Union Jack club after being discharged and was seduced into spending a long week-end at Rochdale watching the rugby. There he met and married Freda, and there he remains a half century later.

Regardless of whether they met their wives back in Fiji on DOMCOL, in the WRAC, in towns near where they were posted in the UK, or other countries;

the longer the men served, and with the arrival of children in most cases, the more pressure of various kinds developed to persuade them to stay in the UK or settle in their wives' homelands. In most cases, the singular attractions were educational and employment opportunities for their children. It did not help that by 1983 these opportunities in Fiji still remained nearly as sparse as they had been in 1961. Many, particularly those without chiefly connections, resented the fact that Fiji's culture was stuck in a colonial time warp and what really mattered was 'not what you know, but who you know'. To be fair, it is unrealistic to expect that much of Fiji's culture, or that of any other developing country, would change significantly in a little over two decades. Many organisations in the developed world struggle with significant cultural change in such a short time frame.

A common denominator in both situations is probably a lack of effective leadership. Conversely, Singapore's Lee Kwan Yew proved the point.

Rabuka's coups delivered a seismic cultural shock in 1987. His leadership and that of one of his successors as RFMF commander, Commodore Frank Bainimarama, eventually changed the political and cultural landscape. Change was certainly necessary, but it is difficult to recognise the net benefit across the country and whether the apparent positive elements, in terms of nation-building, will be sustained in the long term against the negative elements of entrenched political autocracy, supine judiciary and now-timid media of contemporary Fiji.

Rabuka's 'bloodless' coups may not have directly resulted in deaths, but they certainly resulted in some arrogant and brutal behaviour by the RFMF as it assumed responsibility for maintaining law and order. The later chapters of Grahame Southwick's autobiography, *Hard Day at the Office*, published in 2011, include a sobering first-hand account of some of the side-effects of Rabuka's coups. Southwick was arrested, assaulted and detained by the army based on unsubstantiated claims that he had fraudulently used Japanese fishing equipment provided in an aid program in one of his tuna fishing ventures[50]. Elements of the RFMF have behaved in a similarly arbitrary and brutal fashion with their later interventions in 2000, 2006 and subsequently.

---

50 Southwick pps. 247-250.

In a letter of 29 May 1987 to Sir William Heseltine, Sir Len Usher observed:

> We still have too much military rule and Ratu Penaia's major problem is to pour Rabuka, and particularly his soldiers who have become arrogant, back into the bottle.[51]

Southwick also describes some of the disastrous lending excesses of the National Bank of Fiji, and the greed and corruption which damaged Fiji's tuna fisheries during Rabuka's subsequent tenure as an elected Prime Minister from 1992-99. John Murray, who served as the Australian Federal Police's South Pacific Liaison Officer throughout the period of Rabuka's and subsequent coups, has described at length the erosion of law enforcement in Fiji after 1987 and the resulting inroads made by serious criminal groups[52].

However honourable his intentions in 1987, and regardless of his record as Prime Minister, Rabuka's tenure in government was eclipsed by the criminal farce that George Speight foisted on the country in 2000 following the election of another FLP government and its first Fiji Indian PM, Mahendra Chaudhry, in 1999. Speight, of Fijian and European descent, has been described as a 'failed businessman' who appeared to have spent much of his life in the US and Australia but he utilised the Fijian part of his DNA for political purposes. The muscle for Speight's coup came from the RFMF's Counter Revolutionary Warfare (CRW) unit, established by Hoss Ligairi who was recalled from retirement to maintain discipline among the RFMF soldiers who supported Speight. Most indigenous Fijians at the time would have had concerns about any PM of Indian descent, but the new PM Mahendra Chaudhry attracted more suspicion than others of his background. Chaudhry had built his political career in Fiji's trade union movement, and as an advocate for the Indian cane farmers who dominated Fiji's sugar production. Chaudhry made no secret of his determination to address the controversial Agricultural and Landlord Tenants Act (ALTA) under which Fijian land was leased to Indian or other cane farmers.

---

51 *Letters from Fiji 1987-1990* p. 28.

52 *The Minnows of Triton* pps. 7-28.

The failure of Chaudhry's predecessors to review ALTA was the cause of increasing anxiety among the cane farmers, as the expiry date approached for their 99-year leases, the first of which expired in 1997. At the level of the Fijian villagers, from whom the land had been leased, there was an expectation that their land would revert to their control with the opportunity of increased rentals.

Cane farming, however, is a precarious industry in Fiji. It is subject to the vagaries of capricious, sometimes extreme, weather in some years and the profit margins for small leases can often be minimal. In the absence of certainty over their leases, many farmers simply walked off their land, abandoning homes and other improvements to seek employment elsewhere. The continuing failure of successive governments to resolve this issue has led to significant urban drift, unemployment or under-employment and the growth of slum 'squatter settlement' areas around Suva and the larger towns.

Chaudhry's arrogant style of government fuelled hostility against him, but the precise origins of Speight's attempt to overthrow the government will probably never be known. Speight, supported by armed CRW soldiers, held Chaudhry and his ministers hostage for nearly eight weeks while the police commissioner, Isikia Savua, a former soldier appointed by Rabuka, sat on the sidelines or colluded with Speight. The situation was eventually resolved, but not to the satisfaction of the CRW soldiers, who mutinied against Bainimarama later in the year when he narrowly escaped with his life. The limits of Savua's competence were all too obvious during the Speight coup, and the following year, during his interference in the investigation into the murder of John Scott and Greg Scrivener[53]. Two years later in 2003, Savua was replaced as Fiji Police Commissioner by Andrew Hughes, an experienced Australian police officer. Savua was then appointed Fiji's Ambassador to the United Nations.

Hoss Ligairi was closely involved with the CRW men holding the hostages and was filmed and interviewed by journalists to whom he expressed

---

53 Described in Owen Scott's *Deep Beyond the Reef.*

his view that the matter would be resolved 'in the Fijian way', which it was, eventually. Hoss retains his usual reticence when queried on his role and will not be drawn much beyond insisting that he had nothing to do with initiating the coup.

Talking about his eventual prison sentence, Hoss observed that 'Indian lawyers are much better than Fijian lawyers', referring to his prosecution and sentencing. Many Fijians credit Hoss's maintenance of discipline among the CRW soldiers during the hostage crisis as more deserving of a medal than a prison sentence.

Bainimarama declared martial law for a period after opposition to his coup was quashed. However, the CRW mutiny left fifteen soldiers dead, four of whom had been removed from police custody by an RFMF detachment on orders 'from the barracks' and later beaten to death at Queen Elizabeth Barracks. No one has ever been charged with these deaths, and a subsequent attempt by then Police Commissioner Hughes to pursue the matter was curtailed when Bainimarama forced Hughes to resign in 2006. Hoss Ligairi might reasonably be expected to have 'strong views' (in diplomatic parlance) on this matter but keeps his counsel. Ligairi learned, however, that prior to Bainimarama's official opening of a new RBL headquarters building in Suva in mid-November 2014, orders were issued in Suva seeking confirmation that Hoss was not in Suva, but was quietly engaged on village business in Savusavu. One must assume that Hoss remains a 'person of interest' in retirement.

Given these developments, it is interesting to reflect on submissions to the multiracial committee appointed by the late Ratu Mara as interim PM in 1990 to review Fiji's 1970 Constitution. Rabuka and other senior RFMF officers argued that Fiji's stability would best be served by an interim military government for the next fifteen years!

Saiasi Baleimatuku decided to return to Fiji in 1983 because he had not been back for sixteen years and his wife Julia, born in Belize where he met her, had never been there. His main concern: 'I wanted my (three) children who were born overseas to know where their father is from and understand the family roots'. They stayed sixteen years with Saiasi working as a senior manager in companies controlled by Jim Ah Koy, a Sino-Fijian businessman who had close links to the former PM Ratu Mara and the eventually-elected PM Rabuka. Saiasi played golf with Rabuka and worshipped at the same Baptist church as Ah Koy who was knighted in 2006 on the recommendation of then Prime Minister of Papua New Guinea, Sir Michael Somare. These connections probably identified Saiasi to many observers as privy to the machinations of *taukei* politics in 1987 and later.

In 1999-2000 however, Saiasi found that Fiji's politics had 'become tribal' and he felt his family would be better off back in England. By that time his daughter Saadia and second son Elgin had already left for England and Saadia had joined the army.

Throughout 2006, Bainimarama threatened the elected government of the day with RFMF intervention if a couple of its more controversial proposals were pursued, including amnesty for those who plotted or supported the Speight coup. Bainimarama eventually removed the Qarase government from office citing manifold instances of corruption and incompetence, for which there was some evidence. Predictably, those countries with the longest ties to Fiji cried 'foul' again with as little effect as they had with Rabuka's coups. In the years that followed, Bainimarama expelled, and refused to accept replacements for, the Australian and New Zealand High Commissioners. He was impervious to criticism from the US, Britain and the EEC, all of which had long supported Fiji's ailing sugar industry. Instead PM Bainimarama pursued a new 'Look North' foreign policy, seeking 'new friends', most notably China and Russia but also, in the margins of his attendance at the UN General Assembly in September 2013, with Iran, Ukraine, Georgia and the Emirate of Ajman.

None of the latter countries have any history of a significant bilateral relationship with Fiji or any other Pacific island country. Memoranda of Understanding signed with Russia included support for counter terrorism, military support to RFMF peace keeping operations, and for the conduct of elections. In April 2014, China also agreed to assist with the conduct of elections later that year. It is arguable that China and Russia were hardly the best countries for the provision of assistance with running free and fair elections.

Over the years that followed, Bainimarama's government by decree (supported by a complaint judiciary partially recruited outside Fiji) attracted a measure of domestic support. When his 'Fiji First' political party eventually faced the electorate in September 2014, it attracted strong support across Fiji's racial divide. But Bainimarama's strongest opposition, then and now, comes from traditional Fijian interests. A multi-national observer group declared the election fair and a reflection of voter preferences—despite Opposition claims about the electoral advantages Fiji First accrued through government-imposed restrictions on press freedom and on the nomination of opposition candidates, amongst other issues.

Two casualties of Fiji's successive coups have been the leadership and influence of the senior chiefs and of the Methodist church.

The RFMF's reputation as a competent military force, trained, led and equipped along British Commonwealth lines, facilitated its selection as a provider of UN peace keeping forces for the first time in 1978. At that time, one of the first trials faced by another generation of Fijians serving abroad was the absence of their staple root vegetable, *dalo*, a large yam, without which expatriate Fijians can be miserable at meal times. The Regimental Medical Officer, Captain Guy Hawley, an ophthalmologist, solved the problem. Guy negotiated permission from Palestine Liberation Organisation (PLO) representatives for him to drive his UN Land Rover ambulance and quarter-ton trailer to pass through a succession of PLO road blocks to Tyre, where he purchased as much *dalo* as he could load to sustain his warriors. The *dalo* was sourced from the Ivory Coast.

Since then, successive Prime Ministers of Fiji have worked hard to secure peace-keeping responsibilities for units and individual staff officers in Sinai, Afghanistan and elsewhere. Detachments of Fiji Police Officers were rotated through tours of duty in Namibia in the nineties. These deployments were welcomed by individuals for the income paid in tax free USD, which allowed a soldier living in a village to save enough money to build a modest house after a twelve month tour of duty. In addition to UN service, many young Fijian men followed the '212' to seek careers in the British Army. The British became cautious about recruiting Fijians after 1987 and there were embargoes from time to time, as HMG tried more coercive methods of persuading coup leaders to respect Westminster traditions of government. There was a peak in the acceptance of Fijian volunteers in 1999 and currently there are more than 1300 Fijians serving with the British Army.

Since the last of the '212' discharged from the British Army, many of Fiji's soldiers who subsequently served with the RFMF, British or other armed forces have followed the example of those '212' who served with 22 SAS, securing employment with private security companies that have needed contracted staff for assorted protective security duties in Iraq, Afghanistan, Bosnia and other trouble-spots. The Olive Group recruited Fijians for security work in Iraq with mixed success (one manifestly overweight and unfit recruit died of a heart attack), and in June 2013 one media report claimed 38 former RFMF personnel with peace-keeping experience were working as security contractors in the UAE with the G4S company. Fijian Solutions Group International (FSGI) claims to be an 'international security risk management company' based in Los Angeles, California. The FSGI website noted in 2014 that the company was:

> ...established in late 2012, by an all Fijian team of military veterans from the U.S. Army, U.S. Marine Corps, Republic of Fiji Military Forces (RFMF), the British Armed Forces and French Foreign Legion. FSGI provides a wide range of personal protective security services consultation, training and manpower staffing solutions to international corporate customers doing business in high-risk environments. Other services include customised training in crisis management, kidnap and ransom negotiation, investigative services, maritime security, international peace-keeping civilian contractor support.

Although FSGI does not claim special forces expertise, the above claims imply such and it certainly lacks any input from anyone who served with 22 SAS.

An idle enquiry to Jim Vakatalai late in 2015 asked how many Fijians had passed selection for 22 SAS since the seven '212' and two of their sons still serving with the Regiment at that time. The answer was 'only one' in the last half century and relatively recently! Jim explained that many who attempt selection seek his advice and he notes that while most of them have the physical fitness, they lack the requisite mental toughness. Something else is at work, however, when the thousands of Fijians who have followed the '212' into the British Army could not come close to their forerunners' collective performance.

It seems unlikely that 22 SAS have raised the bar on their selection procedures to such a degree that it precludes many more Fijians joining the Regiment.

The main reason why so many expatriate Fijians are now earning their income abroad is that the repatriated proportion of their incomes (a prospect that first attracted many '212' to enlist) is now Fiji's second biggest source of foreign exchange after tourism. Twenty years ago, sugar and gold exports held these distinctions. A significant proportion of current remittances must come from the tens of thousands of Girmitiya descendants, alienated by successive RFMF interventions and supporting aged parents or others who were not allowed to emigrate with them to Australia, New Zealand, Canada or elsewhere. But a growing proportion of this income must come from expatriate RFMF or former RFMF staff representing Fiji around the world.

Service in the British Army, and marriage to a British citizen, no longer guarantee indefinite right of abode in the UK, as enjoyed by many of the '212' who sought it. Isimeli Baleiwai, who served thirteen years in the army, including service in Bosnia and Afghanistan, had an army court martial conviction for fighting another soldier which later hampered or blocked his application for British citizenship. He was judged unfit for continued residency in the UK, despite his marriage to a British citizen.

The current generation of expatriate Fijians serving in the British Army (excluding the sons of the '212' and others who followed in the sixties, seventies and eighties) seem to lack the 'code of conduct' of the older generation. The '212' were not saints, and several paid for their repeated unacceptable behaviour with dishonourable discharges. The journalist who noted 'a lack of good conduct medals' at the Dortmund parade (Chapter 5) exaggerated somewhat as those on parade that day were soldiers any army would have been proud to claim. Allowing for the 'this generation is not a patch on ours' syndrome, this study has revealed many disturbing accounts of unacceptable behaviour at social functions by young Fijians in the British Army since the Falklands campaign—behaviour of a kind that would have been unthinkable and inexcusable among the '212,' who were educated in a different era.

Joe Tuwai retired in 1997, but in his last years of service and since has received many telephone calls from COs who served as Subalterns with him in his later years as a Colour Sergeant, seeking advice on how to best deal with fractious young Fijians. Joe is no admirer of military intervention in Fiji's politics, and has a thesis that the RFMF's 'coup mentality' has resulted in younger Fijians accepting the model moulded by Rabuka, in the first instance, that 'one does what one feels is right' because everything will be exorcised by a decree forgiving any apparent transgression, not least potential charges of mutiny or treason. Joe may exaggerate his appreciation (as, one may argue, Rabuka did in 1987) but if he is anywhere close to the truth Fiji's current and future leaders, and the wider electorate, have a problem to address.

CHAPTER 9:
END NOTES

Many of the '212's lives, second careers and eventual choices of final settlement changed because of the 1987 coups and subsequent developments. Some who were bitterly disappointed by 'the events of 1987' emigrated to Australia or New Zealand or went back to the UK. A few like Jim Masuwale or Jioji Areki returned years later. Others who had been long-term residents of the UK eventually returned to a warmer climate. Of the five who had remained with 22 SAS, only Hoss Ligairi returned to Fiji shortly after his discharge. The remainder stayed in Hereford or elsewhere in the UK, finding ready employment in assorted security capacities, either with their own companies or as sub-contractors. It was lucrative work, but sometimes hazardous. Fred Marafono and Sek Takavesi found themselves on 'two-way ranges' in their sixties in Sierra Leone and Iraq, respectively.

Azam Ali and his wife, from Tavua, returned to Fiji after his 24 years in the army but the ill health of their young children, aged three and two at the time, forced them to return to the UK. The children did not respond to treatment for conditions caused by flies and mosquitoes. He was disinclined to stay because Ratu Mara and others still classified him as 'Indian' rather than 'Fijian'.

In 1980 **Sam and Muriel Tamata** moved to Australia and Sam was the Free Church of Scotland Minister at Taree, New South Wales, until 1983. He spent 1983-85 effectively as a missionary in Suva, attempting to establish the FCS in Fiji. From 1986-92 Sam ministered to a parish in Lochinver on the west coast of Scotland, followed by transfer to a parish at Strathpeffer near Inverness from 1992-98.

On a subsequent visit to Kadavu, Sam was amazed to recognise a former Caledonian McBrayne ferry, with the company name painted over, that had been recycled as an inter-island ferry in Fiji.

In 1998 Sam returned to Australia to a FCS ministry in Raymond Terrace, Newcastle. He has visited Fiji twice in more recent years, including for his sister's funeral. Sam and Muriel have four children. A son is in Glasgow, a daughter serves with the NSW Police, and their younger daughter taught English in China before returning to Australia. Their second son Tevita lives

Sam Tamata accepting his certificate of Australian citizenship from Cr Glenys Francis, Acting Mayor of Port Stephens, June, 2002. Photo: Sam Tamata

nearby in Newcastle, and Sam's brother Willie Tamata moved to Sydney in 1994. A cousin, Laitia Tamata, was a legal adviser to Laisenia Qarase and has been denied employment in the Fiji government because of this and his human rights activism.

Sam became an Australian citizen in 2002 and later retired from full-time parish responsibilities but did occasional locum relief work for the FCS in NSW until major surgery slowed him down in late 2015.

———————†———————

Jale Vuiyasawa needed no exhortation from his Prime Minister to return to Fiji and use his skills and experience at home. He found employment as the personnel manager at the Emperor Gold Mine (EGM) at Vatukoula in 1985.

In February 1991 however, a strike by the miners turned ugly and the South African general manager[54] of the mine asked Jale to raise a locally-recruited guard force for the mine to assist with controlling future unrest. This proved more complicated than might be imagined, as only four of the 132 local volunteers keen for 'security' employment spoke anything other than the local dialect. Other than the four who had some service with the RFMF, none spoke English, Hindi or even the Bauan dialect which Ratu Sukuna popularised through insistence decades earlier, forming the basis of the commonly understood 'Fijian' language. Jale eventually whittled his security force down to eighty.

As the strike became protracted, with unrest from hundreds of miners who were sacked, the mine manager provided transport for Fiji Police Force assistance[55] and contacted a specialist security firm who sent a

---

54 EGM was originally Australian-owned and had some colourful and influential director/ shareholders in the decades after its initial development in 1933, including newspaper magnate Sir Frank Packer, boxing promoter John Wren and former Queensland Premier E.G. Theodore. It is now owned and managed by PRC interests and has never been a model of 'best practice' in industrial relations.

55 Fiji Police Force mobility became increasingly limited after the Australian government cancelled $200,00 worth of new vehicles following the May 1987 coup.

couple of Singapore-based staff with 22 SAS experience to advise Jale. Jale recognised the advisers as having served with him on one of his tours in Northern Ireland and established a good rapport with them, but the mine owners preferred his low-cost solution to the expensive security fence, watch towers and patrolling guard dogs recommended by the consultants. Jale's employment at the mine on expatriate conditions was resented by many other Fijians working there who labelled him *kaivalagi loaloa*, literally a 'black Englishman', which he weathered. He stayed with the mine until he retired at age 55 but in 1999 he returned to the UK to watch the World Cup rugby and stayed for three years working for a security company in Manchester before returning to Fiji.

———— ✝ ————

Bill Vodo's early life, his twenty-two years in the RA, and the immediate years that followed are summarised in Appendix B. His lifestyle in the army and afterwards contributed to a couple of health scares in 1996-97 and Bill became a 'born-again' Christian, abandoning his life-long association with the Methodist Church for the Assemblies of God (AOG). Bill volunteers that he 'thought he knew God' prior to his health scare.

At the time Bill was significantly overweight at 120 kg, smoked forty cigarettes a day and was partial to a few drinks with friends and sessions around the *kava* bowl with other Fijians. He recalls offering a prayer from his hospital bed along the lines of 'Lord, if you want to use me, take these cravings from me and I will be your voice on earth'. Bill's prayer was answered, and he found the strength to master his cravings and eventually reduce his weight to 93kg.

In 1998 Bill first preached for the AOG, and the following year he was ordained as a pastor of the church. He preached in Hawaii on his sixtieth birthday in 2003. In 2004 Bill was ordained as a Pastor in the Church of God, another Pentecostal church.

Two of Bill's favourite passages in the Bible are Matthew 11.28 and Matthew 28.18-20. In recent years the Church of God has sent him to preach in several countries, including Israel and Patmos in Greece. He notes he is a very different man to the one who left Fiji in 1961, and wants to be remembered 'as a man who never knew God but became a man of God'. This is a man clearly devoted to his new vocation.

———†———

After many years in New Zealand and the UK, **David and Wendy Lelo** accepted an appointment in 1998, intended to be for eighteen months, teaching genealogy in New Zealand and throughout the Pacific. They enjoyed the work and the appointment took them back to Fiji every six months for the ten years it eventually lasted, taking them to a total of sixty-five centres in New Zealand, Fiji, the Cook Islands and Tahiti.

———†———

Panipasa (aka Joe) Luva retired after seventeen years in the RAC, and on the understanding that there were few opportunities back in Fiji migrated to Melbourne initially with Australian wife Liz. Fiji beckoned, however, when Joe retired in 1998. Joe and Liz leased land in Deuba/Pacific Harbour and built a cottage on the beach overlooking the nearby island of Beqa. Joe loved the idyllic life there where he could fish and 'be out of the rat race'. Joe was plagued by serious health issues in his last years and died of a heart attack back in Brisbane in 2013.

———†———

After leaving the army in 1978 **Jone Tuisovuna** worked as a fitter/machinist and as a Youth and Community worker. Jone met his second wife, Andrea, at a function at the Fiji High Commission to celebrate ten years of independence in 1980. In 2008 Jone and Andrea returned to Fiji and retirement at Pacific Harbour.

———†———

Kim and Barbara Yabaki spent most of their married life in England, but returned to Fiji in 2000 to build and manage a resort in his home village of Tiliva on Kadavu. They achieved their aim and the 4-5 star rated resort provided employment training and lease money to the village before they sold it to a foreign buyer in 2014 when they returned to live in England for health care that was unavailable in Fiji.

———— ✝ ————

In 1992 **Dr Fred Dewa** was elected an MP for the Naitasiri Fijian electorate, in Josefa Kamikamica's party which was a forerunner of the National Alliance Party. Fred served for five years, including as parliamentary leader of the party after Kamikamica lost his seat. In retirement Fred founded and was a director of the Vutikalulu Centre for Sustainable Technology and Development—a Charitable Trust managed by Fred and wife Julie on village land, experimenting with permaculture and aiming at sustainable development.

———— ✝ ————

Back in Savusavu in retirement, **Ben (aka Peni Levaci) and Barbara Temo** are active in encouraging animal welfare, including the de-sexing of stray dogs in the absence of an SPCA organisation. As '*Kuku*' (grandfather in the local dialect) Ben is also in demand as a 'man of the world' to assist local school teachers with sex education in schools, as this remains a subject rarely discussed in rural Fijian households. The resulting ignorance contributes to a high rate of unwanted pregnancies. Girls often seek help at the local hospital for concerns about their menstrual cycle not discussed with mothers, and boys have little idea of how to use condoms. Ben used a carrot to explain how to apply a condom in one class where the first question was 'Sir, what do we do if we do not have a carrot'? When Ben used his thumb to roll on a condom in another class a boy asked: 'So we are safe if the condom is on our thumb, eh?' Ben despairs of a society in which boys and men watch pornographic movies, but are embarrassed by any suggestion that girls and women might enjoy such films.

———— ✝ ————

Keith Zoing stayed with R Signals until 1985 and spent the next six years as a Foreman of Signals for the Sultan's Armed Forces in Oman, and later with Siemens Plessey in Singapore.

In January 1991 Keith returned to Fiji to manage Nukubati resort near Labasa for relatives, until a kidney ailment forced his return to the UK in 1996 where he and Mary had restored a farm house outside Harrogate. Keith died in 1999, but his son now lives in the house and Mary lives in the converted barn on the property.

———✝———

Mike Yasa was sustained by his faith after 1987, when he continued to preach to Fijian and English-speaking Methodist congregations in and around Auckland. In 1989 he was persuaded to join the Methodist ministry by Reverend Stan Andrews, who had served in Fiji and spoke the language.

Mike enrolled in St John's Trinity Theological College, was ordained in 1990 and was posted as minister to St Andrew's Uniting Parish at Motueka on

Rev Mike Yasa with wife Sereana and son Tevita outside his first ministry, St Andrew's Uniting Parish, Motueka, New Zealand, 1990. Photo Mike Yasa

New Zealand's South Island. In 1995 he transferred to St Stephen's Methodist Church in Christchurch, before another move to a rural parish near Palmerston North in 2000. Mike retired from full-time parish responsibilities in 2003 but was subsequently appointed chaplain of Suva Grammar School for 2004-5. Mike and Sereana settled in Pukohohe outside Auckland to enjoy their grandchildren, but he continued to preach to Fijian congregations for another decade.

In July 2005 Michael Tillotson wrote the authorised biography of Field Marshall The Lord Bramall. One of Mike's most treasured possessions is the copy he received from the former 2IC, later CO, 2RGJ inscribed:

> 'To my good friend Mike Yasa, may you continue to do God's work in a Rifleman-like manner' and signed Dwin Bramall, FM, July 2005

APPENDICES

Each soldier's career, to the extent that it could be determined from individuals, their colleagues or surviving relatives, is summarised hereunder within the first of the regiments in which they served.

Appendix A: Ironsides Cavalry and Armour

Most of the 200 men had little idea of what army service really involved, beyond what they had been told by members of the recruiting team which did not have a representative of an armoured unit. A few, however, were clear that a 'third class ride (in a tank or a truck) is better than a first class walk' in the infantry. One such was John Riley, a twenty-two-year-old who wanted to serve in an armoured unit and drive a tank. He was disappointed to be allocated to Royal Signals in the first instance. John and others may have been influenced by the post-WWII films made in Hollywood or Pinewood Studios, showing advancing infantry protected by tanks in the days before Apache helicopters, drones and laser guided weapons made riding in a tank less appealing. Many would have seen Audie Murphy playing himself in *To Hell and Back* in 1955. None would have been aware at the time of Murphy's later struggles with PTSD.

4/7 Royal Dragoon Guards

The regiment's website lists deployments throughout the years of '212' service, with regular rotations between England and Germany. Two squadrons were deployed to Aden in 1965 and a squadron to Cyprus in 1966 as part of the UN forces. There was also a two-year tour in Omagh in Northern Ireland, from 1966 to 1968, following which the regiment returned to rotation between the UK and Germany.

Centurion tanks of the Royal Scots Greys, Sek Kong in Hong Kong's New Territories, 1963. Photo:Bob Dass

Isireli Vakacegu BUADROMO

Isireli was born in the chiefly village of Lomaloma, Vanuabalavu, like Sek Takavesi and former Prime Minister Laisenia Qarase. He was the eleventh of thirteen children. Apete Sokovaqone married his sister and Isireli considers Takavesi a 'cousin'.

His father was a Methodist minister. A Methodist minister uncle was chaplain to the Fiji detachment that attended the WWII Victory Parade in London. An older brother served in Malaya and was later CO 3FIR.

When the recruiting team appeared in Suva, Isireli was a final year apprentice with two months left to qualify but decided there was no future in Fiji. He served twenty-two years in the 4/7 RDG, discharged as a WO2 and was known as Sam or Vak.

He trained at Catterick and was posted to BAOR, Munster, in 1962 with subsequent service in Aden (1965-66), Sharja, Northern Ireland, Cyprus (UN), Germany, Catterick again and Tidworth. He became a driving instructor for tanks and armoured vehicles.

Isireli's wife is from Kabara and her mother from Beqa. They married in 1977 when she was a qualified nurse. He was not persuaded to return to Fiji by Ratu Mara's speech at Dortmund. His eldest son was born in the UK and his four other children were born in Germany.

Isireli has no regrets about his army experience, and after being discharged he worked in the engineering department of a large nursery near Hereford maintaining machinery, later doing similar work for a poultry farm. In retirement he plays golf twice each week.

Josefa MANAWALALA

Joe was from Somosomo, Taveuni and attended Wairiki Primary School and St John's College Cawaci. He was working on his father's farm when the recruitment team arrived in Savusavu. He felt a 'traditional commitment' to serve in the army and such service appealed to his sense of adventure.

Joe served with 4/7 RDG in Germany, Cyprus, Canada and the Middle East for sixteen years, qualifying as a driving instructor on armoured vehicles.

He married Linieta when he returned to Fiji, working for the Public Works Department, initially as a supervisor at the Vaturu dam and later as an accident investigator until 1998 when he became a driving examiner for the Land Transport Authority. Joe and Linieta's son, Charles, joined the British Army in 2001. Joe died in November 2002, after a long illness.

Josaia USUMAKI

Joe was another finishing school when the recruiting team arrived, and subsequently served fifteen years before settling in London. He married twice, first to a British woman and then to a former nurse who had been the first wife of Dr Timoci Bavadra, a medical practitioner who won the 1987 election for the Fiji Labour Party/National Federation Party coalition.

Joe is a quiet fellow who keeps his own counsel and is naturally disinclined to discuss his life. He was remembered fondly in 1993 by his former troop Corporal in the RDG, G. A. Ellis, who saw an item in the regimental journal about this project and recalled Joe as the wireless operator/gunner in his tank. Ellis served with Joe in Aden, remembering him as a good sportsman who was very sceptical of tinned apple pie when he encountered it on his first exercise with the 4/7.

Joe worked as an electrician/maintenance officer after leaving the army.

The Queen's Own Hussars

Panipasa LUVA

Panipasa was born on Ono-i-Lau, educated at LMS and in 1961 was working as a clerk in Suva with (the then-named) Burns, Philp and Company Ltd, an Australian company active in shipping, merchandising and the copra trade throughout the Pacific. While Panipasa had no relatives with military experience in WWII or Malaya, the idea of military service had more appeal than clerking for 'BPs' (Burns Philp & Co, otherwise nicknamed 'Bloody Pirates' by older generations of Fijians) and he was attracted to the idea of serving in the RAC.

Panipasa became 'Joe' during his seventeen years in the QOH as a tank Commander and gunnery instructor, serving in Aden, Hong Kong, Malaysia, Denmark, Belfast and Germany. He met his wife Elizabeth, a former missionary's daughter, when he was on DOMCOL and she was on holiday in Fiji in 1966 after completing her studies in early childhood education with Adi Davila Uluilakeba, youngest sister of the future PM of Fiji. They corresponded and then married, celebrating with two wedding ceremonies, one in Johore Bahru and the other in Singapore in February 1969. Liz subsequently found employment in early childhood education during Joe's QOH postings in Singapore and Germany.

Joe served in a different squadron to Joe Tuwai, and after accepting redundancy in 1977 he visited Fiji to assess opportunities, subsequently advising his friend Joe that there were very few. Australia offered more for Joe and Liz Luva and their two young children. They first settled in Melbourne, before moving to Brisbane where Joe worked as a supervisor and transport manager for the Amcor Ltd paper mill and packaging business. He had no further military service but was tempted to offer his services again during the Falklands conflict in 1982. Thirty years later, Liz recalled that Joe never had any regrets about his decision to join the army and his years of service were the happiest of his life.

Liz Luva's father Arthur Pocklington was a missionary with the China Inland Mission on the border with Tibet prior to WWII, and her mother had worked in Ethiopia as a nurse. Apples do not fall far from the tree, and Liz's daughter Salote studied theology for her second degree and her son Daniel did volunteer work with a missionary group in Africa before resuming his career as a maths and physics teacher. The link to Fiji continued with Salote's marriage to Ilivasi Tamanivalu, one of Fiji's more celebrated rugby players who was a member of Australia's Wallabies as well as playing in Japanese and Fijian teams. Ilivasi, usually known as Ilivasi Tabua in the rugby world, had the nickname 'The Human Skewer' in his days as a flanker with the Wallabies in the early to mid-1990s.

Naibuka QARAU

Naibuka Qarau transferred to the QOH after nine years with DERR, during which he injured an ankle so badly that it interfered with foot-soldiering. When he transferred, there were seven other '212' in the QOH including his brother in law, Levani Tamani. His service with DERR is covered in Appendix E and he appeared in Chapter Five.

Levani TAMANIKAIRUKURUKUIOVALAU

Lepani Tamani, as he was known in later life –not surprisingly due to the length of his name–was one of the three oldest '212' and almost certainly lied about his age to be accepted. He enlisted as Levani T. Kairukurukuiovalau, which was probably as complicated as the recruiting team could master in 1961 but his full name was as shown above. A family name of 24 characters was beyond the capabilities of computing systems used by the army in those days, which refused to recognise and service the name. By 1983 the army systems had accommodated Sgt L. Tamanikairukuru, which was how he paraded at Dortmund. The literal meaning of his full name is 'father of the Rukuruku people who lived in Ovalau' and refers to his family origins on Ovalau.

Lepani's first military service was with the Fiji Royal Naval Volunteer Reserve (FRNVR), in which capacity he was part of a detachment that visited

Christmas Island (today's Kiribati, the 'Gilbert' half of the former Gilbert and Ellis Islands) in the wake of Britain's nuclear tests there (Operation Grapple). Those familiar with the testing of nuclear devices on Christmas Island comment on the high number of those who visited the island who later died of various cancers, including Lepani, and Fiji's former Governor General and later President, Ratu Sir Penaia Ganilau. The FRNVR was disbanded in 1959 and when he joined the army Lepani was apparently unemployed, according to the *Fiji Times*.

Lepani also misrepresented himself to the recruiting officers as a single man and was not the only one to do so. He was almost certainly married when he enlisted and brought his wife, Kalera, and at least the first of their four children, to England in his first couple of years' service, according to some in his cohort.

Lepani served twenty-two years with the 10th Hussars and the QOH, and was known to his comrades as Tom Tamani. He returned to Suva following his discharge in 1983, settling in Samabula, Suva. He was one of the directors of the ill-fated Bolatagane Motors venture and finished his working life in a security capacity with the Reserve Bank of Fiji. Asiveni Lutumailagi advised in June 1993 Lepani had died. Lepani/Tom was recalled fondly in 2018 by Joe Tuwai as 'a great Hussar'.

Josaia TUWAI Lausiki

Joe was born in the Waiyevo hospital, near Somosomo, Taveuni in 1942, the eldest of three sons. His father was a school teacher and Joe's early education was spread across several schools as his father was posted around Fiji. Joe's father was from Somosomo and his mother from Nakobo near Buca Bay on Vanua Levu. Joe notes with a wry smile that he is closely related, in Fijian terms, to 1987 coup leader Sitiveni Rabuka because of the proximity of Rabuka's village, Drekeniwai, to Nakobo. A younger brother, Emitai Boladuadua, has had a distinguished career in Fiji's civil service, including as Fiji's High Commissioner in London.

Joe's father, who began his career as a technical teacher, first taught at the Saweni school for boys before it became Adi Cakobau school for girls.

Historian and educator R. A. Derrick, a revered figure in early 20th century Fiji, taught Joe's father at the Davuilevu Mission School which later became Lelean Memorial School or LMS, alma mater to many of the '212'. Derrick (1892-1960) was the author of the definitive 20th century Fiji history *A History of Fiji.*

Joe's first school was the Nakobo village school and his first teacher was Kolinio Rabuka, father of the future coup leader. From 1954-57 Joe attended Niusawa Mission School before moving to LMS, DAV College and finally the Sangam School in Suva.

While none of Joe's family served in WWII, or in Malaya, the army offered an opportunity for well-paid employment and a chance to see the world. Together with several mates he indicated a preference for an armoured corps unit as 'something different' and more exotic than being in the PBI or 'poor bloody infantry'. Joe got his wish and joined the QOH together with Joe Luva and Tom Tamani. Six others joined the 10th Hussars and 65th Lancers. Joe became an instructor in small arms and tank gunnery, the latter on Centurion and later Chieftain tanks. He saw operational service with the Centurions in Aden and helped cover the humiliating withdrawal of the last British forces from the former coaling station, using Saracen and Saladin armoured cars as the troops boarded HMS *Fearless.*

Joe's other operational service was in Northern Ireland where he was on patrol at 5 am when advised by radio that his wife had given birth to their elder son in the British Military Hospital, Hanover. An animated exchange took place before Joe learned the gender of his first child.

Joe served until 1997 as a S/Sgt on the Long Service List (LSL) and 'Extra Regimentally Employed' (ERE). When he finally left the army as its longest continually serving '212' and hung up his spurs, he found a niche for himself with the Cambridgeshire County Council as administrator of the Hollywell (CE) Primary School in the village of Needingworth. He was required to be on duty for only 37 hours per week, but the old ways stayed with him and he liked to be the first on duty to open the school and the last to leave.

Joe saw his long hours, that might have been paid as overtime, as partial repayment to the UK for the opportunities he enjoyed in the army and the education his sons received.

Joe and Adi Vasemaca Lagilagi Raiwalui, known as 'Lagi' to most Fijians, bought a house in nearby St Ives and Lagi was engaged by Queen's College, through which Joe enjoyed taking the college punt around the Backs with visitors to Cambridge while Lagi was at the college. Lagi died in 2007.

Joe came from the same village as Seci Drika's wife, Adi Elenoa Lalabalavu, a high chief from Somosomo, and when Adi Elenoa died in 2014, Seci and Elenoa's daughter asked Joe to assist with the burial.

Soropepeli VUNIWAQA

Known as Soro or Sam in the British Army and nicknamed 'Soqe' by other '212', after Fiji's barking pigeon (*Ducula latrans*). Soro was a student at RKS when the recruiting team arrived. He was a late addition to the '212' after some of those named in the *Fiji Times* were found to be ineligible or changed their minds.

Soro was born and raised in Kadavu, a cousin of Kim Yabaki, but identified with Qalikarua on Matuku in the Lau group, where his grandfather was born. Enlistment offered the opportunity to see the world, and Soro saw plenty of that in his sixteen years in the QOH and 16 Parachute Heavy Drop Company. He saw service in Germany, Singapore and Northern Ireland and was discharged as a Corporal.

Soro met his wife on DOMCOL in Fiji and their three children were born in Hanover, Changi and Tidworth.

He accepted voluntary redundancy and returned to Fiji to enlist in the RFMF, initially as a Territorial but as a 6FIR regular after 1987 and was commissioned. He saw service on RFMF peace-keeping operations, but died on duty at the age of 54 while undertaking a fitness test in 1993.

Soro's daughter Keleni, known as 'KB', is the office administrator for the RBL, Fiji, and married to an RFMF Warrant Officer.

The Royal Hussars (Prince of Wales Own)

Sitiveni BERAQUSA

Sitiveni was an 'apprentice, Walu Bay' when he enlisted, probably with the PWD. He was born on Nairai in the Lomaiviti group and was a classmate at RKS with Isikeli Maravu.

Sitiveni died in a car accident in Germany on 31 December 1974 with his three children. His English wife Valerie was not in the car and survived them. According to Apakuki Nanovo, Sitiveni's father in law and the child of another soldier in his regiment were also killed at the time. Sitiveni was driving a right—hand drive car at the time and it was assumed that his view of an oncoming vehicle was obscured as he attempted to overtake a truck which may have been in front of him blocking his view of the road.

Perhaps the saddest sight in the Hanover military cemetery is the grave of Sitiveni's three children, aged 8, 6 and 4, who also died in the accident. Sitiveni's headstone is marked as 'Sgt S. Bonaqusa'.

Levani Naucusou DAMUNI

Levani enlisted under his second name and lied about his age in order to be accepted, according to wife Donna. He was born in 1943 but claimed to be born in 1941. Joe Tuwai recalls Levani had origins in Mokani, Tailevu and attended LMS with Tom Waqabaca a year or two ahead of Meli Vesikula. He was listed in the *Fiji Times* as 'Levani Naucusou, apprentice, Tailevu'.

Levani featured twice in the *Fiji Times* coverage of the recruitment drive. He appeared in a front-page photograph on 14 November 1961, being inoculated at Queen Elizabeth Barracks. He didn't look too happy about either the inoculation or being photographed. He was also quoted as saying: 'I am glad I am going to join the British Army but think I will be homesick'.

Levani did not maintain contact with many of his cohort after his service, and did not mention much of his service to his wife and children beyond serving in Germany and Singapore and qualifying as a parachutist. He never mentioned any family members serving in WWII or Malaya but also never expressed any regrets about his army service.

Levani's last visit to Fiji was shortly before the elections and military coup of 1987. In the late nineties, following a health scare, Levani and Donna visited Israel where he tried to contact an old comrade serving with the RFMF on peace keeping duty with UNIFIL. He was unsuccessful, but a chance sighting of what appeared to be Fijian soldiers proved correct and a happy exchange took place.

Levani died in Worcester, Massachusetts in 2005.

Akapusi Valati KORO

Akapusi's names were juxtaposed in the *Fiji Times* of 6 November 1961, when his occupation was listed as 'insurance clerk, Suva'. Akapusi, also known as Semi, from Lau, attended Lelean Memorial School and joined the 10th Hussars who were stationed in Germany in 1967. On the night of 28 August Akapusi and two friends, Jioji Mate, another '212', and Epeli Buliciri, who followed his brother in the '212' to join the Green Jackets in 1962, were returning to their base from visiting John Riley and his wife at Hilden, near Dusseldorf. According to John, Mate (the non-drinker) was driving at the time of the accident and Epeli was asleep in the rear seat. Jioji and Akapusi were killed instantly and are buried near one another in the Hanover Military Cemetery at Niedersachsen.

The cemetery records list 'Cpl A. Valati' but the headstone reads 'Cpl A.V. Koro'.

Semi VOLITIKORO

Semi was employed as an assistant forest guard in 1961 and served two years with the 11th Hussars before being medically discharged.

Wilfred Vono WHIPPY

Wilfred, who was known as Ben in the army, was unemployed in Suva when he enlisted and is remembered by many as having feet too large to be accommodated in army issue boots. He thus drove 10th Hussars tanks either in his bare feet or plimsolls, depending on the story-teller. Ben took an early discharge and returned to Fiji, and in 1992 was teaching at a school in Nausori.

16/5 Queen's Royal Lancers

This regiment spent most of the Cold War deployed in Germany, with tours in Northern Ireland, Cyprus, Aden and Hong Kong. During this time, it was mainly operated as a battle tank regiment.

Charles Andrew GIBLIN, BEM

Charles was born in Suva in 1942, the third youngest of the six sons and three daughters of John W. Giblin who migrated from Tasmania to Savusavu and married Elizabeth Maybir.

Charles attended Suva Boys Grammar School from 1953-59, finishing in the same class as Harry Powell, Cyril Browne and David Lelo. In 1961 he was a storeman with Miller's Ltd and hated every minute of the job. He earned £3/14/4 per week; the basic army pay was £6/5/4 per week with board and lodging, so the decision to enlist was not difficult. Thirty years later, he recalled 'there was nothing in Fiji for our age group'.

After surviving the bitter cold during his basic training, Charles was posted successively to Osnabruck in Germany, Singapore, Aden, Germany again, Northern Ireland in 1971, Hong Kong, and a further six years in Germany. He finished his original commitment to the Queen at the armoured school at Bovington, Dorset as a SQMS. In this capacity, he prepared NBC kits for units deployed in the Falklands campaign. All this service was with QRL. Very early in this service Charles became 'Charley'.

After completing his twenty-two years Charley was appointed Non Regular Permanent Staff (NRPS), serving a further eighteen years with 72 Ordnance Company, eventually retiring on 15 October 2002.

Charley has some vivid memories of his service, beginning with his selection as one of sixteen British soldiers chosen as an honour guard for President Kennedy's visit to Berlin in June 1963, when he met LtCol Sir Vivian Dunn, who conducted the band of the Royal Marines on that occasion. In 1975 when Charley was based in Germany, his father died in Fiji and there was no leave allowance for the '212' who had to deal with such an emergency need for travel. In the first instance the USAF, RAF and RNZAF all offered assistance, which proved unnecessary when it was learned that his father's dying wish was that Charley stay in Germany. The MOD, to their credit, subsequently decided to provide an immediate return ticket to Fiji for any '212' needing such emergency assistance. His last memory of his service was the two 'dining out' dinners at Mandy Barracks, Cardiff and at the Donnington Territorial Army Centre, where he was farewelled 'like a General' with the regimental pipes and drums at one of these dinners.

Charles met his life time partner Carol in the market town of Shifnal, Shropshire, and they later settled with their two daughters near Telford.

Peni Koroituku WAQA

Peni (Ben) was born in late 1943 in Tavua, where his father was employed at the Emperor Gold Mine. His father was from Kadavu and his mother from Bua, Vanua Levu. Ben was the youngest of seven children, and the family had moved to Suva by the time he was at secondary school. Ben attended the Methodist School in Toorak and later MBHS with Jim Vakatalai, Bob Dass and Arthur Lee.

Ben's father served in the FMF Naval Reserve in WWII, stationed in Fiji. Ben was also a member of the FMF Naval Reserve and visited Christmas Island after Britain's H-bomb was tested there.

Ben was allocated to the 16/5 Queen's Royal Lancers and served 22 years, retiring as a WO2/SSM. He started as a driver of armoured fighting vehicles, later specialising in communications and gunnery. He became known as Ben, but also answered to 'Tooks' and Tuku. He accompanied the last twelve schoolboys to leave Fiji for the UK and thus did his basic training in QRL by himself. He has a vivid memory of travelling to Darlington by train from London and transferring to three-ton trucks for the final journey to Catterick.

He did not have long to wait for his first operational deployment in Aden in 1963. Isikeli Maravu and Ted Wilson served in Aden at this time, as did Labalaba and others with 22 SAS. B and C squadrons of the QRL did three-month rotations with the resting squadron in Bahrein. The QRL also served in Northern Ireland in 1971-72, and had several subsequent deployments to BAOR, Osnabruck and the training range at Medicine Hat, Alberta, Canada. One of his more memorable postings, in retrospect, was with 48 Brigade in Hong Kong in 1973 when a RFMF (N) Lieutenant named Frank Bainimarama, on secondment, played with Peni for the army rugby team. Around this time another capable rugby player was seconded from the RFMF to Hong Kong in the person of Sitiveni Rabuka. It is tempting to speculate whether there was something in the air or the sauce on the noodles in the Wan Chai food stalls that influenced these future coup leaders in Fiji.

Ben loved sports—he played rugby and squash and boxed in the army. He was the light heavyweight champion for Southern Command in the mid-seventies and played squash at county level. In the 1980s Ben became interested in SCUBA diving and has enjoyed exploring the waters around Taveuni and Savusavu in recent years.

Rugby influenced Ben's choice of life partner. Ken Wilks played 'in the backs' with Ben in the QRL team and invited Ben home to meet his family after a game, where Ken introduced Ben to his sister Kay. They married in Ben's early years of service, and he was thus not eligible for DOMCOL to Fiji in 1966. The marriage produced two sons and two daughters.

For his pre-discharge training, Ben had opted for a course in fire management in Surrey. After his return to the UK he found a niche for himself in this area and worked there for twenty years until his retirement at age 65. He and Kay had bought a family home in the village of Madely Heath, outside Crewe, where locomotives were once built and Bentleys still are. Madely Heath became more famous as the home of a train driver assaulted by a bloke named Biggs. Ben was attracted to the idea of buying the licence for the nearby Crewe Arms which was a focal point for serious pigeon racing. Kay talked him out of the idea, for which he was very grateful in his later years.

Ben has absolutely no regrets about any aspect of his army service beyond the racism he experienced, on the assumption that he was of Jamaican origin, in his early years in England.

Jone OBA

Jone was among those not listed in the *Fiji Times,* but was a late substitute for those who were listed and later found unsuitable, or who changed their minds. He was one of the twelve students who were allowed to complete their senior Cambridge exam and arrived in England shortly before Christmas, 1961.

Jone was posted to 16/5 QRL where he served ten years. He later transferred to QOH for seven years and discharged from Dortmund as a Corporal with a redundancy payment. Jone returned to Fiji and found employment in the civil service, but died in 1985 after a heart attack.

Royal Tank Regiment

George CHUTE

George was born in 1938 in Labasa and raised in Nakula near Udu Point, the north-eastern tip of Vanua Levu. His father Alick was a copra planter and

HMTQ inspecting RSDG at Holyrood Barracks, Edinburgh, 1971. Sgt George Chute third from right. Photo: George Chute

boat builder, the great grandson of an Irishman who had made his way to Fiji. William Burley Chute was born in county Kerry, the illegitimate son of a Catholic priest named John and a woman named Burley. William later named his son after his father. A dark Chute family legend, not mentioned during George's childhood, suggests that W. B. Chute was probably a 'Blackbirder' who was involved in the kidnapping of other Pacific Islanders to serve in Fiji's pre-Cession plantation economy through a 'labour exchange' in Levuka.

The first European settler at Udu Point was a German named John Bullinge, after whom many Fijian children have been named Jone Pulini. George was the fourth of eleven children, and his Fiji-Irish ancestry includes a part-Chinese maternal grandmother from the Ah Tuck/Artack family in Levuka, who asked for one of her grandsons to be baptised a Methodist.

George's schooling began during WWII at the Udu Point village school, where its ten young pupils learned to write in wet sand, graduating to a slate when they showed progress. During George's childhood, there was only one radio program in the Fijian language each week and villagers from nearby Bekama Island swam to Udu Point to listen.

George progressed to Labasa European Primary School, where he was the school's first head boy. The newly-opened CSR sugar mill was coal-fired, and the cane farmers transported their harvest to the mill in carts drawn by donkeys, mules and Clydesdale horses. There were only three taxis in Labasa at the time, and no buses. The primary school was established by CSR and did not admit Fijian or Indian students, based on the sugar industry's experience of the mixing of the races in Barbados and elsewhere in the West Indies.

As a thirteen-year-old, in 1951 George was sent to Northland College near Kaikohe above NZ's Bay of Islands for four years. The flight to Auckland took 11.5 hours in a Sunderland flying boat from Laucala Bay, during which time breakfast, morning tea, lunch and afternoon tea were served. The school had an 800-acre farm, and the boys were required to speak Maori at all times.

George was thus one of only four of the '212' recruits to have been outside Fiji before their departure for 'Bolatagane', as Britain was known. He returned from school to help on the plantation. He does not have a clear idea of why he was interested in joining up, but suspects he was influenced by the films and comics of the time. His father was reluctant to see him enlist but did not try to dissuade him—as indicated in George's poem at the end of the first chapter. He was not closely related to any other '212' and had no relatives who served in the Solomons or Malaya. Some family members were merchant seamen.

George was allocated to the armoured corps, 5RTR which was disbanded in 1967 and he transferred to the Royal Scots Greys. In 1971 the RSG amalgamated with 3 Welsh Carboniers to form the Royal Scots Dragoon Guards.

Among these Scottish regiments George became 'Big Geordie'. Some of his '212' comrades heard rumours of George playing the pipes in the regimental band, but this was based on his son Alick's achievement winning a piping competition after being coached by one of the regiment's pipers.

George's first posting to Germany was for six months in 1962, at the Spandau Barracks in Berlin where WWII wreckage remained in abundance. He subsequently completed four more two-year 'tours' in Germany. Another two years in Singapore and nine months in Borneo followed. He later served four tours in Northern Ireland, based at Armagh, Newry, Omagh and Gosford Castle. Another twelve months was spent with Italian mountain troops in Malles Venosta, assessing damage caused by the Red Brigades.

George marvelled at the varied diets he encountered in some places; curried cat in Borneo tasted like chicken, tired donkeys found themselves plated up in Italy, and in Herford, Germany, horse meat was often served.

The highlights of his career included being presented to HMTQ as the youngest Commander of a Chieftain tank, in 1967 at Reinssaleode in Germany. George finished his service as the Chief Testing Officer for all armoured vehicles at Catterick. Fifty years later, he still recalls the cylinder firing sequence for starting a Centurion tank and the model number of the Rolls Royce V12 engine. George delighted in meeting the monarch a second time in 1971, around the time the Duke of Kent was his Squadron Commander. He also met the Queen Mother and Anne, the Princess Royal, and had the honour of driving a Land Rover for Princess Margaret for an inspection of Girl Guides. A photograph of the latter occasion, and another of being inspected by the Queen remained two of the most treasured possessions decorating his home outside Labasa in 2014.

George served sixteen years, taking early retirement as a sergeant on a full pension. He returned to Fiji at the insistence of his Scottish wife who had serious health issues at the time. She sadly lived only eleven weeks after their return to Labasa in 2014.

George's grief at the loss of his wife almost led him to 'squander everything' and he contemplated suicide at one point. He was fortunate that Fiji Forest Industries (FFI) was seeking experienced managers as supervisors at the time of his return and he soon found himself gainfully employed. In 1992 he was the training manager and the company had sent him to NZ and Australia to study management and plywood production.

In his dealings with Fijian villagers on FFI matters, George worked closely with three senior chiefs, Ratu Aisake Kubuabola (a cousin of the current Defence Minister), Ratu Tevita Vakalalabure, and Ratu Iloilo who later served as President.

While baptised a Methodist, George had little interest in religion during his army service, but in his sunset years he worked for the local Methodist church whose minister is a convert named Lal Mohamed who speaks fluent Fijian. George married again to Mere, from Wasavulu, several kilometres south of Labasa, where her older brother is the Chief and where stone monuments from the pre-Christian period were declared a national monument in 1969.

George delighted in recording aspects of his life in verse and kindly gave permission to reproduce two relevant poems in appropriate sections of this text. His involvement in 'the events of 1987' was dealt with in Chapter 7.

George lost his struggle with the ailments of age in early July 2017.

Eseroma RAUSUVANUA

Eseroma was still at school in November 1961, and on arrival in England found himself allocated to 1RTR. During his basic training with the RAC at Catterick, however, he found it extremely difficult to cope with the cold and was given a medical discharge. George Chute recalls taking advantage of eight blankets at night to keep the cold at bay.

Eseroma returned to Fiji and found employment with the Ministry of Health in Suva.

Jack SHEPHERD

Jack was listed in the *Fiji Times* in November 1961 as 'electrician, Suva', and has proved one of the more elusive of the '212'. He is remembered by several of his former countrymen as serving briefly in either 1 RTR or another of the armoured regiments, but was apparently given a medical discharge very early in his service. Maciu Vatu recalls 'a versatile chap' with acting and fashion ambitions. 'He had training and even had parts in a popular TV series in the late 60s'. Jack claimed Bauan chiefly links through a grandfather. He apparently married an English woman named Dinah, had three children and settled in London without returning to Fiji.

Tom SORBY

Tom was born in Namata, Tailevu, in 1938 to a Fijian mother and a part-European father. In 1961 he described himself as a 'junior shift boss' at the Vatukoula gold mine, where the general manager prohibited the recruiting team. Consequently, Tom was interviewed at Rakiraki. He had been educated at Vatukoula and MBHS in Suva.

He served twelve years with 5 RTR and QOH in Borneo, Germany (including Berlin-Spandau) and Northern Ireland. He married an English girl and returned to Fiji in 1974, working at Vatukoula for another thirteen years. By 1992 Tom was living back in Nausori/Suva and his wife had returned to the UK. At that time, he had a son in the Royal Navy, and his daughter had married and also returned to the UK. Tom died before 2011.

Louis TING

Louis, who became Bob, was another who enlisted from school, served about twelve years and is remembered by other '212' as serving with the RTR and last noted 'managing a hotel in Earl's Court years ago'. Naibuka Qarau remembers Bob as 'a good singer and guitarist.... a light/heavy weight boxer, who married an English woman and was last heard of in Australia'.

APPENDIX B: GUNNERS

The Royal Regiment of Artillery

Twenty of the '212' served with RA units, with a disproportionate number serving initially with 34 Light Air Defence Regiment, providing a significant injection of talent into the Regiment's rugby and other sporting teams.

Royal Horse Artillery

Iliesa KADAVU

Iliesa is the younger of two sons of a Naweni, Vanua Levu, subsistence farmer. He enlisted directly from RKS in Suva while his elder brother Mateo Rokovesa was interviewed in Savusavu and allocated to the RUR.

Iliesa served with the Regiment for nine years in Malaya, Cyprus, Sharja and the UK, qualifying as a parachutist in September 1965. He returned briefly to Naweni in 1968 on Domcol, but then settled in the UK and has not maintained close contact with his older brother.

Kalioni RATUNABUABUA

Kalioni was a larger than life character and great practical joker, believed by many of his '212' cohort to have been one of the oldest recruits. They thought he had probably lied about his age, and had most certainly lied to the recruiting team about being a single man. These commentators were half right: Kalioni was a little older than many of the group, but was by no means among the oldest. His eldest child, Mere Ratunabuabua, has confirmed that he was born in 1940; that he was married to her mother, Asenaca; and that Mere was born in Fiji before he enlisted. Kalioni arranged for his wife and daughter to join him in England after he completed his basic training.

Kalioni was born in Nadi, but his father was head of the mataqali of Vunamoli in Nadroga, where Kalioni received his initial schooling. In November 1961, he was a school teacher in Nadroga but was also involved in training villagers in developing business opportunities through cooperatives.

The people of Nadroga have a collective *tauvu*[56] relationship with those of the neighbouring island of Kadavu. Kalioni was very friendly with Nic Naico's father and promised to look after his son, an undertaking Nic described retrospectively, in 2014, as 'like a fox looking after the chickens'. Nic and Kalioni were allocated to the RA, served together in 34 LAD for several years, and remained close friends throughout the remainder of their respective careers in other RA regiments.

Kalioni spent much of his service with 7 Parachute Regiment RHA, and was a Provost Sergeant with 1 Field Regiment, RHA when discharged in 1983; like most British Army Gunners of his years of service and since, he served all over the world. He represented successive regiments in rugby and athletics teams. He was a keen sprinter and enjoyed the shot put and discus. Kalioni's wife, a community nurse also from Nadroga, was not immune to Kalioni's practical joking. According to Nic Naico, she was often presented with bunches of fresh roses collected from the cemetery en route home from the pub in Hohne, Germany. Asenaca and Kalioni had three more children, the youngest of whom, Sivo, followed her father's footsteps and became the first Fijian woman to serve twenty-two years in the British Army.

---

56 Gatty: 'People of certain geographically separated tribes who in legend derive from the same ancestral spirit (*vu*) or have been united anciently by chiefly marriage. They are inclined to make jokes, play tricks against each other, playful insults, sometimes obnoxious'.

On completing his service, Kalioni joined the UK Prisons Service and later worked with security companies until he retired. The family settled in Weymouth, and apart from Mere, remained there after his death in 2010. Asenaca and their son Sitiveni hosted Isaia Labalaba's visit to the UK in 2009 for the unveiling of Talaiasi Labalaba's statue in Stirling Lines, Hereford. Talaiasi, who was killed in action in Oman in 1972, was Kalioni's nephew.

Mo Beg recalls that Kalioni had a 'brilliant' funeral in Guildford Cathedral 'with trumpeters and all the trimmings'. Nic Naico attended the funeral and was so haunted at the time by his old friend's perpetual practical jokes that he was cautious about giving the deceased a farewell kiss 'in case the bugger laughed, threw his arms around my neck and advised he was not really dead'.

Kalioni defied the traditional Fijian preference for burial and left instructions that he be cremated, but some of his ashes were returned to his village. Mere recalled that the death notice in the *Fiji Times* concluded by noting that Kalioni 'will be sadly missed by publicans along the south coast of England', or words to that effect. His grandchildren in the UK still recognise the pubs *'Tai'* (grandfather) patronised!

26 Field Regiment

Mikaele BALEITILAGICA

Mike was another late substitute in 1961 and was not listed in the *Fiji Times*. He had family roots in Macuata but finished his schooling in Lautoka.

After his basic training as a Gunner, Mike was posted to 17 Battery, 26 Field Regiment, with whom he served 22 years, initially in Malaya in 1962 and Cyprus in 1964. Subsequent postings rotated between Hohne and Dortmund in Germany and the school of artillery at Larkhill, Wiltshire.

Mike was discharged as a S/Sgt and returned to Fiji with his family late in 1983.

The following year he joined the then Fijian Affairs Board (now the Taukei Affairs Board) and was posted to Macuata Province as the Assistant *Roko Tui* (District Officer). In 1989 he was transferred to the Board's Suva head office as a training officer, serving there until 1993 when he returned to

Macuata as the *Roko Tui*. He retired to live in Lautoka in 1999.

In his later years, Mike chose to use the family name Rabaro.

Jonasa Nasau JANG

Joe was born on Nayau in the Lau group in October 1939, to a Chinese father and Fijian mother, the second of their four sons. The couple also had four daughters. Joe's father was a shop keeper who spoke very little English, but had mastered Fijian after emigrating from Canton/Guangzhou. Joe attended primary school in Lau before moving to Suva in 1950 to attend the Chinese school in Flagstaff, where the headmistress, a Miss Jennings, spoke Chinese, having previously taught in China. Joe was known as Sam Chang at school but as Nasau to his parents and siblings.

Joe was one of the very few '212' who had travelled abroad before their enlistment. In his case it was to play in a rugby tournament in New Zealand in 1959. He considered himself 'quite an adventurous type of person' and the prospect of seeing the world and the army pay of about seven pounds and ten shillings a week allowed scope for remitting money to his family. Joe was a clerk with the Shell Oil Company in Suva in 1961 and nominated a preference for the Royal Artillery, possibly influenced by Captain Hardcastle, the 2IC of the recruiting team who was a Gunner.

Joe was discharged as a WO2 with the Proof and Experimental Establishment at Shoeburyness and remained living nearby. For the next nine years he operated a mobile fish and chip shop emblazoned with a Union Jack and exhorting potential customers to 'Buy British'. He then operated a courier service until his retirement.

Lote KAITANI

Lote was born in 1943, the fourth of six children of a Methodist minister serving on Matuku in the Lau group. His mother was from the village of Naroi, Moala, but Lote identifies with his father's birthplace on Ono-i-Lau. An uncle returned from service in the Solomon Islands on the day that Lote's younger sister was born; consequently the girl was named Talebuamaisolomone, or 'returning alive from the Solomons'.

Lote started school at Naroi, with Semesa Naivalu and Sotia Ponijasi, but at the age of ten was sent to Suva to live with an uncle and continue his schooling at Nabua District School and DAV College. He was in his final year at the latter when the recruiting team arrived in Suva and he saw the army as an opportunity to see the world. Lote's subsequent twenty-two years with 26 Field Regiment included service in Cyprus, Malaya, Christmas 1972-73 in Salala, Oman, Canada and the inevitable tours of duty in Northern Ireland.

Early in his service Lote married Jennifer, a WRAC he met in Shoeburyness, was thus never eligible for DOMCOL, and did not return to Fiji until 1983. Their daughters were completing their schooling when Lote discharged from the army and the family settled near Jennifer's home town in Wales.

Throughout his army service, Lote specialised in the regimental signals section. He played regimental rugby until his mid-thirties, representing the (army) Gunners a couple of times, before giving more attention to hockey. Lote had difficulty finding agreeable employment after the army and initially worked with Jennifer's brother as an industrial roofing contractor in Somerset before moving closer to home as a taxi driver, and eventually as a supervisor for the taxi company.

In his retirement Lote does not regret not returning to Fiji. He says he would do it all again given the opportunity, but perhaps avoid the smoking and drinking that took their toll until he quit both. He feels the cold more as he gets older but has no recollection of being bothered by cold weather during his army service.

Kitione LALAKOMACOI

Kit was another recruit who escaped mention in the *Fiji Times,* and according to the late Apakuki Nanovo and others he was one of the best sportsmen in the intake, excelling at rugby and athletics. He was born in 1941 in Mokani, Tailevu, and may have been the youngest in a large family as his eldest brother married Ratu Sir Lala Sukuna's sister.

Kit served with 26 Field Regiment and had the unfortunate distinction of being the first of the '212' to die in the UK, from deep vein thrombosis or DVT in August 1965. He is buried in Colchester Cemetery.

Romano NACEVA, MBE

Romano was born in his grandfather's house at the Catholic Mission Station, Savarekareka, near Savusavu. He was named after his grandfather who was a practitioner of traditional Fijian medicine. Romano was educated at St John's College, Cawaci, Ovalau. He described his occupation as 'planter' to the recruiting team when interviewed at Yaroi but was unemployed at the time, having left school a year before. He was seeking good employment and adventure and recalls Captain Hardcastle, RA, on the recruiting team persuading him that Gunners added some class to conflicts that would otherwise be unseemly brawls, or some similarly persuasive line recommending a career in the RA.

His subsequent service with 26 Field Regiment provided adventures in Malaya, Canada, Cyprus, Germany, France, Belgium, Holland, Australia, New Zealand, the USA and Iceland. Romano's terminal posting was at Dortmund, where he was a pivotal figure in the organisation of Exercise 'Fijian Farewell' in 1983 (dealt with in Chapter 5) where he was presented with his MBE for services to the community in the BAOR.

Romano met his wife Bulou in England, and when she returned to Fiji with him on DOMCOL in 1966 they were married. Bulou was one of seven Fijian women originally working in a cigarette factory in Fiji who were brought to Basildon in Essex for experience. The couple had five children. One of their three sons followed Romano into the army, a daughter married another soldier, and a second son settled in Holland. Romano returned to Fiji to be at home with his family. Subsequent employment included assistant *Roko Tui*[57], Lomaiviti.

Kaliova NAIVALARUA

Kaliova was born in Vunisea on Kadavu, where his father was a doctor. He attended the local provincial school before going to QVS. He has a vivid memory of Fiji's 1953 tsunami. He was at Rakiraki returning from a school excursion with Sam Tamata, when Sam's father's dinghy was wrecked. The tsunami generated waves of two metres in Suva and five metres at Nakasaleka in Kadavu. Fortunately, it struck at low tide and only five lives were lost. Kaliova

---

57 *Roko Tui:* top Fijian administrative officer of a province.

was working for Burns Philp in Suva in 1961 when approached by an RFMF liaison officer for the recruiting team. The RFMF liaison officer asked Kaliova to take the selection tests as a substitute for a last-minute withdrawal by one of the men listed in the *Fiji Times* on 6 November. The liaison officer had served in the Fiji Battalion's intelligence section in Malaya with two of Kaliova's older brothers, and later became a *Roko* on Kadavu. Kaliova has vivid memories of his service with 26 Fd Regt in Malaya as part of 28 Commonwealth Brigade in the early sixties. He was conscious of Britain's involvement in SEATO at the time, and its attempts to contain the spread of communism in south east Asia. Kaliova hoped that he might eventually see service in Vietnam. At the time, most Western governments and news media referred to the People's Republic of China (PRC) as *Communist* China, while Taiwan (the Republic of China) was accepted in the UN and elsewhere as representing nearly one billion Chinese.

On his return from Malaya, Kaliova's regiment was billeted close to the Ministry of Defence Proof and Experimental (P & E) establishment at Shoeburyness. After a rugby match one afternoon Kaliova was introduced to Janice, 'the most beautiful woman I had ever seen', a WRAC then serving with the P & E establishment. Kaliova and Janice married a year or so later and eventually settled in Janice's home city of Bristol. The couple raised four sons and a daughter during Kaliova's remaining twenty-three years in the army, serving in the Middle East, Canada and Northern Ireland. After he left the army Kaliova worked as a security officer for a bank in Bristol until he retired.

Kaliova's intention had always been to return to his homeland, but he has visited only three times since 1961, once with two of his older boys. He returned in 2000 to bury his youngest son, Joeli, in the Tavuki cemetery on Kadavu. Joeli followed his father into the army, joining the RE, but he and another Sapper died of asphyxiation while searching the Philippine-owned *Diamond Bulker*, carrying Colombian coal to Londonderry in Lough Foyle. The ship was searched under the UK's prevention of terrorism legislation, but exactly what the search party was looking for has not been revealed. Joeli had always wanted to be buried with his forefathers in Kadavu. Kaliova has been a widower since 2010. His eldest son, Richard, served in Afghanistan with REME.

Inosi RADIO

Inosi was recorded as 'clerk, Suva'. He had attended either RKS or QVS and returned to farming in Tailevu after his army service.

100 Field Regiment

Ralph Wallace LALABALAVU

Ralph was a student at Levuka Public School in 1961 but he had Cakaudrove origins. He served twenty-two years in the RA, initially with 26 and later 12 Field Regiments and was discharged in 1983 as a Sergeant with 100 Field Regiment. He chose to remain in London with English wife Valerie.

29/95 Commando Regiments, Royal Artillery

Roger AFRETE

Roger was a student at LMS when he enlisted and among the twelve who departed after the two main groups of recruits. He enlisted as Roger Afrete but was later known as Alifereti and as Roger Wale. His family background was Rotuman. Roger's initial RA service was with Nic Naico in 34 LAD Regiment, but he volunteered for RA Commando and completed and signed an application for Naico without telling him. The first Nic knew of his imminent transfer was when his CO advised him his application had been successful. Roger served about twelve years and died while back in Suva on holiday. He is erroneously noted on a website of distinguished Rotumans as 'Roger Afrete–British SAS Officer.'

Apisai TOKAIQALE aka Nic NAICO

Apisai, aka Nic during his army service, was born in the Vunisea hospital, Kadavu, in July 1942, the younger of two sons of a farmer. Both parents came from Namuana village in Tavuki district of Kadavu. Nic's early education was at Namalata village school and Vunisea provincial school before attending RKS, at Lodoni (pron. *Londoni*) in Tailevu. Nic recalled seeing the young Queen Elizabeth when she visited Fiji in 1952 and thinking 'what a small woman'. When he found his next school was located near a village named Lodoni he thought he might see the Queen again!

The Principal of RKS at the time was an Australian named Donelly, but Nic's most vivid memory of a teacher who made an impression was Mr Coupon, a New Zealander, who frequently threw chalk at young Apisai to disrupt his dreaming or staring out the window.

When the recruiting team arrived in Suva, Nic was finishing his general certificate and worried by pressure from an uncle teaching at RKS, who was encouraging Nic to become an architect. Jone Buakula was a classmate at RKS where the students had access to all the tools necessary to prepare building materials for housing. Nic's father survived the Solomons campaign in WWII, and three uncles served with the Fiji Battalion in Malaya from 1952. Nic saw the army as an avenue to escape the pressure to perform well academically. Fifty years later Nic admits that some of the movies he had seen as a teenager probably influenced his decision, particularly remembering *To Hell and Back*, about the wartime exploits of Audie Murphy, the US's most decorated WWII soldier.[58] Nic nominated the Parachute Regiment, the infantry and armoured units as his preferences but accepted the decision to allocate him to an artillery unit. Following his basic training, Nic served with 34 LAD briefly in Hong Kong before operational service in Aden and Borneo. Subsequent service took him to Oman, Singapore, Norway, Denmark, Holland, Canada, Australia and Thailand but not Northern Ireland—he volunteered twice while serving with 148 Amphibious Observation Unit which was not suited to the Northern Ireland operations, partly because of its specialised role and small size. Nic was discharged as a Sergeant in 1984. Roger Wale's covert transfer of Nic to 95 Commando Light Regiment is described above (page 111). In April 1965, Nic underwent Commando training at Plymouth and was based at The Royal Citadel. Legend has it Sir Francis Drake whiled away the hours at this site before setting out to defeat the Spanish Armada, prior to the construction of the Citadel.

In February 1970, during his second posting to Singapore, Nic qualified as a parachutist at a course run at RAF, Changi, on the site of the present

---

58 The movie starred Audie Murphy (as himself).

international airport. From early contact with Australia and satisfaction with an army career, Nic decided that service with Australia's Pacific Islands Regiment (PIR) in pre-independent Papua New Guinea would suit him. In 1966 he submitted documentation applying for a transfer and became anxious as his date for re-enlistment with the British Army approached. It was not until the eleventh hour that he learned that the adjutant had discarded his application under instruction from the CO, who was keen for Nic to stay with the regiment (and probably, the rugby team).

Nic met his first wife Esther on his second posting to Singapore. Esther's older sister Shelly had married another '212', Wainikiti Vosabalavu. Nic's first marriage did not survive the difficulties of ineligibility for married quarters and temporary housing in caravan parks.

Before the arrival of their son Ifiremi (named after Nic's older brother) Esther gave Nic an ultimatum—'the army or me'– which did not help his efforts to pass selection for 22 SAS. Ifiremi was born in Singapore in 1972. Nic found initial employment at a difficult time in Germany as a security officer, but a chance meeting with one of his early rugby playing COs led to a succession of civilian appointments in support of the BAOR. One of Nic's most treasured possessions is a plaque presented to him on his retirement in 2007, inscribed 'For Services to the British Army and Army Rugby'.

He and his German wife Anne live in an apartment in Monchengladbach, and Nic has played a lot of golf since retiring.

Ifiremi lives near Munich with his family and is now thoroughly 'Bayerische', according to Nic, and has forgotten his Fijian. Ifiremi's son Timoci is named after Nic's uncle, the village chief at Namuana. Both Nic and Ifiremi have remained British citizens. Nic has no regrets about his decision to enlist, beyond concern that perhaps he should have taken better advantage of some of the opportunities the army offered.

Filipe RAVUOCO

Felipe was born in a village outside Nausori in October 1944, the youngest of four children of an overseer with the Ports Authority of Fiji.

Felipe attended Nabitu District School and RKS before finishing at DAV College with Jale Vuiyasawa and Etuate Qio. He and his similarly under-aged classmate, Jale Vuiyasawa, were very keen to enlist but frustrated by the concerns of the education officer on the recruiting team who told them when they first applied that they were too young.

Jale and Felipe were not easily dissuaded however, and took advantage of the recruiting team's need to cope with hundreds of applicants for the initial quota of one hundred recruits. Both passed the intelligence test but failed the initial interview. As they reappeared at subsequent venues around Suva they were recognised by the recruiting sergeant from a highland regiment who appears to have recognised their determination and may have suggested that what they needed were birth certificates showing them to be a year older.

Regardless of the origin of the necessary fraud, Jale's sister was working in the government Registry Office and was tempted by the suggested reward of a sewing machine if she helped the boys with their problem. A half century later Felipe was asked whether they found the promised sewing machine, and he said: 'We are still shopping for it!'

Felipe spent most of his seventeen years in the Commando Brigade, RA, qualifying as a parachutist and specialising in the preparation of vehicles for fording rivers and for beach landings. His service took him to Hong Kong after his basic training, to South Korea in 1962 and then to Aden on HMS *Ark Royal*—where he encountered a New Zealand couple farming prawns, as one does!

Later service took him to Germany, Norway, the Middle East, and several tours of duty in Northern Ireland. Despite his initial shock at the extreme (for the UK) cold in the winters of 1961-62 and 1962-63, Felipe grew used to freezing temperatures, and volunteered for a three-month winter survival course in Austria. Only 150 of the original 300 volunteers finished the course, during which Ted Qio lost his toenails to frost bite. Felipe eventually found himself 'the only black guy' on the course and was determined to finish it. He enjoyed it immensely and it remains his favourite memory of his army service. Felipe returned to Fiji on DOMCOL twice during his service, once in 1966 and again in 1970 for his father's funeral. He met his future wife in Wales where he was sent for a training course prior to his discharge. There he found the environment very welcoming and laid back, citing cars stopping for the drivers to chat as they passed. The training course to qualify as a plant fitter did not suit his lifestyle at the time, and he eventually made use of his truck driving experience in the army to secure employment as a long-distance lorry driver. He preferred, however, to restrict his journeys to the UK

Light Air Defence Regiments

For reasons best known to those who allocated the '212' to different regiments in 1961, fourteen of the twenty allocated to RA were destined to serve initially with 34 LAD. The regiment was disbanded in 1970 after a farewell parade at Napier Barracks, Dortmund in September 1969. With perhaps more Fijians than any other regiment in the army, it was not surprising that the unit was prohibited from fielding all-Fijian teams in rugby sevens competitions. The fourteen new gunners did their initial training at the RA training camp at Oswestry, Shropshire. In March 1962, the Regiment deployed to Hong Kong and the following year to Aden.

Etuate QIO Ledua

Etuate (Edward) was a student when he enlisted as Uate Qio which evolved to Ted Ledua by the time he left the army, but many '212' still refer to him as 'Q ten', a play on his enlisted name. Ted was born in the village of Liku on Nayau in the Lau group, but the family moved to Suva for his education and he attended Draiba Fijian School, followed by DAV College where Jale Vuiyasawa and Felipe Ravuoco were classmates.

While Captain Hardcastle, RA, on the recruiting team may have had an influence on Ted's preference for artillery, he did not say that in correspondence in 1993. But he did say that he 'had more chance of going' and as his mates Jale

34 LAD Regt in Hong Kong 1962 with 40/70 Bofors Gun.
L to R: Timoci Rokosule (later Ulaiasi), Mikaele Silivale (kneeling) and Jale Vuiyasawa
Photo Ulaiasi Ravela

Vuiyasawa and Felipe Ravuoco had expressed the same preference, he wanted to stay with them. All three were slightly under-age for recruitment but either lied about their birthdays or were accepted because they had made an impression. Ted met his future wife in 1963 when she was thirteen years old and married her in 1970. He served twenty-two years, qualifying as gunnery instructor and radar operator class one. He was posted to Hong Kong and Germany, had active service in Aden and completed four tours in Northern Ireland. After the army Ted settled in Dorrington, near Lincoln, and worked as a supervisor with a US tyre manufacturer until he became disabled in 1991.

Aminiasi RATULOALOA

Aminiasi's occupation was listed as 'messenger, Suva' in 1961. He began his twenty-two years with the army in 34 LAD and was discharged as a Bombardier with the RA's Depot Regiment in 1983. Alex, as he was known in the army, came from Kadavu, served with the FRNVR prior to 1958, and was among those who served on vessels at the Christmas Island nuclear test site in the nineteen fifties. He was diagnosed with terminal cancer while serving with BAOR in Germany and died a few weeks later. He and his wife Mua had no children.

Ulaiasi RAVELA

Ulaiasi was born in Nakelo, Tailevu, the youngest of five children of a PWD shipwright at Walu Bay. He attended Nakelo district school, and later Nausori Central Fijian Secondary School with Lote Kaitani. When the recruiting team arrived, he was working for Millers Ltd, a pest control company. He quickly became known as 'Bob' Ravela in the army.

Bob had no relatives serving in WWII beyond an uncle who was a reservist. A total of four '212' came from Nakelo or a neighbouring village; Manasa Talakuli (RAOC/RLC) was the son of the Tui Nakelo, and Naibuka Qarau (DERR/QOH) was Bob's nephew. Jim Masuwale (RSigs) came from a neighbouring village. Jone Tuisovuna, who was claimed by the RE, is also from Nakelo and a cousin.

Bob completed twenty-two years in the RA, initially with 34 AD Regiment, serving as a Sergeant Detachment Commander responsible for radar operations. His last posting was as a PSI with a TA unit, 21 Worcestershire Battery. One of Bob's more memorable postings was with Felipe Ravuoco, on secondment from their regiment's service in Hong Kong. The two Fijians were selected to form part of the British Army component rotation to the UN Commander in Chief's security detachment in Seoul, ROK, during the Cuban missile crisis in November 1962. At the time, all units in South Korea were on high alert in case the crisis erupted into conflict with the DPRK and China. The Western Allies' concerns about Communist China and its intentions were not eased by a border conflict between India and China along the McMahon Line agreed between Colonial India and the Tibetan government in 1914. Fortunately, both India and China lacked nuclear weapons in those days.

Bob also had two operational deployments to Northern Ireland. He played rugby for the army Gunners team. In his later years he played golf until health issues slowed him down.

During his army career, Bob married and divorced two Fijian women before marrying a widow in 1991 who had been at school with in Nakelo. After leaving the army, Bob attended college in Durham for twelve months before working in London for ten years and returning to Worcester to work until his 65th birthday.

Mike SILIVALE

Mike's birthplace is the village of Koroivonu, in the Tunuloa district of Cakaudrove. He was the eldest of five children of the local chief and enlisted under his father's name of Ratusili. Mike had been educated at St John's College on Ovalau with Romano Naceva and Alex Kubu, but was helping his parents in the village in late 1961 as he awaited the outcome of an application for teacher training. He was seized by the opportunity offered by the British Army and gave his occupation as 'planter' when interviewed at Yaroi outside Savusavu. A grandfather had served in WWI and other relatives in WWII.

Mike was initially posted to 34 LAD and served twenty years, eleven of them with 95 Commando in support of the Royal Marines. He was keen on athletics, winning many trophies for javelin, discus and shot put before discharging as a sergeant with 16 LAD. His father died while Mike was training in Malaysia with 95 Commando, and he was expeditiously returned to Koroivonu for the funeral where he met his future wife, Pipa, who was teaching at the local school. Mike and Pipa married in Singapore in 1971 and had three children before returning directly to Pipa's homeland in New Zealand and settling in Auckland.

Mike started a second career as a security officer with the Ford assembly plant in Auckland until the plant foundered against Japanese competition, when he transferred to working for a Ford subsidiary parts manufacturer and later a specialist security company. He and Pipa remain in Auckland but visit Fiji occasionally. Asked whether he has any regrets about his decision to enlist, Mike's answer is like that of many other '212': 'None whatsoever—I would do it all again tomorrow'.

Timoci Rokosule ULAIASI

Tim was born in Naloaloa, Wailevu, Cakaudrove where his father was a Methodist minister. He was educated at Batibalavu District School, Naqelekule Bible School and Davuilevu Bible School in Suva. When he enlisted Tim was a student at the latter awaiting posting as a 'trial pastor'. Tim is nuggety fellow with a shaven head, a neat, greying Van Dyke beard and an infectious laugh. He volunteers that the big challenge in his probationary year after completing his bible college studies was to 'keep his tie on'. He laughed when his biographer suggested it was more important to keep his sulu on, volunteering that he 'took his tie off' a few times in Hong Kong! As a boy, Tim prayed to be able to see the world beyond the sea. A cousin's husband had served in Malaya. Tim regarded Ilisoni ('Hoss') Ligairi, from a neighbouring village, as an uncle. Hoss was his father's cousin.

Tim's early service was in Malaya/Singapore, Hong Kong and Aden (Chapter 3). He also served in Germany and did several tours of Northern Ireland. After 34 LAD was disbanded in 1970, Tim became a Rapier detachment Commander in 22 AD Regt. He served for a total of twenty-two years and was discharged as a Bombardier.

Nakaleto VAKAVODOKINAIVALU aka Bill VODO, BEM

Nakaleto's birth name under which he enlisted was too much for the army's computers to record or the drill sergeants to master. He quickly became known as Bill Vodo. Bill was born in Suva in April 1943, and his second name translates as 'going to war', a reflection of his father's departure for the Solomons at the time. His first name honours his mother's brother in Levuka (Ovalau) but his father came from Kadavu.

Bill is the youngest of eight children, and attended Nabua Fijian School together with Seconaia Takavesi, Joe Usumaki and Apakuki Nanovo's wife, Kalesi. In November 1961 Bill was a part-time labourer, building a wharf in Walu Bay.

Bill's father survived WWII and became a minister of the Methodist church. Bill was allocated to the RA and did his basic training in Shropshire and Wales, before posting to 34 LAD whose primary air defence weapon at the time was the Bofors gun. Bill served with the regiment in Hong Kong for the next four years. His subsequent service included Malaya and Singapore, but not Borneo. When 34LAD upgraded their Bofors guns to the Rapier ground-to-air missile, Bill was the first NCO to qualify as an instructor. Bill later served in 22AD regiment with Timoci Rokosule Ulaiasi and John Riley who was attached to RA from RSigs. He later served with 16 AD regiment and was discharged as 'S/Sgt Vakavodokinaiva' from the Depot Regiment, RA, in 1983. Bill's service took him on four rotations to Northern Ireland, where he had a lucky escape in 1971 shortly after the 'Bloody Sunday' incident. Bill was relieved as detachment commander on duty at his camp observation post and his replacement was shot by an IRA sniper several minutes later.

Bill represented his regiments in rugby and athletics (sprint, relay and long jump) but his passion was golf. He managed to reduce his handicap to one at his peak, but it blew out to five in his last years of service when a back injury limited his game, playing for Dortmund Garrison Golf Club and in the BAOR and Combined Services golf teams. He coached many officers in the game, including several generals who were happy to be on first name terms with the Colour Sergeant coach on the greens. Bill partnered Prime Minister Ratu Sir Kamisese Mara against a couple of senior army officers in the golf tournament that was part of 'Operation Fijian Farewell' at Dortmund in 1983. The PM's enthusiasm for the game extended to developing a course on his home island of Lakeba, where he offered Bill the position of resident professional, coach and manager when he returned to Fiji. Bill declined the offer for the sake of his children's education.

Bill was awarded a BEM for his contribution to army sport and for his work in the Fijian community. Bill met and married Amelia, from Levuka, while on DOMCOL in Fiji in 1966. Amelia sang in the choir of the Centenary Methodist church in which they were married. Their elder daughter was taking her final school exams in German in 1983, and all three children elected to settle with their parents in England. Bill's son won his golf club championship at fifteen, when his handicap was five, and subsequently played for the Kent County team.

Two grandsons play both rugby codes at a high level. After his discharge Bill sold insurance in Kent for the first few years and is remembered by the daughter of one of his peers as being very successful—a natural salesman. He then drove taxis for another eight years before starting a taxi company, eventually controlling thirty-five cabs in the towns of Chatham and Medway.

He found the administrative skills acquired in the army were useful in the private sector. Bill had several health scares in 1996-97 which triggered some changes in lifestyle and a major refocussing of his life, dealt with in Chapter 9.

Jale VUIYASAWA

Jale (Charles or Charlie) was born in Toorak, Suva but his father was the *Buli* (administrator) for the *tikina* of Yale and associated villages on Kadavu. Jale was the third youngest of eight children and finished his schooling at DAV college in Suva. He was one of the youngest to enlist and was still at school when the recruiting team arrived. His father had served with the FDF in WWII, but his battalion did not get rotated to the Solomon Islands to evict the Japanese. Joe Kamanalagi was also from Yale and Jale's mother and Matereti Vuiyale's mother were sisters.

Jale's twenty-two years with AD regiments took him to Hong Kong in the first instance, followed by operational service in Aden for eight months and two further tours of active service in Armagh in 1976 and West Belfast in 1981. Jale's battery was sent to Cyprus in 1974 for three weeks' adventure training, which morphed into six months of peace-keeping duties after the sky filled with Turkish paratroopers on 20 July. When his regiment had its Bofors guns replaced by the Rapier surface to air missile, Jale became a detachment Commander and he was discharged as a Sergeant in 1983. Jale married Elenoa, also from Kadavu, in 1975 and their two daughters were born in Germany. Jale has no regrets about his army service. He returned to Fiji permanently in 2002. His two daughters graduated from the University

of the South Pacific and now work for the UNDP and the Australian High
Commission's aid section in Suva.

34L AD Rugby Sevens Winning Team Hong Kong 1971/2.
Winners of the Artillery Cup, Rhine Area Cup, BAOR Cup and two other trophies
Rear L to R: Ulaiasi Ravela, Ted Ledua ('Q10') and Aminiasi Ratuloaloa
Front: Jale Vuiyasawa and Bill Vodo. Photo: Ulaiasi Ravela.

Appendix C: Sappers

The Royal Engineers

Jioji AREKI

George, as he was known in the army, was another graduate of St Columba's and MBHS who saw the army as an opportunity to see the world and develop his interest in engineering. In November 1961, he was an apprentice mechanical engineer.

George was born at Matanagata, Vatukoula, where his father was a miner but throughout his life he identified with his parent's village of Tubou on Lakeba in the Lau group. Both George's parents were of Japanese extraction and the family moved to Suva in the early years of WWII to look after his mother's younger siblings, after his maternal grandfather was deported to Japan via Sydney as an enemy alien[59].

George's service in the RE took him to BAOR, Aden and Singapore. He qualified as a combat engineer, specialising in EOD and was involved in trials with a new APC. He represented BAOR as a sprinter, and met and married his Danish first wife, Lyla, in Germany. After six years, however, he felt he had gained what he needed from the army and responded to parental requests

---

59 Jill Waterhouse has recorded that Colonial Fiji deported German passport holders and their families, as enemy aliens, in WWI to internment camps at Canberra's Molonglo Settlement and Bourke.

for him to return to Fiji. He returned with his wife and two young children and resumed his engineering career building roads for the PWD before becoming self-employed for ten years. Despite his mother's Japanese/Tongan extraction, George was steeped in Fijian tradition and protocol. His son Jone, from his second marriage, notes that:

> This mixed heritage in my view led my father to maintain certain views that were pretty unpopular amongst his kinsmen from Lau. He didn't agree with any form of preferential treatment for the i-Taukei except that Government should employ and deploy dedicated teachers into the rural and maritime provinces of the country. He believed that education was the key to resolving much of the challenges facing the i-Taukei.

These views did not win Jioji too many votes when he stood against Felipe Bole in a Lauan electorate in 1987, by which time he had remarried a Samoan woman with whom he had two sons. In 1992 a group of '212' returnees engaged by their biographer in Suva advised that George had been a candidate in the 1987 election 'for the wrong side' (ie the Fiji Labour Party). We dealt with his brief foray into politics in Chapter 7, dealing with 'the events of 1987'.

Michael Shiu CHARAN

When Michael enlisted he gave his occupation as 'teacher, Taveuni', which he almost certainly was because many of his '212' comrades addressed him as 'Master' throughout his service. Few of the surviving '212' seem to have kept in close touch with him but from those who remembered him it is clear he served twenty-two years and was discharged as a Sergeant. He married a Malaysian Indian woman from Malacca, returned to Fiji after his service but eventually settled in Farnborough, working in the officers' mess at Aldershot. Michael died in the early 2000s.

Iliesa Nabalarua KORODRAU

Iliesa is remembered by a classmate in Verata House, QVS, as from Noco in Rewa. He was an apprentice when he enlisted, married a woman from Vanua Vatu in the Lau group and settled in the UK. One of their two sons joined the RAF and served in Afghanistan.

Atunaisa LAQERETABUA

Atu was born in Namata village, Bau, Tailevu, and educated at the village school until 1953, followed by RKS (1954-56) and QVS (1957-61). He was a Technical Apprentice (Roads) with the PWD when he enlisted, seeing the army as an opportunity to 'see the world and learn a trade or two'. Atu qualified as a survey engineer, class 1, as the specialist skill expected of each Sapper of the day as well as being a combat engineer.

In 1994 Atu was asked which village he considered 'home', if not his birthplace, and replied 'St Mary Bourne, Hants (outside Andover) where I made real friends'. His sixteen years' service included 9 Para Squadron, RE, and many years later four of his 9 Para mates came to Fiji with their wives for his 70th birthday. He was known in the RE as Charlie. His RE service took him to Aden on his first operations in the Radfan, with later service building roads in Kenya (1974-76), Cyprus and to Canada for a parachute 'water leap' exercise and building more roads and bridges. Atu left the army as a Sergeant. He met his wife Asilika in 1966 when a full plane load of '212s' returned for 61 days home leave. They returned to Fiji ('no place like home') soon after his discharge, where Atu found a surveying position with the preliminary survey for the Monosavu Dam, 1977-78.

He later joined the Fijian Affairs Department as a provincial administration officer and contributed to the department's Fijian language publication *Na Mata* (The Eye). Atu also served with the RFMF as a platoon sergeant in UNIFIL in 1980 before being commissioned, and completed a tour of duty with MFO Sinai in 1982-83.

Atu and Asilika had three sons and a daughter. The sons returned to England as adults and all settled in Kent, but none followed their father into the army.

Given his Bauan origins and *bati* (warrior) status, Atu played a prominent role in the 1989 funeral for Ratu Sir George Cakobau, the last *Vunivalu* of Bau. Atu retired in 2000 as the *Roko Tui* for Namosi province. He died in July 2017 and was buried back at Namata.

Freddy MUA

Freddy was born in Suva, which he considers 'home', to Rotuman parents who separated when he was young. He was raised by relatives, including an uncle who was a senior winch driver at the Vatukoula gold mine. Freddy's education thus traversed the Toorak Methodist and Vatukoula Fijian schools before he finished at LMS ahead of Tom Waqabaca, Meli Vesikula and others. Freddy's uncle helped him get an apprenticeship as a welder at the Vatukoula mine, but Freddy had taken a few weeks leave in late 1961 to visit an aunt in Suva where he encountered the recruiting team. A couple of his uncles had served in Malaya and Freddy had long entertained an ambition to be a soldier. He expressed a preference for the infantry but found himself allocated to the RE.

Two Rotuman 'cousins' who enlisted with him were Fred Marafono and Roger Wale. As a Sapper Freddy specialised as an internal combustion engine fitter and served nine years, much of it in the 'Far East' of the day, in Singapore, Malaya, Hong Kong and in Thailand working on the 'Operation Crown' airfield in Ubon Ratchathani Province bordering Laos and Cambodia. Two English wives and four daughters kept Freddy from returning to Fiji, and living in Rochdale suited as a base for continuing to see the world. After his discharge Freddy returned to work as a fabrication welder for the rest of his working life. He lost his second wife in 2013.

Isikeli MARAVU Nacamavuto

Isikeli enlisted under his father's family name of Nacamavuto, was initially known as 'Naka' in the army but then came to be known as Kelly/Keli. He was born in his father's village of Qaravu, one of sixteen villages on Gau in the Lomaiviti group of islands to the east of Viti Levu. Keli was brought up in the next village, Navukailagi, his paternal grandmother's village. His father was a farmer and a Methodist minister whose main source of income came from copra.

As a child, Keli played only soccer (football), and in the post-WWII years rugby was unknown on Gau. Keli was not exposed to rugby until he moved to RKS on Viti Levu with a scholarship worth thirty pounds a year, a sum his father could never afford. At the time there was no secondary school on Gau. Keli has many happy memories of his school-days but hated leaving the village at the end of each holiday break to return to boarding school. One of Keli's classmates at RKS was Sitiveni Beraqusa, from Narai, Lomaiviti, who died in a car accident with his three young children in 1974.

Keli has only favourable memories of colonial Fiji and finished his schooling at QVS where three of his classmates in Verata House were subsequently selected for the British Army: Sam Barokei, Iliesa Korodrau and Kalioni Naivalarua. Nearly sixty years later Keli recalled with great affection his most positive memory of QVS, a New Zealander he remembered as John Roose, from Waikato, who was the rugby coach.

Keli's interest in army service was stimulated in part by tales an uncle told of his experiences in New Zealand and the Solomons. His uncle, a SNCO with the Fiji Battalion, was the first man in the village to go abroad and Papakura (a training depot in New Zealand) featured frequently in his recollections. When the recruiting team arrived in Suva, Keli was a trainee surveyor with the PWD and hoped to become a draughtsman. He had left QVS a year or so earlier and had not lacked opportunities, having rejected an apprenticeship offer with CSR in Lautoka and a brief stint at the Teachers' Training College at Nasinu. Keli is remarkably frank about his reason for being desperate to leave Fiji in October-November 1961. He had been keen to become a teacher, but was expelled from the Teacher Training College for breaking into a store in order to sell goods for some extra cash. He was convicted in court and still on probation for the offence when the recruiting team arrived. Keli was thoroughly ashamed of this incident and desperate to leave Fiji's small-town environment and the embarrassment of facing friends and relatives. His minister father had died before the burglary. Keli thought honesty the best policy and declared his conviction and probation to the recruiting team. He was advised that he could be accepted only with an endorsement from his probation officer. Keli first wrote to the Chief Probation Officer, a New Zealander named

Wright, seeking his endorsement and in desperation visited Mr Wright at his home. Wright is also remembered very fondly for agreeing that Keli had learned his lesson and was suitable for the army.

Keli served nine years in the army, then discharged as a Sapper having qualified as a combat engineer and plant fitter. He later spent many years working on oil rigs in the North Sea until sustaining a back injury from a loose drill. Subsequent surgery aggravated his back condition, leaving him spending much of his later years in outer London in a wheel-chair.

Maika QARIKAU

Maika was another apprentice snaffled by the RE in 1961. He is remembered by Tom Morell as the second of the '212' to qualify as a parachutist for 9 Para Squadron, RE but appears to have accepted a redundancy in the late seventies and returned to Fiji with his British wife. Former colleagues remembered in 1992 that the couple 'could not settle' in Fiji and in 1994 they were living in Stockport, Cheshire.

Isoa RABOLA

Isoa was born in Naloaloa, Wailevu East, Vanua Levu, as the second of three boys. He was in his final year at RKS in 1961 and was encouraged to enlist by his teachers. The army appealed to his sense of adventure and he was in the second contingent to leave. Isoa was related to many of those who enlisted from Vanua Levu, including Hoss Ligairi, but his farmer father did not serve in WWII. Isoa served nine years in the RE, qualifying in field engineering skills and was discharged as a Sapper. He never intended to serve the full twenty-two years for which the recruiting team may have hoped. His service took him to South Arabia/Aden and elsewhere in the Middle East, Gibraltar, Kenya and other countries on adventure training. He did not serve with the RFMF on return to Fiji. Isoa returned to marry and settle in his wife's village, Dreketi, became a farmer and had two sons and two daughters. Isoa later became a pastor for the Lutukina Assemblies of God congregation from 1976-2003 and for the Batiri community from 2004-14.

Anare RADRODRO

Anare (Henry) was born in the Waiyevo Hospital, Taveuni and educated at RKS. He was in his second year as an apprentice motor mechanic in 1961.

Henry's father served in the Solomons as a Corporal, and Henry wanted to join the army and see the world. Henry's first choice of corps was RASC as a driver and he had RE as his third choice but that is what he got and served twelve years, finishing as a L/Cpl, vehicle mechanic class A2 and a heavy plant fitter, class A3. He served in Aden, Sharja, Kenya, Belize and Munchengladbach.

Henry married a Lancashire girl who was teaching in Ripon near Harrogate, but the couple divorced in 1980 with no children. He remarried after his return to Fiji in 2010. After the army he spent a year with Dowsett Engineering, another year with 'UMO' a Soviet trade delegation, then CIG Engineering Ltd as a 'cementation ground engineer'.

Tevita ROSA

Tevita is the Fijian rendering of David and he was known as Dave throughout his army service. Rosa, however, is not a Fijian name and Dave's father named him after a former employer, David Rosa, scion of an established settler family who owned the Laucala Island estate, north of Yacata where Dave was born. During his mine clearance work after the conflict in the Falkland Islands Dave signed his letters home to wife Ann as 'Tevita' but she also addressed him as Dave.

Dave was born on 21 October 1942, on Yacata, his mother's island, but identified throughout his life with his father's birthplace of Kabara, Lau, noted for its builders of large ocean-going outrigger canoes. Dave was the eldest of eight children and left school at fourteen. By November 1961, he had completed four years and seven months as an apprentice boat-builder with the Public Works Department marine shipyard in Walu Bay.

Dave's practical orientation was nurtured in the RE. As a young Sapper he was soon engaged in the construction of a forward airfield and the Dhala road in Aden, and in 'minor engineering works' such as the development and improvement of village wells and water holes. Subsequent service had him involved in the construction of a jetty and electrification of Lantau Island in Hong Kong, an airfield in Libya, and Bailey bridges in Zaire and Bangladesh. He also played rugby for his corps and for combined services teams. His remittances supported his parents and helped educate his younger siblings.

Dave specialised in explosive ordnance disposal (EOD), including as a compressed-air diver, and while he served in Northern Ireland, the final challenge in his service was oversighting the clearance of Argentinian mines at the cessation of hostilities in the Falklands Islands in 1982-83. Dave's wife Ann was well aware of his dedication to his RE EOD work before they married, but was rudely reminded of it when their honeymoon in Scotland was interrupted on the second day with a summons back to duty to assist with dismantling an IRA bomb at Bristol docks.

In common with many conflicts before and since the Falklands campaign, one or both parties left a mess with their defensive minefields, that were improperly mapped or not documented at all. As recently as 2013 an FCO visitor reported the following:

2001 Reminder of Argentina's 1982 attempt to reclaim the Falkland Islands.
Photo: Nick Beer

> After the 1982 conflict, there were 25,000 land mines on the islands, 20,000 anti-personnel and 5,000 anti-vehicle. Right after the end of the conflict, a de-mining exercise took out the most dangerous devices and those remaining are on unused pastures and shorelines, well-marked and monitored.[60]

At the time it was estimated that about 18,000 of these devices remained where they had been laid or nearby.

During his sojourn in Port Stanley, Dave wrote to his wife Ann about twice weekly and his letters revealed much of the unique operating environment, inclement weather and problems of cleaning up the mess left by the Argentinians. His most frequent complaints related to the RAF, which he termed 'Crab Air', primarily for frequent pilot failure to manage air-to-air refuelling, and especially for interruptions to mail deliveries. Newspapers were usually delivered within three days of printing 'if Crab Air flies'. His letter of 12 January 1983, referred to a visit by Prime Minister Thatcher arriving in a C-130 Hercules equipped with a Portacabin (including a double bed) but the aircraft became unserviceable and the PM was obliged to return in a second aircraft. In early February the airfield was not usable for three days after a RAF refuelling aircraft landed without withdrawing its refuelling snorkel, which ripped up the surface of the runway. At the time the sappers were working seven-day weeks. The mail issue was clearly a source of concern over the Christmas period when Dave referred to letters and cards from his mother, old friend John Maidment and from Nat Ledua, Kim Yabaki, Sikeli Vakalala and other serving or former '212'. He boasted that his unit (49 EOD Sqn, RE) had made 'the biggest man-made tree in Port Stanley'. Dave's role with 49 EOD Squadron featured in an article on the 'Fijians' Farewell Year' in an early 1983 edition of *Soldier* magazine.

Dave's missives to Ann included passing references to oddities such as a reference to a Fijian seaman, named Nikola, on a visiting cargo ship, and on 21 November he reported the arrival the previous day of 'the first tourist

---

60 Thais Nogueria, employed at Britain's embassy in Brasilia in 2014/15, on an FCO blogsite.

WO2 Dave Rosa with a presentation from his EOD comrades, a cane topped with a brass mortar bomb, Port Stanley 1982. Photo: Ann Rosa

boat' with retired Americans en route to Antarctica. In mid-January Dave met a New Zealand couple with a farm in the North Arm, East Falkland, visited by Fred Marafono with a 22 SAS patrol during the conflict.

A couple of Dave's letters to Ann at this time indicated that he was running out of patience with army bureaucracy and clearly looking forward to returning to a new career back in Fiji. Dave was part of a contingent of '212' senior NCOs and WOs who paraded at the Royal Tournament in Earl's Court in July 1983 and met the Queen Mother. In September, however, he was completing a resettlement training course in business management and did not attend the farewell parade at Dortmund where Prime Minister Ratu Sir Kamisese Mara exhorted those on parade to return to Fiji.

Dave needed no encouragement from his PM. He knew well that his skills and experience could be put to good use back in Fiji. He met Ann on a skiing holiday in Scotland in 1970 and had always made it clear that he wanted to return to Fiji after completing his twenty-two years. They married in 1974 and Ann's preparation for settling in Fiji included supplementing her degree in physical education with an honours degree in geography and history from the Open University. A couple of visits to Fiji, including Kabara, ahead of their eventual settlement in Suva helped Ann's appreciation of Fijian village life and the future importance of Dave's role as the head of his *mataqali* (clan). There were thus no surprises when they returned. Ann was also happy to give up her British passport and take Fiji citizenship which helped her secure employment as a physical education teacher at the International School, where she later taught history and geography, and as an instructor at Polaris Edge fitness centre.

Dave chose to retain his British passport as neither country allowed dual citizenship in 1984. Ann obtained another British passport after Dave's death and eventually returned to live in the UK.

The late John Maidment worked for the Shell Oil Company in Borneo and Irian Jaya for twenty-five years, but usually took leave in Fiji en route to his home in Bournemouth. John first met Dave and several other '212' when transiting Brunei in 1967 and developed close friendships with many of them in the decades that followed.

In late 1993 John recalled the circumstances under which a Taiwanese *beche-de-mer* (sea cucumber) project collapsed. Dave discovered that the project's earnings from sea slug exports to China were being paid outside Fiji, and that the principals were preparing to leave Fiji without paying the staff wages and bonuses owing. Dave visited the Taiwanese manager's office twice without the promised wages being paid. On the third occasion he took a Fijian war club with him, locked the manager's door, banged on the man's desk with the club and promised that if the wages were not paid on the spot the manager would die in his office. The wages were paid but Dave lost his salary and the Fiji government lost the FD50,000 it had invested in the project.

Dave's last appointment was as Operations Manager for the Tai Kabara inter- island shipping line, but a productive life was cut short by diagnosis of acute myeloid leukaemia in 1993. Dave was admitted to Royal Prince Alfred Hospital in Sydney and underwent a bone marrow transplant from his sister Teisa but developed complications and passed away on 24 November 1993. Filimone Jitoko and Adi Litia Samanunu, wife of Ratu Manasa Talakuli, were among those who delivered eulogies at Dave's funeral. Several returned '212', including Hoss Ligairi and Nat Ledua, were among his pall-bearers. His daughter Asenaca later married Taniela Balenivalu who was among the second generation of Fijians to follow the '212' into the British Army.

Ram SAMUJH

Ram gave his occupation and address as 'Electrician, Suva' in 1961. Decades later Pramod Tikaram recalled that Ram grew up in Navua, served about nine years, married a woman from Fiji and opened a nursing home in the UK where he died.

Iliesa SAQUSAQU

Iliesa was another young man from Kadavu who found the army more appealing than his apprenticeship and served in the the RE for twenty-two years. His service included 9 Parachute Squadron and he was discharged as a Corporal from 28 Amphibious Engineer Workshop in 1983. He returned to Fiji the following year and found satisfying employment as an instructor at the Centre for Appropriate Technology and Development (CATD).

Apete SOKOVAGONE Latai

Apete was born in Vatukoula, where his father was a carpenter at the gold mine, but he considered Naikeleyaqa village on Kabara, Lau, as his home. His mother was from Bega. Apete attended RKS before joining the PWD as an apprentice shipwright in the marine department of the government shipyard. He wanted to see the world, further his education and develop his trade skills. His father's younger brother served in the Malayan campaign and Apete's younger brother has since served with the RFMF in Lebanon. His sister Vika Usumaki married Sireli Buadromo, another '212' in 4/7 DG, a tank regiment. Apete served only two years in the RE, in UK and Germany. He was trained in carpentry and joinery and boat building at Marchwood Port Regiment and was known as 'Latai'. He suffered 'shell shock' during a RE training exercise and spent three months in hospital.

He returned to Fiji to look after his parents with his sister and to complete his training as an apprentice shipwright. Apete worked in ship building for thirty-two years, finishing at age 55 as chief ship's draughtsman, working to naval architects until the Fiji government sold the shipyard in 1996. He then spent his last two years working for a private company. He had no subsequent service with the RFMF. Apete died in the CWM Hospital, Suva, in November 2016.

Emani Naqura TABALILI

Emani was born in the village of Dagai, Nabukelevu on Kadavu, Fiji's fourth largest island. He attended the Vunisea Provincial School before RKS and was still a student when he enlisted at nineteen. Emani was never asked about family members who had served with Fiji's military, but gave his reason for enlisting as a desire to see the world. He expressed a preference for the RE in order to learn a trade.

Emani was known as 'Tab' in his twenty-two years as a Sapper, mainly serving in England and Germany, apart from three tours in Northern Ireland. His last posting, however, from 1979-83 was as a sergeant with the MOD sales team demonstrating British weaponry and other equipment including a short runway with 'ski jump' made from RE bridging materials, for the RAF's Harrier VTOL aircraft. The list of countries this took him to makes interesting reading: Brazil, Canada, Colombia, Denmark, France, Germany, Greece, Hong Kong, Iceland, India, Iraq, Kuwait, Nigeria, Puerto Rico, Saudi Arabia, Sierra Leone, Spain, Sweden, Tunisia, USA and Yugoslavia. This is probably more countries than any other '212', apart from those who served with 22 SAS.

Emani's English wife and two daughters did not embrace life in Fiji and returned to the UK (Chapter 6). He settled in his second wife Makareta's village and died in December 2009, survived by Makareta.

Roi TAMANALAILAI

Roi was born on Vanuabalavu, was a relative of Jioji Areki, and attended the Adi Moapa government school there before transferring to Lelean Memorial School outside Suva. He was working as a carpenter in 1961 when he enlisted as a '212'. He served with Isikeli Maravu at Osnabruck, BAOR, before a posting to Singapore as a Corporal where he received a bad head injury in a brawl in a restaurant. He was operated on three times in England before reporting for a posting in Berlin. Roi sustained a further head injury in a rugby match and died soon afterwards on 22 November1968. He is buried in the Commonwealth War Graves Cemetery in Berlin. The epitaph in Fijian on his headstone reads: 'Deepest love from your beloved mother Oripa Matatai and all your family'.

Jone Seru TUISOVUNA

Jone was born in Nauluvatu village in the Nakelo district of Tailevu in eastern Viti Levu. He attended Nakelo district school, RKS and QVS. Jone enlisted because he 'wanted to see the world and out of loyalty to the Queen and to the UK and the Empire—we were all very Royalist at the time'. His paternal grandfather had served in France in WWI, and his elder brother served in the Malayan campaign. Ulaiasa Ravela, a cousin from Nakelo, also enlisted.

At the time Jone was an apprentice mechanical engineer in the PWD which may have influenced the army's decision to allocate him to the RE. His army service enabled him to further his education and he also qualified as a fitter machinist class 1, and a combat engineer class 1 in his seventeen years' service. He served in Germany, Gibraltar, North Africa and Northern Ireland.

Jona Raogo TUNIDAU

Jona was born in the CWM Hospital, Suva but considers Dakuniba, Cakaudrove, his home. He was educated at Suva Methodist Boys School and LMS. At the time of his enlistment he was a heavy diesel plant apprentice with the PWD. Jona had no relatives who had served in WWII or Malaya, but he 'loved the promise' of action and adventure in the British Army. A RE corporal in the recruitment team advised him to become a Sapper.

The corporal conducting one of the first parades of Jona's basic training had trouble pronouncing his family name and agreed with Jona that he could be addressed as 'Private Scouse', regardless of the lack of connection to Liverpool. The name stuck and over thirty years later another Sapper named Peter Dratwa recalled meeting a Fijian known as Scouse serving with 6 Field Support Squadron in the late seventies. A few years earlier another sapper returning from a year of roadworks and other construction work in the Caribbean with Jona insisted on introducing him to Liverpool to give substance to his nick-name.

Jona discharged as a Corporal, after becoming a general heavy-duty plant technician. He served in Aden (1962-65), Libya (1968-69), Anguilla (1972-73), BAOR (1973-75) and Sierra Leone in 1983. The RE work in Sierra Leone reflected HMG's gratitude for assistance during the Falklands War and prevented Jona's attendance with younger brother Tomasi at the farewell parade at Dortmund. 'Home sweet home' brought him back to Fiji where he married for the first time but lost his wife in 2009. Jona continued in 'the old trade' with the PWD.

David WHEY

David was born and raised in Suva where he attended St Columba's Primary School and Marist Brothers College. At the time he enlisted, David was a storeman in the motor division of Morris Hedstrom in Suva. His father was an Australian-born '3/4 Chinese' and his maternal grandfather was a German named Schmidt, who married a Polynesian woman. David never knew his father, who died when he was very young. The *Fiji Times* noted David's enlistment as 'John Whey, alias David Michael Yen' and he was known as D. M. J. Whey in the RE. Members of David's mother's family served with the Fiji Battalion in the Solomons.

David served with 11 Independent Field Squadron from 1963-66 on 'Operation Crown', the SEATO-sponsored construction of Loeng Nok Tha airfield at Ban Kok Talat, near Ubon in north eastern Thailand. After six years in the army, David delayed his departure from the UK and intended to return to Fiji via Sydney where his younger half-brother Vernon Yen had settled. He lived for a while in Kings Cross and acquired permanent resident status with Vernon's assistance, before working for a mining company in Papua New Guinea. He persuaded his old girlfriend in England to join him in Sydney and they married and had a daughter. The marriage failed after a few years and his wife returned to England. David tried a number of different occupations over the years before retiring in suburban Brisbane. One of his treasured possessions that has stayed with him over the years is an excellent annotated photographic record of his service with Operation Crown, which he intends to pass to his daughter and her children.

Operation Crown. David Whey, 'being technical', with 11 Independent Fd Sqn sappers Andy Wilson and Frank Robinson, building the airfield at Loeng Nok Tha, near Ubon, north eastern Thailand, between November, 1963 and January, 1966.
Photo: David Whey

Edward WILSON

Edward was another apprentice recruited into the RE in 1961. He served in Aden in 1963, with 11 Independent Field Squadron at Terendak in Malaysia, and later with Operation Crown, building the airfield at Loeng Nok Tha in north eastern Thailand in 1966. Ted made his mark as a middle-weight boxer in the army, and migrated to Sydney on completion of his service.

Kemueli (Kim) YABAKI

Kim was born in the village of Tiliva, Kadavu and attended the local village school before Vunisea Provincial School and DAV Boys School in Suva. In 1961 he was an apprentice shipwright with the PWD in Suva. Thirty years later he recalled:

> At that time it was the chance to go abroad—it was a big thing for our age group—I just followed the flow of things, overall (hoping) to do better.

Kim qualified as a basic field engineer but specialised as a diver seaman and marine engineer, supporting operations in Borneo from Labuan and Singapore. He loved being in Borneo: 'It was just like Fiji, the weather and fishing.'

An incident in Singapore resulted in Kim's early separation from the army, causing him regret in later life, but he settled back in the UK in an engineering workshop, later marrying Barbara from county Sligo. Kim returned to Fiji for the first time in 1992 with Barbara and their son. Between 2000-14 they developed a successful resort in Tiliva.

William Sing YOUNG

William was listed as 'Assistant engineer, Suva' in 1961. Former colleagues recall he served more than fifteen years, after which he settled in Germany.

He died in 2006 in Osnabruck, where a son now survives him. The main War Office file on the recruitment of the Fijians included a unique reference to '23890207 SP William Sing Hong Young' of 30 Field Squadron, 35 Corps Engineer Regiment, as agreeing to have one pound per week deducted from his pay toward an outstanding income tax obligation in Fiji'!

APPENDIX D: SIGNALLERS

I n 1961 one of the British Army's main recruitment shortfalls lay in recruiting those suitable for skilled trades. Probably unexpectedly, they found a rich source of those they needed most among the Fijians. Royal Signals and REME required the best and brightest for maintaining army systems increasingly dependent on the latest technology.

Joeli CAGILABA

Joeli, who enlisted under his full name, is frequently confused with Joseva Mae Cagilaba, who enlisted under his first two given names but also came to be known as 'Joe Cagilaba'. Joeli was born in Naceva on the island of Beqa, finished his schooling at RKS and was another who left an apprenticeship to serve twenty-two years in RSigs where he made his mark in rugby. Joeli returned to Suva to work for the *Fiji Times* in the first instance, but finished his career as a publications officer with the Fijian Affairs department. He is remembered by some who served with him as more serious than most about his Christianity.

Robert Sant Kumar DASS

Bob was named Sant Kumar at his birth in Suva. Dass is his father's name. He adopted Robert after he was christened into the Catholic church at fourteen. His parents were adherents of the Assemblies of God, but his father

'212' Signals basic training course, Catterick, early 1962
Rear row: L to R Sefton Erasito, Lorima Vula, Matereti Vuiyale, Harry Powell, John Riley,
Joeli Cagilaba, Bob Dass, Alex Kubu
Middle row: L to R John Mason, Isimeli Degei, David Lelo, Fred Dewa, Joseva Mae
Cagilaba, Tom Morell, Keith Zoing, Frank Madden, Sailosi Soqo
Font row: Felix Lockington, Koroi Koto, Bob Thaggard, Officer and
Sgt instructors, Mike Thoman, Sam Pillay, Usaia Masuwale
Photo: Sam Pillay.

had no problem with him becoming a Catholic and Bob chose the Christian name Robert himself. He attended St Columba's Primary School, followed by MBHS, Suva, where he was known as Robert Kumar. The *Fiji Times* listed his full name as Robert Sant Kumar Dass.

Bob's father was a French-polisher of very modest means, an employee of the Fiji government, who ensured that each of his children received a good education. Bob's parents were both fluent in Fijian. Bob's mother grew up near Nailillili village in Rewa where there is a Catholic mission. His father spoke the Rewan dialect, 'Cakobau's Fijian', and knew Ratu Sir George Cakabau through being masseur to the local rugby team. Bob is the second son of ten children. His older brother died in a work-site accident at seventeen.

At MBHS Bob played rugby with his good friend Jim Vakatalai and when the recruiting team arrived in Suva Jim was very keen to enlist while Bob was indifferent but curious. Bob had no family history of military service. Enlistment was a spur of the moment thing, encouraged by classmate Jim when they skipped class ('Latin, or some other shitty thing') to talk to the recruitment team. Bob was allocated to RSigs, served six years and was discharged as a L/Cpl. He married a coal miner's daughter from a broken home who took Valium for her depression and could not cope with army life in Germany without the support of village social life in Bishop Auckland, Darlington, near Catterick, County Durham.

Bob regrets he married so young and without an older adviser/mentor to help him cope with early married life. One of Bob's daughters from this marriage became the first in his family to obtain a university degree. Bob returned to Fiji in 1967 working briefly for Fiji Airways, before moving to Melbourne for five years with AWA, working with aircraft, as his marriage deteriorated.

By 1977 he was a licenced aircraft maintenance engineer in Iran, highly paid, partly as a reflection of the strength of the Australian dollar at the time, servicing aircraft radios and avionics for Iran Air.

Bob returned to Melbourne in the early eighties and opened Sando's Restaurant ('Sando' is a nickname based on his second name) in Brunswick St, Fitzroy. Sando's was very successful and was sold for a substantial profit to invest in another restaurant in Park St, South Melbourne. This venture could not compete, threatened to lose earlier profits and was terminated. Bob then opened Shanti's, with cooks from Southern India, which thrived during a recession in Brunswick's cafe society. Both Sando's and Shanti's appeared in *The Age* Good Food Guide. Bob's second wife Padma was born in Nadi, of South Indian origin. Bob met her in Melbourne after she decided not to return to Fiji from a 1987 visit. Their son Sachin is named after Indian cricketer, Sachin Tendulkar.

Bob's five brothers and two sisters now live in Canada and a brother David also lives in Melbourne.

Isimeli DEGEI

Isimeli, or Semi, born in Bavu village Nadroga, finished his schooling at LMS in 1957. He joined Fiji Posts & Telegraph the following year and was trained as a radio telegraphist. In December 1959 he was posted to Sigatoka. He enlisted as Isimeli Vuki and was clearly destined for RSigs.

By the end of his basic training course, however, he had clarified his identity and was known as Degei, eponymous with Fiji's legendary ancestral snake god of Western Viti Levu. Semi was stationed at Blandford in Dorset for his first six years, after which he served in Swaziland, Aden and Brunei. In 1967 he was stationed in Singapore and served in Thailand with an RE unit working on the airfield for Operation Crown. Postings in Germany consumed the next five years and in 1969 he married a student nurse from Namata, Tailevu. Subsequent postings included an attachment to the RAF's Technical Communications Wing, service in Northern Ireland and instructor postings to the Army Apprentices School and the Honourable Artillery Company (HAC). Semi found the HAC posting his most interesting, serving with a Territorial unit manned by lawyers, bankers and stockbrokers from the City of London whom he recalled would have 'a very different role in war'. Latter day 'Baker Street Irregulars', perhaps?

Semi completed twenty-two years with RSigs and was listed as a Staff Sergeant with the 3rd Armoured Division HQ and Signals Regiment at the Dortmund parade. In March 1992, he said that it had been his hope that his four children would return with him 'to help Fiji' but the children, born in Fiji, Germany, Northern Ireland and Southampton, had decided to stay in the UK. Semi regretted that they 'had no Fijian thinking' which was probably a bit harsh given their ages at the time. Semi returned to Fiji and in May 1987 was one of the directors of the ill-fated Bolatagane Service Station Ltd. He was more successful with his own company, GMS cleaning services in Lautoka. Isimeli died in February 2009, and is survived by his second wife, Voli, who sold GMS several years later.

Fereti Seru DEWA, BSc, Dip Ed, MA, PhD

Fereti (Fred) was born at the CWM Hospital in Suva in 1940. His father was a teacher from Navuso in Naitasiri, and Fred attended Navuso School, RKS and QVS. When he enlisted, Fred was an accounts clerk with Carpenters. Fred enlisted to see the world and get an education. He obtained New Zealand University entrance in 1957 but his parents could not afford to send him abroad. He had earlier attempted to enlist with the FMF for service in Malaya. Fred remembers travelling to Nadi in the back of a truck as part of the first contingent and being among those who went to see boxing at Madison Square Garden while they were in New York.

Exposure to British mid-winter conditions was a shock, and Fred recalls the rearranged beds around the coal fire in the centre of their barracks room each morning. Most British soldiers had been given Christmas leave, and the new recruits were put to work shovelling snow off the main north-south railway line. The Chaplain stopped this and provided Christmas lunch for the Fijians.

Probably because of his exposure to severe cold, Fred was diagnosed with TB and hospitalised for a year until he was cured, albeit with a collapsed left lung. He declined a medical discharge and was later judged fit for active service but was cautioned against boxing. When queried in 2013 on how a man with a collapsed lung could still play competitive rugby, Fred explained that in 1962-63 very few black men played rugby, but many were prominent in boxing, and Fred continued to play because the medical officer had not advised against rugby! Fred nonetheless left the army with a disability pension.

Fred served ten years as a Squaddy with RSigs after completing his basic training. He served in Germany, Cyprus (9/64—4/65 PKO), Hong Kong and Singapore, specialising in electronics. He later became a member of the British Computer Society and a member of the Society of Information Systems Engineering. The final comment by the CO, 8 Signals Regiment comment on Fred's discharge certificate/record of service is worth noting: 'A well-built, fit soldier...good moral standards...played an excellent game of rugby.'

Fred's first wife Molly owned a pub and drove a Bentley in which she collected Fred from rugby matches. They met in Darlington while he was serving at Catterick and had two sons, the elder of whom was an architect in Qatar in 2013, the other an IT consultant in the City of London. Fred was an early graduate of the Open University and later acquired a Dip Ed from Durham, an MA from USP and a PhD from Loughborough University of Technology in 1988.

After earning the first of these degrees, Fred taught at schools in East New Britain and elsewhere in Papua New Guinea in the mid-seventies before returning to an unpaid teaching position in Nabua, Suva. On one occasion Fred advised an Australian colleague that his language with the students was abusive and offensive. The Australian did not get the message until the head boy chased him out of the school wielding a cane knife!

After Fred's return to Fiji, Professor Don Joyce, head of the Maths department at USP, sought out the former British soldier with a degree from the Open University and found employment for Fred at the university. Fred claimed his USP employment was later terminated unfairly due to discrimination by expatriates and Indians against Fijians. In May 1987, some returned '212' were unsuccessful in seeking Fred's support for the coup. At the time he was teaching at USP.

Molly died in 2000 and in 2003, Fred met his second wife Julie through an internet dating site. Years later Julie liked to joke that she was attracted to Fred's online profile of himself, despite being outside her age bracket and his distant home at the time, in deepest darkest North Yorkshire! Fred's only regret about his army service is the good friends that died. Fred lost most of his photographs of his army service when a piece of his luggage was stolen while travelling. Fred passed away in February 2016. His funeral at his birthplace was delayed by Cyclone Winston, the worst storm in Fiji's recorded history.

Seci DRIKA, BEM

Seci advised in early 1994 that Naivaka village in Bua province of Western Vanua Levu 'will always be home to me'. He was educated at Buculevu on

Taveuni and at RKS. When the recruiting team arrived, he was a wireless operator in the Posts and Telecommunications Department in Suva. He wanted a career in radio and modern telecommunications and was delighted to be given his preference of RSigs. He also wanted 'to see the world and serve king (sic) and country'.

Seci served the full twenty-two years as a radio technician, primarily in the UK and western Europe, and discharged as a Sergeant. He represented the BAOR in rugby and his corps in rugby, tennis and golf. Seci was awarded the BEM in 1982 for his service in the army headquarters in Germany. On DOMCOL leave in Fiji, he met and married Adi Elenoa Lalabalavu, from Cakaudrove. As Adi Elenoa's father was deceased and Seci was a commoner, the future *Tui Cakau*, or high chief of Cakaudrove, Ratu Penaia Ganilau, had to approve what became a very successful marriage.

Seci remembered the farewell parade at Dortmund as a key moment in his life, and proceeded from Dortmund to Oman to spend the best part of the next five years supporting communications in the Sultan's Armed Forces. Seci and Elenoa wanted to return to Fiji when the children finished their education. By early 1994, son Nigel was at university and Adi Tui was finishing her schooling. Seci gave no indication of health problems in correspondence with his biographer and died from bone cancer in November 1994. Tragedy struck again ten years later when Adi Elenoa was diagnosed with early onset dementia. Adi Elenoa passed away in 2014 and was buried with Seci in the Fort Pitt Military Cemetery in Kent, together with other soldiers of successive sovereigns dating back to the Crimean War.

Sefton ERASITO

Christened Sefeti Vindo Erasito when born at Mt Kasi Gold Mine in Vanua Levu, where his father Dr Aisea Erasito was a doctor in October 1938, Sefton was the second of four children. Sefton was a good student, excelling at mathematics at Levuka Public School, by which time his father was a house master and his mother, Marietta, the matron for the whole hostel at the co-educational school. Sefton transferred to Suva Grammar School after finishing form five in 1955.

Sefton's grandfather was chief of the Malhaha district of Rotuma, and a descendant of one of the Rotuman chiefs who ceded the island to Queen Victoria on 13 May 1881. Sefton's grandfather had attended QVS and was one of the first three Rotumans to qualify as a doctor. Sefton was awarded a Rotuman community scholarship, the first to study science at Sydney university, and was encouraged by his father to enrol in medicine which did not appeal to him. He wanted to study arts, but returned to Fiji an academic failure after two years. He was however recognised for his prowess on the rugby field. His father was livid and lobbied the recruitment team to take his second son and make something of him.

At the time, Sefton gave his occupation as 'reporter, Levuka' but the family historians have lost track of which newspaper may have employed him. Sefton had no forebears who had served in WWII or Malaya, and any special attraction he may have had to the British Army, beyond his father's exhortations, are lost to family or other memory. Sefton was expected to be best man at his older brother Terence's wedding in Levuka on Saturday 18 November 1961, but as part of the first detachment to leave for the UK on 21 November, Sefton was confined to QEB with the rest of his detachment. About twenty of the wedding guests made the journey to Nadi the following Monday to farewell Sefton, who Terence and his new wife Mary did not see again for twenty years.

Terence Erasito became a teacher in 1959, later studied at Exeter University and became an early TESL teacher in Fiji. He died in 1995. Sefton served sixteen years in RSigs, specialising in radio technology and was discharged as a Sergeant. He was known by his first name in the army but other '212' referred to him as 'Rotuma'.

Sefton was a good correspondent throughout his army service, and maintained regular contact with his mother and siblings. He had been a keen sportsman at school, excelling at rugby at university and in the army and also enjoying cricket and tennis. Sefton married Ann, from Penzance, whom he met while she was a WRAC driver, and they produced four children. He enjoyed his army service which included postings to Cyprus and Germany but wanted to return to Fiji. His eventual decision to return to Fiji was influenced in part by a cassette recording his mother sent to him in the Rotuman language pleading with him to come home, and he accepted an offer of redundancy. Sefton returned to Fiji with Ann in 1977 and lived initially in the family home in Delainavesi before moving to Lami. Sefton worked initially with former colleague Harry Powell but was a great lover of the outdoors and later managed a quail farm for a German woman at Pacific Harbour. Sefton's boisterous life ended in February 1996. Sefton's son Terence runs a very successful engineering business in Suva.

Eroni KORO Turaga

Eroni enlisted under the name Turaga but was known as Eroni Koro. He was a student at Fulton College with classmate Jese Maimanuka who was rejected on age grounds. Eroni served for about seventeen years, married a German woman and settled in the UK where he died around 2014. He is remembered by Alex Kubu as a 'great rugby player—solid man'. Many Fijians would be happy with that as their epitaph.

Lepani KOROI, later known as Roi KOROI and Roi or Koroi KOTO

Lepani Koroi, whose name, like that of many other '212' evolved during his army service and in later years, was listed by the *Fiji Times* as 'unemployed, Davuilevu' but is frequently confused with Eroni Koro above. Roi was one of the older recruits and may have lied about his age to be accepted. In his last years he had to cope with Alzheimer's disease, which has not helped resolving his various *nom de guerre*.

Saiasi Baleimatuku recalls Roi as the eldest of four recruits who were attending the bible school at Davuilevu with him in 1961. Others recall Roi as one of the recruits who struggled with English in his first months in the army. Roi was one of the first of the '212' Signallers to volunteer and qualify as a parachutist, and later served with 216 Para Signals Squadron.

Roi regarded the tiny island of Fulaga, or Vulaga, in the Lau group as 'home'. The island is noted for its wood carvers, a hobby that Roi maintained throughout his life, including two months as Artist-in-Residence at USP in 1987. During his seventeen years with Royal Signals he married Marja (known as Maria) from Finland, and eventually settled at Middlesborough near Harrogate. Roi completed a course at an art college and taught part time after his army service. He also supplemented his pension with security work and driving buses. Roi lost his struggle with Alzeimer's in November 2016, and in his later years preferred to communicate in Fijian. He was visited by Marja, the Kubu family and Mary Zoing in his last week, and their repertoire of Fijian songs elicited one of the beautific smiles for which he is remembered on the cover of this book.

Aleksio KUBU

Alex Kubu was born in Suva but moved to Levuka, his mother's family home, at an early age. Kubu is his mother's family name and he became the eldest of twelve children. His biological father was a boat builder named Gibbons. Alex attended the Sacred Heart College in Levuka and later St John's College, Cawaci, Levuka, and finished school in 1958.

He was recruited into the Civil Aviation Administration at Nadi Airport by a New Zealander named John Horsefield. When the recruiting team arrived in 1961 Alex was training as an apprentice technician maintaining communications to aircraft in the Pacific region. Horsefield brought the recruiting team to Alex's attention and encouraged him to apply. Alex's father and his mother's younger brother had served in the Solomons. His stepfather's younger brother was Livai Nasilivata who won a MC in Malaya. One of Alex's most treasured possessions is an inscribed photograph Livai gave him on 21 November 1961 before leaving Fiji for England, of Livai and Ratu Sir George Cakobau in uniform together. Livai Nasilivata served in the RFMF, including service in Sinai, rising to Lt Col. On 31 December 1985 he was awarded an OBE as Minister for State Cooperatives.

Petro Kubunavanua was Alex's mother's youngest brother and represented Fiji in cricket. He also served in the Solomons and Malaya and became RSM of the FMF. Petro left the army to become 'RSM' at the Fiji Police Academy which took over the old FDF/RFMF Nasova training camp. Tomasi Kubunavanua was a younger half-brother who also served in the RFMF and was ADC to Ratu Sir George Cakobau as Governor General, and in that capacity accompanied Ratu George to the ill-fated wedding of Prince Charles and Lady Diana Spencer.

After completing his basic training, Alex was posted to 7 Signals Regiment in Germany where he played rugby for the BAOR team. He served twenty-two years, specialising as a radio relay technician, and was discharged as a WO2. His best posting was as CSM of the Army Apprentices College at Harrogate, where he possibly contributed to the maturity of many young men who occasionally got into trouble with the police and invariably looked to 'Big Daddy' to bail them out. Several were later commissioned, and a couple reached General rank but still addressed Alex as 'Sir'.

He passed up a posting to Hong Kong to take the Harrogate posting on promotion. Most of Alex's fond memories and entertaining anecdotes of his army service concern rugby. He enjoyed a close relationship with Mike Campbell-Lamerton of DWR who captained the British Lions. He also blames his involvement in rugby for delaying his promotion to senior NCO rank, as he served in 7 Sig Regt under four Colonels, each of whom considered it necessary to advise the then L/Cpl Kubu that they deemed it in the Regiment's interests to extend his posting, so he could continue to be a bastion of the regiment's rugby team.

In 1977-78 Alex was encouraged by Andrew Hickling, then serving in Hong Kong and Captain of the Hong Kong rugby team, to seek a posting to Hong Kong where a young RFMF captain and promising rugby player named Steve Rabuka was serving on attachment to the RGJ.

Alex's wife Erika was born in Silesia, east of the current German border with Poland, and her parents were refugees from what became the Soviet satellite state of East Germany. Alex's decision to marry Erika raised eyebrows in the tram-tracked minds of those responsible for vetting the backgrounds of the wives of British soldiers but the then CO 7 Signals Regiment was Archie Birtwistle, one of Alex's early rugby mentors. Birtwistle directed his staff to expedite the clearance and ensure that Cpl Kubu had leave to get married and return in two weeks to the regiment, in time for the BAOR rugby tournament!

The wedding reception was held in Jim and Mereoni Masuwale's married quarters. Birtwistle rose to Major General rank and became Master of Signals in the army. Years later, as CSM of the apprentice's school, Alex over-ruled recommendations from his staff to discharge a rambunctious young soldier he valued on the rugby team, and after some forthright counselling up against the wall of the CSM's office the young man mended his ways.

Alex was on parade at Dortmund and considered returning to Fiji as he was attracted to coaching rugby at home and had developed a business proposal with several other '212'. The proposal eventually foundered on personality and management issues, but his children were also at a critical stage with their secondary education. Alex played a lot of golf in the army, reducing his single digit handicap to two at one time but his rugby days caught up with him eventually and he now has titanium knees. He has no regrets whatsoever about his army experience.

Arthur Eric LEE (see also p214)

'Big tall Arthur', as he was remembered decades later by former classmates at MBHS, served at least nine years with RSigs, partly with the RTR. After completing his service Arthur migrated to Australia and remained unlocatable in West Ryde, Sydney, until October, 2020.

David Louis LELO

David was a salesman with Morris Hedstrom in Suva when he enlisted. He was nineteen at the time and his parents tried to dissuade him but accepted his decision. Like many others David was attracted to the opportunity to see the world outside Fiji. His father was a manager at the Vatukoula gold mine. David was a middle child and 'pet' of eight. He was raised a Methodist, but his parents had converted to the Mormon church by the time he enlisted.

David was remembered by former comrades in Suva in 1992 as having served in RSigs for six years and having moved to New Zealand. Tom Morell thought the family name was unusual, not Fijian and probably Samoan in origin. David explained in 2013 that a Scottish forebear, named Laidlaw, had traded in the Pacific in the late nineteenth century and married a Samoan woman with whom he had seven children. The wife did not fancy accompanying her husband back to Scotland and jumped ship in Suva with the children and hid until the ship departed. When asked for her name the woman's answer was recorded as 'Lelo'.

David described his forceful mother as 'domineering' and one who always insisted that her name was 'Viti Georgina Lelo'. David later discovered that her birth certificate recorded Flora Lelo and makes the point that researching Fijian ancestry is complicated by the tradition of childless couples adopting a child of a sibling.

David was assigned to RSigs and after his basic training in 1962 was posted to 39 Infantry Brigade at Lisburn outside Belfast in Northern Ireland, well before the 'Troubles', and was posted to the Brigadier's staff. At the time the IRA were targeting British Army armouries. The Brigadier (later MGen), C.H. 'Monkey' Blacker OBE, MC, was a strict disciplinarian and insisted that soldiers salute his vehicle with the Brigadier's pennant even if he was not in it. David's wife Wendy was also serving with the WRAC/RSigs in Lisburn at this time, and they met when two groups of friends were celebrating birthdays in a pub and later shared a cab back to camp.

David's family in Fiji were recent converts to the Church of Latter Day Saints and a Mormon missionary contacted David in Northern Ireland soon after his arrival. Wendy shared David's curiousity about Mormon beliefs, but meetings had to be held in rooms above pubs that the missionaries had rented for their living quarters. When the landlord discovered they were Mormons they were quickly tossed out as one had to be either Catholic or Protestant in Belfast at that time and Mormons were frowned upon. David and Wendy were baptised into the Church and married in 1963.

In 1965, and with a two-year-old son, David was due for another posting and transferred to peninsular Malaya where he served the remaining two years of his enlistment as a Corporal. During this time 39 Inf Bde spent several months clearing the land at Ubon Rachathani in NE Thailand on Operation Crown (chapter 3). The British Army at the time lived on tinned Irish stew and David's comrades were envious of the US soldiers when they arrived with their chicken and salad diet. After returning to Fiji and living in New Zealand for some years, David and Wendy returned to the UK in 1978 where Wendy completed a course in genealogy and he established a new floor sanding business. His main client was an Emirati businessman who earned US$3 million per month from oil royalties and owned several properties in London.

David had problems returning to New Zealand in 1984 on a New Zealand passport which stated that he was a 'Fiji citizen'. He was assisted by another Mormon and David later served a second term as a bishop of the Church of LDS. David retired in 2006 and has no regrets whatsoever about his decision to enlist.

Felix Patrick LOCKINGTON

Felix was born in Suva in 1943 but identifies with Namaka near Nadi where he grew up in the home of his uncle, Tom Henry, as Felix's father died when he was very young. He attended St Mary's school in Nadi, and St John Bosco at Lautoka. Felix's grandfather George Lockington had served in WWI and Tom Henry served with the Fiji Battalion in the Solomons. Tom's son, Joe Henry, was also keen to enlist and Felix volunteers that he 'followed like a sheep'.

In 1961, Felix was an apprentice electrician working on refrigeration systems at Nadi airport where Tom was a building supervisor. He expressed a preference for the RE which he thought might allow him to develop his interest in engines, but found himself allocated to Royal Signals at Catterick for basic training with 11 Signals Regiment. Felix served nine years, which included ten months with the Joint Communications Unit in Borneo during Confrontation with Indonesia and five years with 7 Signals Regiment in Herford, Germany, specialising in radio relay operations and aerial propagation.

Trainee Signallers, Catterick, 1962: Harry Powell (L) and Felix Lockington.
Photo Tom Morell.

He volunteers that he was 'not much good at rugby' but enjoyed playing guitar in the regimental pop group. In 2014 Jim Masuwale recalled Felix as 'a brilliant guitarist'. Felix and the army were unlikely to bond after he presented himself drunk at his first posting to a unit at Verden in Lower Saxony and much later had a fall from a third-floor barracks building in Germany while under the influence of too much beer. He was very lucky not to have been killed or more seriously injured in this fall, as he missed both the concrete path around the building and the kerbing, landing in the flower garden where he fell asleep in the snow until found by a patrolling guard.

While an initial medical examination after he had sobered up did not detect anything amiss, it soon became apparent that Felix had fractured his spine, requiring a body plaster cast and tight confinement to his bed for the following nine months. His eventual reappearance back in his local NAAFI was greeted with incredulity as many of his mates believed a rumour that the fall had killed him.

Frank MADDEN

Frank, from the old capital of Levuka, enlisted as 'clerk, Suva' and served twelve years. According to Semi Degei, Frank married a German woman and was managing a hotel in Germany in 1992. Many of Frank's '212' comrades recall him as a very strong swimmer who swam for BAOR teams and the city of Lippstadt, but he died tragically when swimming alone, apparently suffering a heart attack, and his body was found on an isolated beach in Fiji, between Nadi and Sigatoka, several days later.

Kit Uluinayau, who also married a German woman and settled in Berlin, recalls Frank visiting Berlin as a member of a Fiji Tourism Authority delegation several years ago, possibly 2009. Kit remembered that at the time Frank was 'running a bicycle shop in Nadi'!

Joseva MAE Cagilaba

Joe enlisted as Joseva Mae, 'laboratory assistant, Suva', and was working with Sam Pillay in the agriculture department at the time. He later became known by the above name but is frequently confused with Joeli Cagilaba (page 132 above.) Joe was allocated to RSigs but transferred to REME after completing his basic training. He served twenty-two years and was listed at Dortmund as 'S/Sgt Cagilaba, HQ REME and 48 Comd Wksp'. Mo Beg recalls that Joe was one of the few to qualify at a REME Artificer's course, known as a Tiffy's course. His son followed him into the army, REME and also qualified as an Artificer. Joe's home was at Cikobia, Vanua Levu. He attended MBHS and was in the same class as Tom Morell and Mo Beg. Joe was an excellent rugby player who married a Dane and died in Denmark in 2012.

John Henry MASON

Mason enlisted as 'assistant mechanic, Suva', and served in R Sigs as a linesman. He married an English woman and returned to Fiji to work with Fiji Posts & Telecommunications. Letters addressed to him at Fiji P&T in Suva in 1993-94 were returned marked 'unknown'.

Usaia MASUWALE

Usaia laughs when asked whether he has ever been told that he closely resembles the late Jomo Kenyata, first President of Kenya and former Mau Mau terrorist leader. But he advises that his close-cropped grey-white hair and goatee beard prompt airline check-in staff and immigration officers everywhere to ask if he has ever been mistaken for the actor Morgan Freeman or the late Nelson Mandela.

'Swinging Sixties' Sigies in party mode and close to fluency in Morse: Jim Masuwale (L) and Sefton Erasito (white shirt). Photo: Terence Erasito

Jim, as he was known in the army, was born in Suva but identifies Nakelo in Tailevu as home. He attended RKS and QVS and was expelled from the Nabarivatu Forestry College earlier in 1961. When the recruiting team arrived, he was working as a market vendor and hoping to attend medical school in New Zealand in January 1962.

Jim's father served in the merchant navy in WWII but none of his relatives served in the Solomons or Malaya. He saw enlistment as an opportunity for adventure and a chance to see the world, despite his mother's objections. Jim served sixteen years as a radio relay technician in RSigs in Germany, Cyprus, Singapore and Northern Ireland before accepting voluntary redundancy as a Sergeant.

In 1966 he married Mereoni, from Naitasiri, a recently graduated nursing sister who later found employment on Jim's subsequent postings, including in Singapore. Their second son is named after Keith Zoing who was one of those objecting to Jim's announcements on the flight to the UK (page 30 above) and served with Jim in the Royal Signals. Jim returned to Fiji in 1978 with his family and worked for the Fiji Broadcasting Commission (FBC) as a broadcaster for the next eight years, varying his dulcet tones according to the nature of the program, with 'a religious voice for Sunday programs'!

He also served in the RFMF as a WO2 territorial, and achieved a degree of notoriety with his attendance at the farewell parade in Dortmund when he and Naibuka Qarau were considered AWOL from UNIFIL, although Jim insists they had valid leave passes and Qarau had resigned his commission. In 1986 the family returned to live in the UK, where Jim attended management courses and was employed as a training officer and area manager for the Family Welfare Association and later the Hackney Council. He also served for ten years as an interpreter for the British Army, assisting soldiers who had enlisted after 1998 and appeared in court. Sometimes he assisted with two to three such cases in a week.

Jim and Mereoni returned to retire in Pacific Harbour in 2014 and paid FJD 3,000 to regain their Fiji passports.

Jioji Lesi MATE

Jioji, commonly known as George, was another apparent substitute recruit not listed by the *Fiji Times* but remembered by those who served with him as having Nayau origins and schooling at RKS. He was most likely named after, and encouraged to enlist, by his uncle who had a successful career with the Fiji Defence Force and later the RFMF. Uncle George Mate won a MM in the Solomons and a MC in Malaya.

The younger George's military career was cut short in August 1967 as a Corporal in a car accident in Germany in which Akaputi Valati of the 10th Hussars was also killed. The two are buried together in Hanover Military Cemetery. Uncle George attended the funeral.

Thomas Karl MORELL, GM

Tom was born at Nasali, Rewa, where his family owned a small farm, growing cane and managing a small dairy herd. The Morells of Fiji are descendants of Horace Edward Morell, who was born in London in 1829, found his way to Fiji via gold mining ventures in Australia and New Zealand and established an inter- island mail service with a steam yacht. Naqara, off Nabukavesi is 'Morell Island', where elements of the family remain.

Tom attended St Joseph's, Nailili Primary and Marist Brothers High School where the Principal, Bro Cassian, was a former RAF fighter pilot, but never spoke of it. In WWI two of his father's cousins enlisted with the Auckland Infantry Regiment and one, Horace Valentine Morel (with one L) was KIA in the battle of the Somme on 23 May 18.[61] Tom's Scorpio star sign may have given him a thirst for service. He served in the Fiji Royal Naval Volunteer Reserve (FRNVR) from May 1958 until July 1959, when it was disbanded. He then became a Special Constable in the Fiji Police until September 1961, shortly before he enlisted in the army. At the time of his enlistment Tom was Fiji's youngest Postmaster, at Samabula in Suva, having mastered both accountancy and the morse code necessary for the radio communications between Fiji's many islands in 1961.

Tom was allocated to Royal Signals but as soon as he finished basic training at Catterick he applied, and was rejected, for selection to the parachute brigade. He was then posted to Germany from May to November with 2 Div Sig Regt, in Bunde, Westphalia, learned German and married Fane Sivoki, one of the twelve women who had enlisted with him. Tom and Fane produced four fine sons, three of whom eventually followed their parents into the British Army, serving with the 2RGJ and 22 SAS.

After eight months service Tom applied again for transfer to the parachute brigade and was 'fronted' to his squadron commander, who sought

---

61 New Zealand based researchers Christine Liava'a and Howard Weddell have both mentioned H.V. Morel in their documentation of Fijians and other Pacific Islanders who served in WWI.

an explanation. Tom told the Major 'I signed up for nine years and one is almost gone. I did not come half way around the world to serve without proper soldiering'. The OC approved his application for 'P' company and parachute brigade selection. Tom was the only one of twenty men on his truck to continue selection after the first week and was among the successful 32 of 140 to finish the three weeks. Tom served in 216 Para Signals Sqn, 16 Parachute Brigade from 1962-68.

After selection with P Coy he could not complete a basic parachute course until the ground thawed from the coldest winter in a century—the drop zone was covered with ice in March. Four of the '212' were already in the Parachute Brigade at this time, including Roi Koroi and Jake Tulele (aka Jake Mateyawa, who enlisted as Sekope Turaga). Tom subsequently saw service in Singapore and Borneo before passing selection for 22 SAS in January 1969. He remained in a protected occupation with Royal Signals on the army establishment until 1975 when he formally transferred to Infantry. The balance of Tom's career is dealt with in Appendix F.

Harold NAIDU

Harold was born in Rakiraki, where his father was a farmer, but educated at the Indian High School in Suva. He was working as a clerk in Lautoka when he enlisted and was quoted in the *Fiji Times* of 22 Nov 1961 as telling the reporter 'what we will be taught in the British Army will be very helpful when we come back to Fiji'. Harold served fifteen years in Singapore, Hong Kong, Germany and at RAF Akrotiri in Cyprus when Turkey invaded in July 1974. He returned to Fiji in 1977 to work for Fiji Posts & Telecommunications. His first marriage to a Muslim did not last. He married again, and a son joined the Fiji Police Force.

Hurricanes Nigel and Eric caused considerable damage in western Viti Levu in 1985, disrupting the Lautoka-Namata microwave link on the Sabeto Range, but Harold was able to restore communications via a temporary satellite link provided by the US military.

The following year Harold and Alex Kubu leased land near the Dogo

Island radio station and planted two hectares of cassava as a joint venture. In the aftermath of the May 1987 coup however, local villagers dug up and appropriated their crop. The *Roko Tui* was a former soldier who had served in Malaya and was not interested in mediating the dispute with the villagers. The experience left Harold bitter and in 1992 he noted 'these were not the Fijians we knew' (in 1961).

Samarasam PILLAY

Sam was known as Bill throughout his army service as Pillay was too exotic in 1961! Pillay/Pillai is his mother's name, a result of a mix up with his birth registration. Sam is the eldest of five children. From 1958-61 he was employed as a laboratory assistant in the herbarium at Rodwell Rd, Suva, for an annual salary of £180 with an eventual prospect of £240. He did not bother to check the army wage and wanted to travel. With his government work Sam got two weeks annual leave and only took one week for three years, hoping to have a month in which he proposed to tour the Pacific islands in a copra boat.

The arrival of the recruiting team offered another option, but he did not tell his mother the real reason for wanting to show his birth certificate to a potential new employer. The army also appealed for other reasons. Many police officers of both races in Nadi and Rakiraki were tough, no nonsense but fair men who had served with the FMF battalion in Malaya and Sam thought there must be something good to be achieved through army service. His (maternal) uncle Manickam Pillai had been Attorney General in Ratu Mara's Alliance government and had served in the FDF/RFMF reserves. Uncle Manickam had volunteered for the New Zealand Air Force but was told his eyesight was too weak.

Sam attended Sri Vivekananda High School in Nadi with Mahendra Chaudhry[62], who later (1999-2000) became Prime Minister of a FLP government, and both gained their senior Cambridge certificate. Sam served six years with RSigs, mainly in the UK and Germany, but visited Denmark

---

62 A December 1961 photograph of the two young men appears on page96.

before returning to Fiji. In 1971 Sam married Anand Loshni and in 1987 he was elected MP for the Tavua/Vaileka Indian communal seat previously held by his father for two terms. His all-too-brief service as an elected representative is dealt with in Chapter 7.

In 1992 he was a teacher at Penang High School, and later worked with disabled children. In his later years, Sam worked at USP as a warden and later became involved with Loshni helping rural Indian women under an AusAID-funded project. He corresponded with other '212' for some years but such contact ceased when he lost his diaries.

Harry Lewis POWELL

Harry was born in Lomaloma, Vanuabalavu in the Lau group and considers himself more Tongan than Fijian. He was educated at Levuka Public School and Suva Boys Grammar School and was a clerk/salesman when he enlisted. Harry was keen to follow in his father's footsteps as Powell senior and two uncles had served in WWI. He expressed a preference for Royal Signals as he wanted to become a radio technician. He married Jacqui in 1965 and served until 1974, retiring as a Technical Sergeant.

Postings took him to Germany in the first instance, followed by Singapore, Malaysia, Hong Kong and Malta. In 1968 he accompanied a Gurkha regiment to Fiji on jungle warfare training. Harry swam for his corps and regiment for ten years and represented both at rugby. Back in Suva, Harry found employment as a technician, sales manager, regional manager and managing director of the local AWA subsidiary. He eventually bought into the business but regretted it, and in later years wished he had put the resources he invested in the company into real estate. In retirement Harry and Jacqui live close to a golf course outside Savusavu, a very long way from Tonga.

John RILEY

John was born in Vagadaci village, near Levuka, Ovalau in 1939. His great-great-grand father was an Irishman who arrived in Fiji via the US selling guns, and was rewarded with half the island of Nagini when he married the Tui Verata's daughter. The family rights to that land were later signed away in disputed circumstances. John was born into a Methodist family and attended LPS, which in the 1950s was restricted to Europeans, part-Europeans and the sons of high chiefs. It later opened up to accept more Fijian students. Keith Zoing and a cousin, Alex Kubu, were at LPS with him. John later attended a Catholic school in Lautoka.

At the time of his enlistment, John was a trainee Post-Master. John's father and two uncles served with the Fiji Battalion in the Solomons. At school John had read widely and saw enlistment in the British Army as a conduit to travel to the places he had read about. John wanted to serve in an armoured unit and drive a tank. He was disappointed to be allocated to RSigs and later transferred to REME, supporting 34LAD Regt in the first instance. John's initial trade was that of 'Radio Technician, Light' supporting VHF and UHF communications. He served 22 years, and was discharged as a S/Sgt. His first posting abroad was to Aden in 1962 supporting 34LAD with its Bofors guns in a direct fire support role. He later served in Singapore, Malaya, Germany, Belize, three tours in Northern Ireland, and Canada. His last posting of four years was to the Army Research Centre in Malvern, UK.

John did not attend the Dortmund farewell, but was awarded a medal by the Queen Mother at the subsequent ceremony at Earl's Court. Two of John's most vivid memories of his army service concern his postings in Aden and Belize. In Aden some of the 34LAD Bofors were situated near Negub in the mountains, and in this unlikely environment an 'Arab' youth arrived to enquire whether any Fijians were serving in the camp. The enquiry originated from a part-European Fijian, like John. This particular expatriate Fijian was working with an oil company exploring the region.

John has a relaxed attitude to his and other '212's' ancestry: 'We are all distant cousins'. He jokingly refers to those of mixed race like himself as 'half castes'. When one of the local villagers was caught stealing fuel from the LAD camp some of the soldiers were invited to witness his punishment, the removal of his right hand. During John's service in Belize, Guatamalan forces threatened the British colony and the garrison was strengthened with a detachment of RAF Harriers, whose appearance at a bridge on the border on one occasion persuaded a troop of aging Guatamalan tanks that they would be safer back in their barracks. A helicopter ferrying John to a task on another occasion was diverted to winch a patrol of 22 SAS from the jungle and Hoss Ligairi came aboard.

John and his Yorkshire-born wife Mada met in Germany, married in 1965 and a few years later bought a house in a village outside Catterick where they have since lived. John elected to take most of his short postings with REME unaccompanied, so that his wife and two children could have a settled life. He declined a job offer with Marconi in the south of England after his army service concluded because the family did not want to move south. In retirement John became a regular on the greens of the Catterick golf club until he required titanium knee joints. He is a regular beater of game birds on the Yorkshire Moors, where much of the bag is shipped to London restaurants by air the same day. In December 2013, an Australian TV network broadcast a program on the Yorkshire Dales, featuring a Fijian festival at the George and Dragon pub in a village near Catterick with a Fijian cook. Fijian squadies from units at Catterick prepared *lovo* and *kava* with Riley playing the role of a visiting chief, because he was the longest-serving resident of Fijian extraction.

Ratu Inoke SERU

Ratu Inoke, from Gau, was unemployed in Suva at the time of his recruitment. He is remembered by some of his colleagues as attending QVS but was one of the few not suited to British Army life and did not complete the first six years before returning to Fiji.

Sailosi Ragasawalu SOQO

Sailosi was recorded as a 'telephone mechanic, Suva' in 1961 so it was a natural progression from that to the Royal Signals. When he discharged in 1983 he was a Sergeant at the School of Signals in Blandford. A group of his former comrades recalled in 1992 that he was from Wailevu, Cakaudrove, had remained single until that time, and that he was best known for Elvis impersonations!

Henry (Bob) THAGGARD

Bob was born in Savusavu and educated at Suva Grammar. He was the second of five children. He was tested and interviewed at Savusavu and did not tell his mother of his application until he found he was successful. She was not pleased. He gave his occupation as 'farmer'. There was little to appeal to Bob in Fiji. Four uncles served in the Solomons and all returned. He was not related to any other '212'.

Bob served twelve years, discharging as a corporal, and returned because his father was ill, and Bob was expected to take care of family affairs. His main sporting activity in the army was water polo and he had no regrets about his service.

On his return, Bob married a Rotuman woman he knew before he enlisted. Their son and daughter emigrated to New Zealand. Bob's last years were hampered by a stroke and he passed away in 2015.

Michael THOMAN

Born in Lautoka, Mike was the second eldest of eight brothers. His paternal grandfather was a Girmitya at Lomawai, near Sigatoka who later moved to Lautoka and became a bulldozer driver for the PWD. Mike's father was a police officer and was one of the first Indian officers commissioned as an Inspector. In later life his father complained of the racist attitude of a CP of Rhodesian or South African origin named Lucanelli who apparently did not want 'native' officers in the mess.

Mike attended St Columba's Primary School and Marist Brothers High School. He returned to the Western Division after school and from 1958-61 was a clerical officer in the District Officer's office under the Commissioner Western. Mike was the registrar of births, deaths and marriages on a salary of fourteen pounds per month. The British Army pay was much higher, and Mike signed on for nine years to get a higher pay rate. He was not related to any other '212' and had no relatives with service in WWII or Malaya.

Mike returned to Fiji on DOMCOL in 1967 and met his wife Ramba, who was studying to be a physiotherapist, and they later married. Two children were born at Rintelen in Germany. Mike became a radio maintenance technician and applied for a job with Fiji P & T before his discharge as a L/Cpl. His wife found employment with the CWM hospital as a physiotherapist. All of Mike's service was in BAOR and he did not join the RFMF on his return home.

Mike was a keen soccer player at school, and for Lautoka and Sigatoka district teams while at school and afterwards. He was a member of the first Fiji soccer team to tour abroad in New Caledonia 1960, an all-Indian team. The Fiji Indian Football Association used that name until the late sixties. In the army Mike played for 7 Signals Regiment, a Corps HQ Signals Regiment and 12 Div HQ Signals Regiment. When he first attended football practice the coach was sceptical: 'You Fijians all play rugby'. Mike subsequently qualified as an army soccer coach and on return to Fiji was active in coaching young players. In 1986 he selected Hoss Ligairi's great nephew, Epi Ligairi, for the Fiji team.

Mike returned to Fiji after his army service and worked for Fiji Posts & Telegraph on radio maintenance from 1970-87. The first three years were spent in Suva and thereafter in the Western Division installing radio communications (VHF radio telephone links) in offshore tourist resorts— including Plantation Village, Mana Island and Castaway. His decision to emigrate to Australia is dealt with in Chapter 7.

Josese TOKAINAQELE

Jo was unemployed in Suva when he enlisted. He was born in Daliconi village on Vanuabalavu in the Lau group and educated at QVS. He completed basic training with REME but opted for a transfer to Royal Signals whilst doing his trade training and became known as Jo Toka. Jo's first posting was to a signals regiment in Germany and he became the first of the '212' to die, aged 21, in an accident on New Year's Day 1964. He was hit by a car after a good night out and died in the arms of Seci Drika. His good friend Tom Morell named his second son in memory of Jo. The son, who followed Tom into the army and 22 SAS, was still serving in 2015, and is known as 'Tok'.

Jo is buried at the Hanover Military Cemetery. The late Sir Timoci Tuivaga, former Chief Justice of Fiji, recorded details of Jo's funeral in his 2014 memoir.[63] Timoci (as he then was) was awarded a Commonwealth Scholarship in 1960 to study law in London, and he and his wife had hosted visits by Jo and Bill Pareti at their home in the village of Old Windsor, Berkshire, in the first year of the '212''s arrival in England. Jo and Bill were cousins of Timoci's wife Vilimaina Leba Parrott Savu. Vilimaina received a telegram from the MOD after Jo's death and was invited to nominate two family representatives to attend the funeral in Germany at the Army's expense. Timoci and Buli Buadromo, also studying in England at the time, attended the funeral and in his memoir more than fifty years later Sir Timoci praised the efficiency, courtesy and hospitality of the escorting army officers.

Eroni TUKAITURAGA

Eroni was recorded by the *Fiji Times* as 'farmer, Tailevu'. Former colleagues recalled in 1992 that he served twelve years and was still in the UK at that time.

Jake TULELE

The first thing another military parachutist notices on entering the living room of Jake's house outside Nausori is the framed motif of the Parachute Training School: 'Knowledge dispels fear'. Jake was one of the first of the '212' signallers to volunteer for selection into 216 Para Signals Squadron, part of the airborne division in 1962. Basic parachute training began with descents from anchored balloons and progressed to double-door exits from Hastings bombers with two files of parachutists exiting simultaneously from doors at the rear of the aircraft. While double door exits are clearly the most effective way of discharging parachutists on operations, they have some unusual Occupational Health and Safety concerns as Jake discovered on his first double door exit with equipment in August 1962. Jake was oscillating wildly under his canopy

---

63 Sir Timoci Tuivaga, memoir pps. 72-73.

immediately after it deployed, and another trainee's equipment passed through Jake's rigging lines. Once two canopies are intertwined like this there is no separating them and Jake's canopy was 'stealing' air from Pte Jock Lamond's canopy, causing partial collapse and increasing the overall rate of descent. Fortunately, both soldiers landed without injury. Jake went on to make many more safe descents from what the RAF love to call 'perfectly serviceable aircraft'.

Jake is an abbreviation of Jekope [Jacob] and he enlisted with Turaga as his surname, but later adopted his great-grandfather's surname of Tulele, from Lomaloma, Vanuabalavu. Many '212' remember him as Sekope Mateyawa at the time of their enlistment.

He was born in Vunuku, Moala but identifies with Lomaloma as his forefathers' home. Jake left Moala for Delana Methodist Mission School on Ovalau as a twelve-year-old. He was Dux of the school and awarded a King James bible which he took with him to the UK but eventually lost his faith. When the recruiting team arrived, Jake was studying for his senior Cambridge certificate at the Indian College in Suva and staying with relatives.   One of his teachers was Irene Jai Narayan, who later entered politics and was Minister for Indian Affairs in Fiji's transitional government of 1987-92 following Rabuka's 1987 coups.

Jake joined the Army for an education, not money, and left on the second aircraft on 19 December 1961, arriving at Heathrow. He had no close relatives with service in WWII or Malaya and assumed he was selected for RSigs because of the intelligence test and his expression of interest in radios. He volunteered for airborne as soon as he finished his trade training. Jake served in 216 Para Signals Squadron, 16 Parachute Brigade, for much of his service and was discharged as a corporal. He volunteers that he was often in trouble for fighting. He had no subsequent service with RFMF. He saw active service in Aden and did a tour in Northern Ireland in 1971. His unit exercised in Libya, Egypt and Ghana and he also served in Germany. In 1963 he had an accident on his motor bike near Farnborough—wearing a helmet for the first time. He has a steel plate in his right tibia as a result.

Jake's extra-curricular activities included the Airborne Forces Rugby Club at Aldershot, and starting the first '212' association with Tom Morell. His first marriage was to Tupou, another Lauan, a student nurse he met back in Fiji on leave in 1967. Tupou was a haemophiliac who remained in Germany working at the hospital in Hanover that specialises in treating the condition. The couple had no children.

Jake elected to do a business studies course prior to discharge. The army paid 80% of fees for part time business studies, which he chose to continue rather than attempt SAS selection. He eventually obtained a qualification from London Business School. Some years later the Fiji Development Bank and Westpac sponsored a small business competition and Jake's proposal won. He later established a successful small business, the 'Drop In Lovo' (a reflection of his parachuting days) selling packets of hot lovo food (cooked in an underground oven) to late night revellers in Victoria Parade, Suva.

Jake's second marriage to Sera produced seven children and over eighteen months in 2001-02 he wrote an autobiographical novel, *Island Boy*, reflecting aspects of his life. Like most first-time authors, however, he has had problems finding a publisher. Jake has always been a fan of Britain's royal family and, as a keen letter writer, he sent a note of congratulations to Prince William when Prince George was born and is very proud of the photograph of the young prince with his parents that he received in return.

Mahendra VIJAYNAND

Mahendra was born in Suva, the youngest of seven children of a school-teacher father. He was keen on scouting and became a King's Scout, retaining his interest in scouting in his last years in the army in Germany. Mahendra completed the Fiji Junior Certificate in 1960 and when the recruitment team arrived he was studying for his Cambridge Overseas School Certificate at Suva's Indian High School.

Mahendra, known as 'VJ' to his army colleagues, took his time finding a bride but on his third DOMCOL as a single man in 1976 was introduced to Sheila, the daughter of a close businessman friend of his father.

They married later that year and Sheila joined Mahendra in Germany after he had secured a married quarter. They enjoyed Germany where Sheila found work in a MOD office as a dependent wife, but had to resign from this position when Mahendra was discharged and they operated a small video rental business for the next two years. Their daughter Nina was born in Germany.

They bought what became the family home in Kingsbury, London, at this time and rented it until they settled in the UK. Mahendra spent the last years of his working life in the security industry before retiring in 2009. He died after a short illness in August 2013. His daughter Nina married a Fiji-born man in 2014 and moved to New Zealand, furthering the émigré trek.

Mika VUIDRAVUWALU/RATUMAINACEVU

Mika was born in Rukua village, but also has familial links to Raviravi, further north on the west coast of Beqa, an island of 36 sq km south of Viti Levu. He finished his schooling at Ratu Kadavulevu Intermediate School and the DAV College in Suva and enlisted from school. His older brother, Filimone Navuso, and a cousin, Jonetani Kucuve, also enlisted. Decades later, when asked why he enlisted, Mika's response was 'experience, put on the British Army uniform and fight for the Red, White and Blue', adding that 'my elder brother Jioji Momo was a wireless operator for (the) FMF during the campaign at Solomon Islands in (the) 1940s and I wanted to follow his step'!

Mika's enlistment was recorded under the surname Vuidravuwalu, but on arrival in England he changed it to his father's surname of Ratumainaceva on advice from the army, and became known as 'Ratu' because his army betters could not cope with the correct pronunciation of his full name. They would not have coped with Vuidravuwalu either. He enlisted for twenty-two years, served in Minden, Germany, but left after only four years, seduced by an opportunity to play for Rochdale Hornets R.L.F.C. Mika married Anne, a local girl, and raised three children in Rochdale. Rugby proved a short second career and Mike became a publican for a while before finishing his working life as a precision machine tool setter. He stayed in Rochdale.

Matereti VUIYALE

Matereti, from Kadavu, and known as 'Buli' to other '212', was a clerk with the GPO in Suva who had served in the FRNVR on Operation Grapple in 1957, visiting the Christmas Island site where Britain tested nuclear weapons from 1956-58. His younger brother, Sakeo Vuiyale, was also listed in the *Fiji Times* but there is no evidence that Sakeo ever left Fiji with any of the three detachments of the '212' men. Matereti was a good rugby player and an accomplished sailor who coached Pramod Tikaram's son. He was a Corporal with 201 Signals Squadron in Germany when he died in tragic circumstances on 6 August 1982, and is buried in Hanover Military Cemetery at Niedersachsen. Alex Kubu read the eulogy at Matereti's funeral.

Lorima VULA

Little could be gleaned of Lorima's background or army service, beyond his listing as 'clerk, Suva' in the *Fiji Times* in 1961, suggesting probable employment in the Fiji government. Jim Masuwale recalled that Lorima was from Kadavu and a year ahead of him at QVS. Charles Giblin recalled Lorima was posted to 1 RTR after his basic RSigs training. Jim Masuwale also remembers that Lorima 'married late' and accepted a redundancy from the army in the late seventies when he returned to Fiji. Jim was already working for FBC/Radio Fiji in 1978 and encouraged Lorima to join the company as a radio technician. When Jim returned to the UK in 1986, Lorima was still working for Radio Fiji. He died some time later.

Keith ZOING

Keith was born in Labasa, the fifth of seven sons of the baker, Lui Kum Zoing, who had migrated from China to Fiji in the nineteen twenties. Keith's mother, Louisa Simmons, was a niece of the former Mayor of Labasa and former president of the Fiji Sugar Tradesmen's Union, Morgan Simmons. Keith's stepmother, Kelera Steiner, presented Lui with a further eight children. Kelera's father was a German gunsmith who had assisted a local chief in a nineteenth century conflict over the Macuata Lai Lai.

Keith was sent to board at Levuka Public School and then to Suva Grammar. When the recruiting team arrived in Fiji, Keith was a technical trainee with the Fiji Broadcasting Commission. Three years after leaving Fiji, Keith asked Mary McFadyen to marry him and follow him to Germany.

Keith served twenty-four years, retiring as a WO2 Foreman of Signals, without active service. Two of his children were born in Germany and the third in Cyprus where he was still serving in 1983. Keith attended the ceremony at Dortmund but did not retire until November 1985. Jim and Mereoni Masuwale named their second son after Keith. From 1986-89 Keith served in the Sultan of Oman's Forces as foreman of signals in charge of the installation and training of personnel in trunk area communications for the Sultan's Forces.

Keith spent the next two years employed by Siemens Plessey Defence Systems in Singapore as their customer support engineer, introducing, installing and commissioning trunk area communications for the Singapore Armed Forces.

Keith and Mary always intended to settle in Harrogate but spent the years 1991-96 managing the Nukubati Island Resort for relatives in Fiji before a health issue forced his return to Yorkshire. Keith died in the UK in 1999 after a six-year illness.

Arthur Eric LEE (addendum)

Further to the brief reference above, Arthur was located in August, 2023, after the Covid pandemic via P.K.Simpson, Albert's (pp312, 317) junior at MBHS.

Arthur was born in the CWM hospital in Suva on 04 January, 1944. He never met his father who was a US serviceman who had been stationed in Fiji. Arthur's daughters did some ancestry research and found he has a half sister in the US but he has no other knowledge of his father and does not know if he survived the war.

WO2 Keith Zoing, Foreman of Signals, 259 Signal Squadron, RAF Akrotiri, Cyprus, 1982, escorting Maj Gen Archie Birtwistle. Photo Mary Zoing

Arthur's mother, Beri King, was 'half Chinese (of Hakka descent), one quarter English and one quarter Gilbertese (Kiribati)' descent. A great grandfather was an Englishman named Lanyon. Arthur was raised by his mother and grand mother before his mother married Eric Lee, a Chinese who owned a bakery in Suva, with whom she had a second child. Arthur was adopted and took the Lee family name. Eric Lee died of TB when Arthur was seven years old. Arthur identifies the village of Vatudamu on Vanua Levu as 'home' where his Gilbertese grandmother's brother owned property where the family enjoyed Christmas holidays.

In November, 1961, Arthur was in his final year at MBHS and, as one of the youngest '212' recruits, did not depart for Britain until finishing his exams. MBHS classmates remember him as 'big tall Arthur' and Lee liked to test the wit of British army interlocutors by giving his height, when asked, as 'five feet fifteen inches'! He served nine years with RSigs and has no recollection of why he was not present when his basic training course was photographed (p184). His early service included 9/12 Royal Lancers in Aden and Sharja and with 4 RTR in Borneo. He has fond memories of serving with Frank Madden, Lorima Vula, George Chute and others in those years. He played in a rugby tournament in Nairobi and later enjoyed two weeks R&R in Mombasa. Arthur was discharged as a Corporal.

Arthur knew his future wife, Betty Betham, during their school years and they met during his army service when he returned to Fiji whilst on leave from Singapore. After qualifying as a nurse Betty travelled to the UK with friends and married Arthur in April, 1969, in the Catholic chapel at Herford, Germany. Lt Col Archie Birtwhistle, CO of 7 Signals Regiment, agreed to 'give away' the bride. Seci Drika was Arthur's best man.

Betty's father, Oscar Betham, served with the FIR in Malaya as RSM with Bill Sorby as a company commander, Captain (later Brigadier) Ian Thorpe as Adjutant and the battalion was commanded by Ratu Penaia Ganilau who was awarded a DSO for the battalion's success on operations and the rugby field.

Arthur's mother and her family migrated to Australia in 1962. Arthur and Betty joined them after his discharge from the army. Arthur spent many years working as an electrician or electrical contractor before spending his last working years with IBM in Sydney. One of his step-siblings became a lecturer at the Australian Defence Force Academy in Canberra.

APPENDIX E: 'FOXHOUNDS'

Foot Soldiers/Infantry of the Line

Most of the two hundred men claimed direct or mixed Fijian lineage, and thus some of the warrior ethos that many believe is in their DNA. The infantry may not have been the first preference of the initial forty-six who served in line regiments, but it was certainly the first preference of several, including Jim Vakatalai, Tom Morell and Meli Vesikula who transferred to their first preference at the earliest opportunity.

Both Meli and Tom had the same response to COs concerned about their wish to transfer from REME and RSigs, respectively—'with respect, Sir, I have not come half way around the world to serve in the British Army and not serve as a proper soldier', or words to that effect. These men identified with Bob Hope's quip in his 1967 Christmas concerts for US troops in Vietnam: 'The Infantry used to win wars—until the Air Force employed a public relations officer'.

Individual soldiers are listed under the names of the original regiments to which they were allocated, many of which have subsequently been amalgamated with related regiments and renamed as the army has contracted, along with Britain's shrinking expenditure on defence.

2 Lt Mike Yasa with 9 platoon, C company, 2 RGJ with the Bramall trophy for best platoon, Minden Barracks, Penang, 1965. Photo: Mike Yasa

The Kings Own Royal Border Regiment

Ilisoni Vaniqi LIGAIRI, BEM

'Hoss' Ligairi, as he later became known, began his service with the KORBR but is better known for his subsequent time with 22 SAS, and then with the RFMF in Fiji (dealt with in Chapters 7, 8, and Appendix F.) Hoss was the best shot in his platoon, having the benefit of previous service with the RFMF.

Seconaia Wakolo TAKAVESI, DCM

In 2014 'Tak' recalled his first three years in the KORBR. He admitted extreme difficulty coming to terms with the way NCOs addressed recruits on the parade ground, and was often unsure whether he would shout back, laugh, cry or punch the NCO. Tak is considered in more detail in the following Appendix F, along with others who passed selection for 22 SAS.

The King's Regiment

Jemesa L. NAIVALU, aka Jemesa N VANAISA

In November 1961, the *Fiji Times* recorded one 'Jemesa L. Naivalu, clerk, Suva' among those who responded to the call to the colours. In 1997, Jemesa, or James, was recalled in Hong Kong as 'Jimmy Vanessa' by the former commander of the Reconnaissance Platoon of the Kings Regiment, later Major John Shannon. At the time, Shannon was assistant political adviser to the last Governor of Hong Kong, Christopher Patton. Shannon remembered with angst that the Kings were allocated only two of the two hundred Fijian men, while other regiments received enough of the talented rugby players to make a real difference to their regiment's success in competitions.

Many years later, Shannon suggested the editor of the King's Regiment magazine, Eric Roper, as one to whom a small advertisement might be submitted to flush out aging Kingsmen with memories of the Fijians who served with them. This initiative produced an email from Jimmy's best mate in the recon platoon, Joe Challoner, now living at Mandurah in Western Australia. Joe was keen to see his old friend remembered, as Jimmy was killed on a training exercise when a Ferret scout car crushed him in May 1970. Joe generously proffered several photographs of his old friend. In April 2018, Joe recalled a Kingsman named 'Duglay', whom he thought was another Fijian, killed by an IRA bomb at Springfield Road police station on 30 May, 1972. An internet search facilitated by Mo Beg revealed that the deceased was Marcel Doglay, a Seychellese, with eleven years service in the army. Doglay was almost certainly recruited in the Seychelles in the months before the '212' were recruited in late 1961.

Jimmy was born and began his schooling in the village of Naroi, on Moala in the Lau group. He was a year younger than Jake Tulele who attended the same school. Other '212' like Tom Morell remembered Jimmy as 'Jemesa Vanaisa' and Jake suggests that the confusion may derive in part from 'Vanaisa' being an alternative name for James or Jemesa in the Viti Levu dialect. Jimmy was buried in Hanover Military Cemetery Niedersachsen as Corporal J.N. Vanaisa.

Once Jimmy had been identified, it was possible to glean a few details of his life from those he served with, or had grown up with, such as Jake Tulele and Vosa Cama who was born on nearby Kabara. Jake recalled that Jimmy attended the Sangam school in Samabula, Suva, but Vosa was at LMS with Jimmy. No one recalls who was employing Jimmy as a clerk at the time of his enlistment, but he cannot have been long out of school, as he was twenty-six years old when he died after more than eight years in the army.

Little could be determined of Jimmy's family background and marriage to Taleka, whom he probably married during or shortly after his only return to Fiji on DOMCOL leave in 1966. Joe Challoner recalls that Jimmy was part of a chiefly line, and Taleka was reluctant to return to Fiji with their young son immediately after Jimmy's death. With the assistance of the Kings' CO, Taleka found employment and accommodation in Minden until she decided the best course. She is understood to have married a German citizen and remained in Germany.

Kiniviliame ('King Billy') NAVUSOLO

Given his first name, Kiniviliame was unlikely to ever be known as anything but King Billy in the army, and he is well remembered as such by those who served with him in 1 Kings. King Billy was born in Narikoso village, Kadavu, in May 1942, and was related to Sam Tamata through their mothers. The two boys received their first schooling at Vunisea Provincial Boarding School before further schooling in Suva. Kiniviliame's father was a farmer, but he was named after an uncle who served in the Governor's residence for several years.

The *Fiji Times* list of recruits accepted into the army did not include anyone named Navuso. King Billy appears to have been a last-minute substitute for the twenty-two recruits the Governor chose to retain in Fiji, or others who failed to maintain their enthusiasm to enlist. His basic training took place at Fulwood Barracks, Preston, after which he was posted to the

1st Battalion of The King's Regiment in Berlin. King Billy served initially in the Signals Platoon before joining the Regimental Police. After Berlin he served in Ballykinler Northern Ireland, Libya, British Guiana (Guyana), British Honduras (Belize), Catterick, Minden (Germany), Weeton Camp and Brunei. He was wounded by the IRA in Belfast in 1972 and discharged in Hong Kong January 1974, after which he returned to the UK.

King Billy quickly became a mainstay of the Battalion boxing team and helped the Battalion win several Army Inter Unit Boxing Championships over the years, as well as many individual titles in the heavyweight division. He also excelled in the shot-put, javelin, tug of war, discus and hammer. Decades after the event, King Billy's platoon commander, John Shannon, recalled the basis for his appointment as a regimental policeman:

> 1 Kings was stationed in Ballykinlar Barracks, close to Downpatrick, in Northern Ireland in the mid-1960s, in the days before the 'troubles' started. Kingsman Navuso got involved in fights most Saturday evenings in Downpatrick, spending Sundays in a cell in the regimental guardroom, having been arrested by the Regimental Police. As he was an up-and-coming heavyweight boxer, it was decided to give him a chance and so he was made a regimental policeman, acting LCpl. He was able to sort out the Saturday night fights in the Downpatrick pubs, often just by attending the scene, whereupon the fighting 'Kingos' fled, knowing King Billy's prowess as a boxer!

King Billy died in Royal Liverpool Hospital on 28 March 2008. His funeral was well attended by former Kingsmen, some of whom escorted his ashes to the Fiji High Commission for return to his family in Fiji, together with his many sporting trophies.

Manoa VOSABECI

In 1961 Manoa was listed as 'teacher, Savusavu' and is remembered by former comrades in 1992 as serving six years with the Kings before returning to work for the operator of the international airport at Nadi. He was related to Peni Lepai, who joined SCLI (page 222), and had returned to live on Taveuni by 2013.

The Royal Anglian Regiment

Asesela WAQAIROBA

Asesela was one of the older recruits, and with Hoss Ligairi, one of the two serving with the RFMF in November 1961. He served twenty-two years and was discharged as a Sergeant with 3 Royal Anglian. He returned to Fiji to a position with the Fijian Affairs Ministry, and in this capacity in March 1992 convened a meeting of those '212' living in Suva at the time, who were keen to assist an Australian interested in recording their collective experiences.

Unfortunately, Asesela was not a keen correspondent and died before the 'Flames' (daughters of several of the '212') assisted the Fiji Museum with a commemorative exhibition to mark the 50th anniversary of the '212''s enlistment, which preceded the resurrection of this collective biography.

Somerset & Cornwall Light Infantry and The Light Infantry

Navitilai KUNADOMO

Navitalai was listed in the *Fiji Times* as 'teacher, Nadroga', the latter being his home province. He returned to Fiji, probably after six years, to join the Fiji Police Force and was serving with the Police Mobile Unit at Nasinu in 1994. He was not a natural correspondent and died before the fiftieth anniversary of the '212' enlistment in 2011.

Peni LEPANI Baledrokadroka

Peni was unemployed when he enlisted to serve 'Queen and country' and spent nine years as a private in the Assault Pioneer Platoon, acquiring demolition skills and experience. He enlisted as Peni Lepai and used this name in later life, but between those times he was also known by the above names. Within the Regiment he was known as 'Lep'.

Peni was born in Toorak, Suva, the son of a carpenter working for the PWD, but he returned to family land at Nakobo, Vanua Levu in 1998 to retire. Peni was the eldest son of a Nakobo chief and attended Suva Methodist Boys school.

His service with SCLI took him to Gibraltar, Germany, Libya and Norway and operational deployments in Northern Ireland and Aden. After his army service, Peni worked as a rigger and in other manual work. Peni married an Englishwoman and has a son and a daughter in England. His partner for the last twenty years, Shirley, met her husband of the previous twenty-four years, Kasiano Qaduadua, in Ballymena when Kasiano was serving with the RUR.

She was still known as Shirley Qaduadua. Peni died in Nakabo in 2014. Shirley died of a stroke in Savusavu hospital early in 2018.

Anare Ravula RAVAI

Anare was an 'auto-electrician' in Suva when he enlisted, and served initially with the Warwickshire Fusiliers, in Minden, Germany. He transferred to the Second Battalion of the Royal Regiment of Fusiliers, and as a Staff Sergeant, was awarded a BEM for meritorious service in Northern Ireland in 1978. He discharged in 1983 as a WO2 with the Queen's Division Regiment. When he retired, Anare served initially as a Yeoman Warder or 'Beefeater' at the Tower of London, guarding the Crown Jewels, before moving to other security work. He died relatively young and is buried in a churchyard in Telford, Shropshire.

Isikeli NAQOVU

Isikeli was a dairy farmer from Navua who appears to have spent perhaps six years before the colours, and was still in the UK in 1992. He died before the fiftieth anniversary of his enlistment.

Meli TABUAVAKA, BEM

Meli enlisted in 1961 as 'Meli Tabua, carpenter, Nausori' and discharged in 1983 as 'Sgt Tabuavaka, 1 LI'. In 1993, the Regimental Secretary, SCLI, Brigadier A.I.H. Fyfe, advised Meli's last known address in London, noting that Meli had served with SCLI before the merger to 1LI. In the Queen's Birthday Honours List for 1983, however, Sgt M. N. Tabuavaka was awarded the BEM for 'meritorious service worthy of recognition by the Crown'. Meli, however, like most of the '212' is a modest fellow who has been unavailable for involvement in this project.

Lasaro TEKULEKA

Lasaro was listed as a teacher from Navua in 1961, and was allocated to the SCLI, which merged with other regiments in 1968 to form the Light Infantry. Former comrades recall he served six years before returning to Fiji, where he joined the Fire Brigade at Nausori.

The Prince of Wales Own Regiment of Yorkshire (PWO)

Seru Vuibau VUNIVALU

Seru, from Tailevu, was the son of Ratu Ravuama Vunivalu, a member of Fiji's Legislative Council who died in 1964. Ratu Ravuama served as a Sergeant in Malaya from 1954-56. Seru served twelve years with the Regiment, returned to Fiji and died in 1987.

Semi KOROTOGA Yaranamua

Semi was born on the tiny island of Nabowalu in the Kadavu group, the youngest of five children of a subsistence farmer. He attended a Methodist primary school and was still at RKS when the recruiting team arrived. He saw the opportunity to serve in the army as a panacea for the lack of opportunity in Fiji at the time. Semi's birth certificate showed his family name as his middle name, Korotoga, rather than Yaranamua, and that was how he was enlisted and remains known. He served twenty-two years with postings in Germany, UK, Aden, Norway, Canada, Australia, New Zealand and four tours in Northern Ireland.

As a single man, he returned to Fiji on DOMCOL in 1966 and again in 1982-83 with his English wife Sue and three daughters to assess opportunities, which he found wanting. Regimental duties prevented him from parading at either Dortmund or Earl's Court in 1983.

Semi tried his hand at managing a pub for his first two years after the army, settling in Essex, and later as a farm worker. He then found a niche in the office of a civil engineering firm until he retired in 2007. Semi has no regrets about leaving Fiji and no complaints about the opportunities he enjoyed in his army service. However, he has strong views on the way recent

British governments have treated the armed services and says he would not serve in today's forces, given the treatment they receive from political leaders.

The Cheshire Regiment

Timoci BUKASOQO

The eldest of three children of a FDF/RFMF Major, in 1961 Tim was a classmate of Bob Dass and Jim Vakatalai at Marist Brothers High School where he first came to attention as a talented athlete. His MBHS long jump record was not broken for twenty-five years. Tim was widely remembered by other '212' as perhaps the best sprinter of the group, representing the BAOR. In 1968 he came very close to an Olympic qualifying time.

His decision to enlist was doubtless influenced by his father, who hosted a farewell lunch for Bob Dass and Bob's father before their sons' departure for the UK. The two boys also drank their first beers with their fathers at QEB during their orientation week. Tim served ten years with 1 Cheshires, describing himself as a 'tracksuit soldier' in later life. He met his wife Helen in West London and chose to remain in England with their two children, working for a number of security firms. He died in Kent in May 2015.

Nacanieli LEDUA

Nat was another who found the prospect of a few years in the army preferable to finishing his apprenticeship. He was discharged as a Sergeant twenty-two years later, having represented the regiment in the athletics team, coached the novices boxing team and qualified as a physical training instructor (PTI).

Nat was born on Kabara, Lau and educated at DAV College, Samabula, in Suva. Like many others he wanted to see the world but had no family members who had served in WWII or Malaya. He served in Northern Ireland, Cyprus, Germany and Canada but had no subsequent service in the RFMF. Nat died suddenly in May 1997, survived by Venaisi and their two sons. One son, Tui, obtained a BA in graphic arts from the University of West England and now has his own animation and illustration business. Their second son Josefa emigrated to Sydney.

Navitalai RATUQA

Remembered as 'Nat' by the regimental secretary of the Cheshires in 1993, Navitalai was a carpenter when he enlisted and served, until October 1977 when he settled in Liverpool.

Simione RAVIA TILALATI

Simione was born in Dravuni, Viria, Naitasiri and educated at RKS. He was still at school in November 1961. He was not listed in the *Fiji Times* and must have been selected when some did not report to QEB for travel to the UK, or other checks eliminated them. He enlisted because he wanted to reprise his father's service in WWII. Two uncles served in Malaya, and one of his sons subsequently served with the RFMF in Sinai PKO. Simione served nine years with 1 Cheshire, specialising as an anti-tank gunner. He trained in Libya, France, Denmark, Belgium, Spain, Sweden and Norway and served on operations in Cyprus in 1964 and Northern Ireland in 1970. He discharged as a Corporal. Simione returned to Fiji and joined the Fiji Police, serving from 1970-96. His last appointment was as an Inspector instructor at the Police Academy before he retired to his farm at Naitasiri.

South Wales Borderers - Royal Regiment of Wales

Six of the two hundred men were allocated to The South Wales Borderers, famed for their eleven Victoria Crosses awarded at the Battle of Rorke's Drift South Africa, in 1879. The Fijians integrated easily into the Regiment and quickly became known as the 'black Welshmen'.

Jone BUAKULA

Jone was born in March 1943 in his mother's village on the island of Mali north of Labasa, but considered Nukulau, Navosa in Nadroga/Navosa to be home.

He completed his schooling at RKS where his father, Taniela Buakula, was the manager of the school farm. Taniela's brother had served in the Solomons, and Jone was one of the substitutes for those named in the *Fiji Times* who did not leave Fiji.

Jone completed six years with 1SWB, serving in Hong Kong, Aden and Botswana, returning to the latter as a firearms instructor for the Botswana police after his discharge from the army. When 1SWB returned from Hong Kong they were based at Lydd in Kent. Jone was the first Fijian to be part of the guard at Windsor Castle when the Regiment was given the honour of Mounting the Guard, normally performed by the Guards Regiments. Jone was particularly proud to have had this honour.

After serving in Botswana, Jone returned to the UK and tried his hand as a professional rugby league player for a short time.

Fiji then called Jone home, where his next employment resulted from a chance meeting in the bar of the Grand Pacific Hotel in Suva. Jone was employed as an assistant manager and bodyguard for the American actor Raymond Burr, whose passion for orchids involved a farm near Nadi now known as 'The Garden of the Sleeping Giant', after Sleeping Giant Mountain, which dominates the Sabeto valley. Burr was a homosexual who had a well-documented long-term relationship, but nurtured concerns about threats from a former lover or lovers. Jone was frequently asked to accompany Burr on first-class travel to the United States.

Precisely why Jone left such an easy job to join the Fiji Police Force as a Constable is unclear, but it probably involved his marriage to Alesi and three children. Jone thrived as a policeman, rising through the ranks to become, successively, OIC in Levuka and Savusavu and retiring as the Commandant of the Police Academy. Jone remained aloof from Fiji's coup politics and associated appointments. In a 1993 letter he advised that an army officer, Isikia (Zeke) Savua, was to join the police as DCP, before proceeding to the UK for 'further police studies.' Savua eventually succeeded Philip Arnfield, an experienced and respected senior British policeman; Jone advised 'mixed feelings within the ranks' about Savua's appointment. Jone should have been a diplomat.

Savua's shortcomings as Commissioner are dealt with in Chapter 8, page 108. Jone maintained his passion for rugby as an administrator and is well remembered for his management and coaching of Fiji's Sevens teams in his later years, including winning the world title in 1997. He died in October 2008 after a short illness.

Jonetani KUCUVE

Jonetani's home was the island of Beqa, south of Viti Levu. He attended the Central Fijian Secondary School and gave his occupation as 'labourer' when he enlisted. He served twelve years with 1SWB before leaving to play with the Rochdale Hornets, a professional rugby league team. He settled in Rochdale but died in 2004. Jonetani was part of a composite platoon Bryan Tichborne took to Okinawa on an exchange programme with the US Marine Corps around 1964.

Tichborne recalls a USMC Master Sergeant saying at some stage how impressed he was with the way that 'your white soldiers get on with the black ones'! Tichborne noted: ' 'Our Fijians' were always accepted by the Welsh soldiery as equals—they even spoke English with Welsh accents at times'!

Sisa Radri MATADIGO

The *Fiji Times* listed Mat (as he was known in the Regiment) as 'student, Suva'. At the time he was a student but at Fulton College, near Nadi, run by the Seventh Day Adventist church. Mat's good friend Jese Maimanuku applied with Mat and was rejected, as he was three months short of his eighteenth birthday. Mat, who was born in June 1944, must have lied about his age to be accepted. Apakuki Nanovo recalled in 2013 that this little 'porky' caught up with Mat early in his service, when 1SWB was based at Stanley Fort in Hong Kong. Mat had to correct the record for pension purposes. Jese Maimanuku and several '212' recall Mat regarded Saqani on Vanua Levu as home. Mat is recalled most vividly by his battalion swimming officer, Bryan Tichborne as lacking the solid build of the other Fijians, but also because 'he was equally tough!' He was the only Fijian in the swimming and water polo teams, excelling in both, and in the annual Cross Harbour Swim, now known as the New World Harbour Race.

SWB swimming team after the Cross Harbour Swim, Hong Kong 1964-65, with the battalion swimming officer, Lt Bryan Tichborne (left rear). 'Mat' Matadigo, front right.
Photo: Bryan Tichborne

Mat competed twice in this race[64] while the Regiment was based in Hong Kong and was among the first to finish on both occasions.

In 1967, 1SWB served in Aden where Tichborne recalls a story about whose truth he is unsure, but which is too good to leave out of this record. Mat was wounded by a chunk of hand grenade in his backside. Whilst in the military hospital, his kind Welsh comrades organised a request for him on Forces Radio—'Ring of Fire' by Johnny Cash was popular at the time. Mat served for eighteen years before settling in Rochdale. He was one of four Fijians who attended a reunion at Brecon in 1990. He died in August 2011, shortly after his former comrade Adama Rokotuni. He is remembered by Tichborne as a gentle, modest man with a shy smile, and by the regimental Secretary at the time of his death as 'a Regimental Icon and a first-class rugby player but also a 'gentle' man and good friend to many'.

---

64 In the years before the renaming of the race, the distance between the shores constricted with land reclamation. The water became less of a health hazard after the government of the Hong Kong Special Administrative Region completed a massive new sewage disposal system.

Adama ROKOTUNI

Adama, from Tailevu, was another MBHS old boy who was an apprentice with the PWD in 1961. He completed basic training with REME but preferred the infantry, and was transferred to 1SWB where he served in the Battalion Signals Platoon for much of his service.

Josefa TABUA

Jo appeared in the *Fiji Times* as 'salesman, Suva'. He served six years but there are few recollections of his service and subsequent life, apart from his eventual emigration to Sydney before 1992 where the trail disappeared.

Kitione Riorio ULUINAYAU

Kit was born in Suva, in October 1943 but identifies with Nayau, Lau where his parents originated. Kit's father was a police officer in Lautoka and Kit was the eldest of five children. He attended Methodist Primary School and DAV College, Suva and was a student at the time of his enlistment/ selection. Kit was not on the *Fiji Times* list of 6 Nov 1961 but was chosen to substitute for one of those who did not leave Fiji.

Kit enlisted out of curiosity, as some of his relatives had served in the FDF/FMF. He apparently preferred the SWB because of a relative's service with the FMF in Malaya. He served fifteen years, discharging in 1977 as a Corporal Signals Instructor. He served successively in BAOR, Hong Kong, Borneo and Labuan, the UK, Aden, the UK again, Canada, and another posting with BAOR, as well as on three tours of Northern Ireland. He was discharged with clasps for Borneo, South Arabia and Northern Ireland on his GSM. In 1966, 1SWB were assigned to the independence celebrations for Botswana but the Fijians were omitted from the contingent because of South African sensitivities at the time regarding 'coloured soldiers'. In June 1969, 1SWB was redesignated 1RRW.

Kit's first wife was a Rochdale girl, and their daughter lives with her mother in England. Kit attended pre-discharge training at the Training Services Agency at Catterick—a 26-week course in Centre Lathe Turning.

He later used this qualification to build a second career in Germany. Kit's record of service noted that he was 'sober, honest and thoroughly reliable'. Kit had planned to work for the Ministry of Works in Germany supporting British bases, but he secured employment with a German firm for the first ten years and then, at age 45, got another job for a further twenty years operating computer-driven lathes. He did not return to Fiji because of his second wife, a German woman who he met in Berlin.

Kit's last visit to Fiji was in 1996 when his mother was ill. Kit has a younger brother in New Zealand and a nephew named Uluinayau played rugby for Fiji. He lost another brother to diabetes and his two sisters live in the US.

Kit attended the farewell ceremony at Dortmund but was not swayed by Ratu Mara's appeal for the '212' to return to Fiji. Kit said it had never occurred to him to return there to live. In 1990 Kit had a minor stroke, experiencing vision problems but drove himself to see his doctor and found a blood clot was the cause of the problem. He has since enjoyed good health. Throughout his army service Kit played rugby, hockey and badminton—maintaining the last until 2010-11. In his declining years he practices yoga.

The Duke of Wellington's Regiment

Ratu Meli BASU, MBE

Ratu Meli was born in 1943 at Ucunivanua village in Verata, Tailevu, on the eastern side of Viti Levu, the eldest son of a senior chief's ten children. Meli was in his final year at Lelean Memorial School where he was head boy and dux of the school. Examination of the War Office recruiting file for the enlistment of the '212' showed he was given the highest assessment score of all the male applicants. Whether it was this high score or his first preference, Meli was allocated to REME in the first instance, as he wanted to study electronics and saw the army as a good avenue for furthering his education.

As one of the younger '212' still at school, he was one of the final twelve recruits to leave Fiji after finishing his Senior Cambridge examination. Meli's full given names of Meli Basukunuvanua Vesikula were too difficult for the recruiting team to manage, and he was listed as 'Meli Basu' and came to be known as 'Sam' Basu, particularly throughout his twenty years with 1DWR. He spent his first couple of years servicing helicopters in REME but became increasingly unhappy ('it was not soldiering') and an astute officer with whom he played rugby arranged his transfer to infantry.

In a 1993 letter, Mo Beg recalled Meli the recent school leaver from the adjacent bed space in the REME billets they shared during basic training, and later at the School of Electronic Engineering. Meli's diligent bible reading and church attendance contrasted with 'the coarseness of barrack room life and the oasis of calm and serenity which (Meli's) bed space represented was something to behold! His relative innocence and earnest sincerity made him a respected friend of everyone.' While Meli coped in later years with the temptations beer brings to soldiering, his faith never left him.

Meli became quite a controversial figure in Fiji after his army service (dealt with at some length in Chapter 7) and many exaggerated reports were published at the time and in books that appeared after 'the events of 1987'. Contrary to some reports, he never served with, or even sought selection for, 22 SAS.[65]

After serving with the Dukes for several years, Meli was nominated for an intensive School of Infantry selection course for sergeants, run on SAS selection lines in the Brecon Beacons. Most nominees were given two years' notice to prepare for the course, but Meli had just twenty-four hours to prepare after another DWR nominee withdrew. One hundred and twenty nominees reported for the course; forty-five survived the initial physical selection; and only thirty passed, including Meli.

His service involved two peace-keeping tours in Cyprus in 1967 and 1975, and six tours in Northern Ireland. Over the next two decades he served in BAOR twice (either side of being based in Hong Kong) and finished his service in Gibraltar as the RSM of his Regiment, the only one of the '212' to reach this appointment. He was also posted as an instructor with a

---

65 Eg *Shattered Coups*, R.T. Robertson and Akosita Tamanisau, p. 100.

Territorial regiment in Sheffield. He was located through the administrator of the DWR website, Eugene Hayes, who had vivid memories of 'Sam's' leadership and care of his men as CSM of Somme company. Eugene recalled:

> He was an army man through and through, the Dukes and all it contained was his family—every serving member was his son, the regiment was his mother and father. He would soon let you know it if you where silly enough to bring the Regiment into dispute (sic) or in some way insult the Regiment or its belongings—a very hard man but I have to say very fair man.

An archetype RSM, it seems!

Meli was the parade RSM for Operation 'Fijian Farewell' at Dortmund in 1983 (Chapter 5). He returned to Fiji with Welsh wife Elizabeth and her two children, more in response to his father's urging and his own ambitions rather than Prime Minister Ratu Mara's exhortations at the parade. Ratu Meli had never been an admirer of the PM, whom he saw as abusing his chiefly position with 'dynastic' ambitions. The two were to disagree and eventually clash in the years to come.

In his final year of service, Meli and several others who were on parade at Dortmund prepared a proposal for a Volkswagen agency in Fiji and had at least interest and support in principle from VW headquarters in Germany. The company was registered in July 1985 as Bolatagane Motors Ltd and Bolatagane Service Station Ltd. *Bolatagane* is Fijian for Great Britain. Two years later the company was placed in liquidation. (See also Chapter 6 pps. 70 and 76, and a number of other references throughout this book.)

Meli was a controversial figure in subsequent years, but in 1993 Meli and his family returned to the UK where for some years he was the chief security officer at Marthyr College in South Wales. In 2000 Meli and Elizabeth returned to Fiji, where Meli became a social worker. Elizabeth died in 2005 and Meli has since devoted his energies to assisting Suva's urban poor, and to the work of the Royal British Legion in Fiji, assisting veterans in trouble and younger men who wish to follow the '212' into the British Army.

Viliame BULICIRI

Bill Buliciri was allocated to the Yorks and Lancs regiment, but later transferred to the 1DWR after the Y & L were disbanded. After his discharge in 1970 Viliame became disenchanted with the army and detached from the '212' fraternity. While he remained in England, he had no contact with his older brother Epeli for fourteen years before his death in 1998. He never married.

Bill is sometimes confused with Epeli who joined the army a year or so after him. While Epeli is not strictly one of the '212', he is mentioned on page 134 above and served with the Royal Green Jackets.

Sotia PONIJASI

Sotia spent his first few years in the DWR before passing selection for 22 SAS in 1969 and later transferring to the New Zealand SAS squadron. He is dealt with at length in Appendix F (on those who served with 22 SAS), and in Chapter 7.

William PARROTT aka Bill PARETI

Bill was born in Daliconi, Vanuabalavu, the youngest of nine children. Two of Bill's older brothers (Josefa Dobua and Alipati Jimi) were doctors and one of them served in Malaya. Bill's father Jese was always addressed as Pareti but signed his name 'Parrott'. Bill's birth was thus registered as 'William Parrott', the name under which he enlisted and was known throughout his army service. Bill's father was a farmer and fisherman who earned a modest income from copra. One of Ratu Sir Lala Sakuna's initiatives was to allocate a percentage of copra income to an education fund for islanders.

Bill's mother was Tongan, and he is related to the late Lady Lavinia Ah Koy through his mother. Bill attended the Malaka District School until Class 8. The principal was a Tongan named Tevita Fa. Getting to school involved a two and a half-hour walk. He then spent a year at the Adi Maopa School on Vanuabalavu before finishing at the Draiba School in Suva. Throughout his later school years, Bill returned to Vanuabalavu for Christmas. At the time of his enlistment and arrival in England, Bill had not yet sat for his New Zealand Higher School certificate so was given the opportunity to prepare for and sit the exam as soon as he arrived in England. Bill and five other '212' were transhipped to Strensall near York (Queen Elizabeth Barracks) to the Training Battalion of the Yorkshire Regiment. He joined the York & Lancaster Regiment on completion of his basic training, and served with the Regiment until it was disbanded in 1968. He transferred to 1DWR when the Regiment was in Hong Kong in 1969. The Dukes were the top Army rugby regiment at the time, and Mike Campbell-Lamerton was a Major in the regiment then. Mike was also Captain of the British Lions Rugby team in the early seventies. Bill remained with the DWR until discharged in 1983 as a Colour Sergeant. He and his wife had four children, and one of their sons served in the British Army. His return to Fiji is dealt with in Chapter 6.

Tom WAQABACA

Tom was born on Ono-i-Lau, where his mother and father were born. He attended primary school there before attending LMS with Meli Vesikula and Sotia Ponijase. He was at school when the recruiting team arrived and was one of the twelve who stayed back to complete their Senior Cambridge Certificate. Tom was the youngest of sixteen children. An older brother was wounded in the Solomons. Tom wanted to see the world—geography was a favourite subject at school. England was a focal point during his boyhood, and his heroes were Robin Hood, Dick Turpin, Churchill and Montgomery. Tom also wanted adventure which started with the flights to Sydney, Singapore and the UK, arriving before Christmas, 1961.

Tom did not think he had been a good professional soldier, not like his schoolmates Meli Vesikula (to whom he was very close) and Ponijase. He got on well with everyone and thought his niche might have been as a community relations officer. Rugby featured prominently in Tom's army service. He was the only one to play first grade rugby for the army, and Huddersfield RLC bought him out of military service in 1965. Tom did not enjoy rugby league, however, and re-enlisted in 1967. In 1969 Tom was stationed in Hong Kong with DWR and injured his knee, requiring a cartilage operation, while playing with a Hong Kong team in Japan. This injury ultimately led to his medical discharge from the army in 1975, but he stayed in the UK until 1982.

He finished his soldiering career as a Corporal.

Tom decided very early in his army service that he could not return to Ono-i-Lau as it was too small—only 7.9 sq km with a maximum elevation of 113 metres and just four villages! During a return visit to Fiji Tom engaged a nephew working in Savusavu to find him 200 ha of land which he then leased for FJ$500 per annum from 1975-82. Tom lamented that he was 'a bad son', explaining that he wrote to his parents only once while he was away. He did, however, send flowers to his mother on one occasion, though it seems likely that the flowers might have wilted somewhat by the time they were delivered. Tom's father was a native magistrate and died while he was away. His mother died the year after his return.

Tom had three daughters with a Yorkshire woman, and two more with his second wife. He returned to Fiji without his wife, and then asked for a divorce as he did not think she would adapt to the life he had chosen for himself in Fiji. He just wanted a (cane) 'knife and fork' to farm with and his hobby was fishing. He lost the little finger of his right hand while fishing by himself, when the anchor rope severed his finger against the gunwale. In 1986-87 Tom had a one-year contract with the National Marketing Authority in Savusavu.

Tom's memorabilia, including all his photos and his medals, were left with his wife (who has remarried) and his daughters in the UK. Tom's service took him to Hong Kong, Germany twice, Northern Ireland several times, Japan, Australia, New Zealand, the West Indies, Puerto Rico, and British Honduras (Belize). He regrets only that he 'did not give his best and could have done more'. Tom thinks his generation was more cohesive and responsible than the current generation.

The Sherwood Foresters

Taniela Sofala TOAISI aka Taufale TOAISI

Taniela, or Daniel/Dan, was not listed in the *Fiji Times* and appears to have been one of the late substitutes for those the Governor deemed could not be released to the army in the interests of Fiji's development. He was remembered, however, by a group of returned '212' in Suva in 1992 as 'Taniela Sofala, an Ellis Islander (or Tuvaluan) who served with the Sherwood Foresters, and died in a road accident in Germany'.

Taniela's niece, Keresi Toaisi, however, confirmed in 2015 that Taniela was also known as Taufale Toasi and that his father was a Tuvaluan named Hollis Toaisi.

The CWGC Enquiry Support Team subsequently provided details of Taniela's burial in the Hanover Military Cemetery, where he is recorded as L/Cpl Taniela Sofala Toaisi who died on 4 April 1966. Subsequent contact with Taniela's youngest brother, Harry Moviki Toaisi, revealed further details of the family's origins and Taniela's life. Harry advised that Taniela's father, Hollis Toaisi, a Tuvaluan crewman on an inter-island trading vessel, met his Fijian wife in Suva and settled in Fiji.

Taniela, the eldest boy in the resulting family of nine children, was born in Suva in 1941. Taniela progressed from Draiba Fijian school to QVS and started his working life at the Fiji Industries cement factory, before following his father's profession as a seaman with the Delfino company operating across the Pacific to South America. In late 1961 however, Taniela was in Suva and was attracted by the prospects of service in the British Army.

Taniela wrote to his family while serving in Belfast before the Sherwood Foresters were involved in peace-keeping in Cyprus in 1963. The regiment was based in BAOR in 1966 when Taniela was killed on duty driving a vehicle in a convoy. Harry Toaisi, who enlisted in the RFMF Territorials in 1969, was recalled to serve after the 1987 coup and again for peace-keeping duty in Sinai in 2002-03, when he had an opportunity to visit Taniela's grave in Hanover while on leave.

The Duke of Edinburgh's Royal Regiment (DERR)

Saiasi BALEIMATUKU

Saiasi was born in November 1943 on Namuka-i-Lau, the youngest of three sons from his father's second marriage. His father was the head of his *mataqali* and wanted one of his sons to become a Methodist minister, a role for which Saiasi was training at Davuilevu when the recruiting team arrived. His earlier education had been at Namuka-i-lau District School, then Gaunivou Methodist School at Lakeba.

Saiasi had thus not had his eighteenth birthday when he presented for recruitment using his friend Laisasa Ratabacaca's birth certificate. His bible training must have pricked his conscience, because he felt obliged to admit his deception to the recruiting sergeant, who was wearing the kilt of one of the Scottish regiments. The sergeant was delighted and said: 'You are just what we are looking for—a chap with initiative who can think for himself'! Queried half a century later in the life of his friend Laisasa, Saiasi regretted that they had lost contact—Laisasa was last heard of in New Zealand. None of Saiasi's immediate relatives had served in the Fiji defence forces. He recalls:

> I joined the British Army as I wanted to see England as at that time every Fijian child wanted to see the Queen and visit England, and this was my opportunity.

He also recalled:

> We joined the DERR as we were under the mistaken belief that by serving in this regiment we would be bodyguards of the Duke and thus more likely to meet or see the Queen'.

Saiasi was discharged from the DERR as a Colour Sergeant in 1983, having served in Malta, Cyprus, Germany, Northern Ireland, Belize (where he met his wife Julia in 1970) and Panama, training American officers in jungle warfare techniques before they served in Vietnam. He was nicknamed 'Prince' because his father was a minor chief as head of his *mataqali* (clan).

During his service he qualified as a Quartermaster, drill and training sergeant, driver/commander of an APC, an anti-tank gunner and in winter warfare survival skills. At the DERR Ferozeshah Parade in 1982 (commemorating an 1845 victory over a Sikh army in the Punjab) Saiasi and Lasarusa Turaga, to whom he was related through maternal links, were the Colour Sergeants carrying the Regiment's colours.

Saiasi's return to Fiji in 1983 is dealt with in Chapter 8. His daughter Saadia Baleimatuku joined the British Army from Fiji in December 1999, and on her 21st birthday the *Fiji Times* interviewed her about the hopes she and about 400 other young men and women had about forthcoming service in the British Army. Whilst she was a British passport holder, she had not lived in the UK in the previous five years and was thus ineligible for consideration in the Intelligence Corps, her first preference, because of the need for a security clearance.

Saadia enlisted in the Royal Logistics Corps and trained to be a Movement Controller or MC. She loved the opportunity the army and service as a MC would provide for travel throughout Europe and perhaps, with rank, to her mother's homeland of Belize. Saadia missed her boyfriend, Michael Elder, an apprentice motor mechanic in Fiji, who joined her in England after a year. Michael's father Richard (Dick) Elder was a civil engineer who had worked in PNG and Vanuatu before marrying Michael's mother, Lite, from Naitasiri, and settling in Fiji.

Saadia loved the army but found few of her comrades had the positive attitude and attributes she remembered of her father's service and of various 'uncles' from the '212' who had served with him. She had little confidence that she could rely absolutely on many of those around her in the emergency and conflict situations for which they prepared on exercises. Saadia also regretted that few of the six thousand or more young Fijians then serving in the British Army showed much of the discipline and dedication of her father's generation.

When offered the option of a medical discharge when she found she was pregnant with first daughter Jade, Saadia elected to leave. By this time her parents had become disillusioned with Fiji's coup politics and had returned to live in Litchfield, UK.

Saadia and Michael remained in Litchfield until after the birth of their second daughter. They decided that Australia was a better place for educating and raising their children, and became the third generation of Elders to live in the family home at Mt Macedon, near Melbourne, in a garden with century-old rhododendrons and other exotic trees. Saiasi died in July, 2018.

Buisena CONIVAVOLAGI

Buisena came from Koro, Fiji's seventh largest island about half way between Ovalau and Taveuni in the Koro Sea, which was devastated by tropical cyclone Winston in 2016. He was listed as 'unemployed, Samabula' by the *Fiji Times* in 1961, and was probably one of the hundreds of aimless young men for whom the army offered a unique opportunity in 1961. Thereafter records of his career are sparse. He is noted as one of the seven Fijians who served with the Duke of Edinburgh's Royal Regiment in David Stone's *Cold War Warriors*[66], and as one of two who 'returned to civilian life ...at the beginning of the 1970s'.

Thereafter recollections of him differ. The late Asesela Waqairoba recalled in 1992 that Buisena returned to Koro after twelve years with DERR 'to assume chiefly obligations'. Naibuka Qarau, however, agreed in 2016 that Buisena served twelve years, that he married an Irish woman, and that they had a son named David who died in a motor cycle accident. Naibuka said that Buisena spent some time in London before returning to Fiji, where his second wife, from Koro, was a teacher at the LDS school in Suva. Buisena remained living in Fiji's capital for several years.

Naibuka Samisoni QARAU

Naibuka was born in November 1942 at the Mt Kasi Gold Mine on Vanua Levu, where his father was the mine's doctor. He claims that while some of his peers were born at the local hospital, he was in fact born inside the mine, because of concerns at the time about a possible Japanese invasion. Naibuka identifies with his father's origins in Nauluvatu, Nakelo, Tailevu South.

---

66 *Cold War Warriors–The Story of the Duke of Edinburgh's Royal Regiment (Berkshire and Wiltshire) 1959-1994*, David Stone, Pen & Sword Books 1998.

He attended Nakelo District School and RKS and was looking for employment when the recruitment team arrived. He gave his occupation as 'builder' as that was what he hoped to do because of the emphasis at RKS on carpentry and other practical skills.

He was attracted by the prospect of travelling to the UK, and throughout the remnant British Empire he had studied at school. His experience in the RKS Cadet Unit also influenced his decision to enlist. Together with five other Fijians, Naibuka found himself in the DERR, where he spent the first nine of his sixteen years in the army becoming known as 'Sam' and was promoted to Sergeant. In 1967 Naibuka attempted selection for 22 SAS, surviving as one of twenty-eight of the eighty who started together but found the final 45-mile (72.4 km) yomp too much. He tried the Parachute Regiment course straight after that, passing selection and later qualifying as a parachutist. His seventeen years service embraced deployments or postings in Malta, Cyprus, Libya, Egypt, Lebanon, Israel, Italy, Germany, Denmark, Luxembourg, Holland, France, British Honduras, Panama and the United States.

In British Honduras in 1969, Naibuka trained with the US army in the Panama Canal Zone preparing GIs for the Vietnam War and jungle warfare. He then became the British Army support company Sergeant at an airport camp near Belize. He also had a tour of Northern Ireland with the QOH in Belfast in 1971. Naibuka took part in an Outward Bound course at Kristiansand at Telemark, Norway which was also attended by Buli Vuiyale (Royal Signals) and Jale Vuiyasawa (Royal Artillery).

A pin needed to secure a badly damaged ankle restricted normal walking and Naibuka's career as a foot soldier. He did not want to be medically discharged and transferred to the RAC, joining his brother in law, Lepanai Tamanikairukurukuiovalau, and seven other '212' at the time in the QOH. Naibuka joined the support squadron, qualifying as a Swingfire anti-tank missile controller on the 438 Armoured Vehicle. He was discharged as a Corporal, with the reduction in rank suggesting at least occasional difficulty with army regulations and discipline.

Naibuka is a man with a fund of entertaining stories about his life, but two of the better ones are recorded by John Blashford-Snell in his book *In the Steps of Stanley*, a record of his 1974 expedition up the Congo River, utilising Joe Tuwai and Naibuka to maintain his forward and rear communications links, respectively. Naibuka bonded very well with a tribe of pygmies encountered by the expedition but terrified them with his party trick of squirting flames of paraffin from his mouth. When Naibuka first met one of Blashford-Snell's staff named Pam Baker, Naibuka greeted her with 'Baker? That's interesting, my grandfather ate a missionary named Baker'! The then Cpl Qarau's jest referred to the unfortunate Rev. Thomas Baker, a Methodist missionary killed and eaten by xenophobic villagers in the hinterland of Viti Levu while spreading the holy word.

Naibuka's service involved three tours of duty in Northern Ireland, on one of which he was injured while involved in riot control.

Naibuka married Makareta in Fiji in 1966, and their three daughters were born in the UK, Germany and Fiji over the next ten years. All eventually settled in the UK. Their youngest daughter Lusia eventually completed five tours in Iraq and Afghanistan as an army medic. On return to Fiji, Naibuka served with the RFMF for six years, during which he attended an officer training course at Waiuru, New Zealand, and was commissioned. He first served with the UN in Lebanon for six months as a Platoon Commander. He later served with MFO in the Sinai Peninsula for two years as Reconnaissance Platoon Commander and Operations officer for the Regiment and Force HQ. He was a Company Commander in 'C' Company Training team for the first Sinai contingent in 1981.

Naibuka also developed a profitable sideline with a small pig farm outside Suva and by selling vegetables at the market and Army Barracks. The Nausori Agriculture Department recommended he apply to the Fiji Development Bank (FDB) for FJD41,000 to enlarge the piggery to a twenty-sow unit with improved facilities. Naibuka paid staff to look after the farm for him while he served with the RFMF. Naibuka recalls bitterly that in Fiji in the early eighties, what mattered most was 'not what you know but who you know' and he was disappointed when the FDB rejected his loan on the basis that a serving soldier could not also properly manage a farm.

He became even more embittered when he was informed by one of the territorial soldiers working at FDB that the loans officer who rejected his loan subsequently approved an identical proposal for a cabinet minister. Naibuka claims that it was at this stage that he decided to leave Fiji and return to the UK, although his eventual departure was triggered under unusual circumstances detailed in Chapter 5.

In London, Naibuka initially found employment as a body-guard for a Dutch multimillionaire. He later worked for the Ministry of Defence as a Family Welfare and Housing Officer, and as a rent officer for Hackney Council. In retirement he became a Circuit Steward at Wesley's Chapel in London. Makareta died in 2010 and Naibuka returned to Fiji in 2014.

Usaia RAIDANI

Usaia (known as 'Nick' in the DERR) from Mokanai village in Tailevu South, was in the the RFMF when he enlisted and returned to them after an incident in Sliema, Malta, in 1965. Nick eventually reached WO2 rank in the RFMF, telling Lasarusa Turaga years later that he had 'learned a lesson'.

Stone's history of the DERR mentions a Fijian named Koroidovi joining the battalion shortly afterwards, but Koroidovi was not one of the '212'. According to Mike Netzler, Timoci Koroidovi, known as 'Jim' in the army, travelled to the UK as a stowaway, like Netzler, and when he was presented to a court the magistrate suggested a choice of deportation or army service—a judicial refinement of the Royal Navy's 'Press Gangs' of an earlier century. Netzler recalled that Koroidovi ended his days in Derby, where he had married an immigrant woman of Indian origin.

Josese RAVU

Joe was born in Naivakacau, Tailevu and educated at the Buretu District School before finishing at RKS. He was working as a carpenter in Tailevu and his decision to enlist may have been influenced by his father's service with the Fiji Defence Forces in WWII. Joe was attracted to the DERR primarily because he heard that the Regiment was to serve in Malta, and any place warmer than the UK appealed strongly. Joe was discharged as a Sergeant after twenty-two years, during which he specialised as a heavy infantry weapons (anti-tank) specialist and a sniper. His service took him to Malta, Libya, Italy, France, Germany, Canada, Cyprus, Northern Ireland and throughout the UK. He was a member of the DERR shooting team at the annual Queen's Medal competition at Bisley.

Joe married Una from the next village. They returned to Fiji because his mother and his wife's parents were still alive, and they wanted their children to know their grandparents. Jo and Una had four children born in Germany, England and Northern Ireland during his postings. All the children returned with them to Fiji.

Joe found a niche at Fiji's Telecommunications Training Centre at Laucala Bay. He has no regrets whatsoever regarding his army service but had no subsequent service with the RFMF.

Lasarusa TURAGA

In Liverpool today Lasarusa is very proud of his Mualevu, Vanuabalavu origins, and has fond memories of his schooling at the Marist Brothers Convent in Levuka and later at RKS. This was where he was one of twelve Lauans in the team which won the inaugural Dean's Cup inter-school rugby trophy, defeating a team from LMS which included Tom Waqabaca. He is very dismissive of the MBHS team of the time, which he recalls had 'too many Europeans and part Asians—all poofters'.

In October 1961 Lasarusa expected to train as a teacher the following year. RKS provided a bus for all interested sixth-form boys to present themselves for interview at Nausori. Lasarusa responded to the recruiting team advertisement 'as a joke'. His Tongan mother wept when she saw his name in the *Fiji Times* as one of those who had enlisted. For the first five years he sent half his net pay back to Fiji to support his parents. This proved far more lucrative than being a teacher. His father was the captain of the *Tui Levuka* trading vessel and died in a fire at sea.

The DERR conducted its basic training at Honiton in Devon, but in the severe winter of 1961-62 this had to be delayed until March. The new recruits from Fiji, billeted in Nissan huts, were fortunate that sympathetic officers and NCOs allowed them to keep their coal fires burning during the day.

The Regiment was moved to Malta in 1962 and Lasarusa subsequently served in Cyprus, Belize/British Honduras and Northern Ireland. In 1972 he was posted as an instructor at RMA, Mons. Lasarusa claims that he and Joe Ravu were the only '212' to represent their Regiment at the annual Queen's Shoot at Bisley. Lasarusa was a member of the DERR team from 1965-82, finishing in the top 100 of thousands of contestants on one occasion. He also claims to have won the 'Cyprus Walk' in 1968, an eighty-mile (128.7 km) orienteering exercise he completed in ten hours and twenty minutes. He trained for this event by running a fifteen-mile (24.1 km) course twice daily.

On one of his tours in Belize, Lasarusa was advised that a visiting General named Baker had asked to meet him. Lasarusa was puzzled by the request and spent extra time cleaning his kit before the appointment. On arrival he was told to sit down and relax, and was asked 'You must have heard of my relative, Dr Baker, in Fiji—he is very famous'? Lasarusa could not recall any medical practitioners named Baker and remained puzzled until General Baker said: 'they ate him'! The General explained that when he retired, he hoped to retrace his ancestor's steps and meet the descendants of those who killed the British missionary Rev. Thomas Baker in 1867, and see his remaining boot in the Fiji Museum!

Lasarusa's anecdote generated a sheaf of correspondence attempting to identify the above 'General Baker'. The Military Adviser at the British High Commission in Canberra in 1993 suggested writing to MGen Ian Baker, CBE, who promptly advised that it was not him and suggested contact with LGen Sir Maurice Johnston, KCB, OBE, who had served as Military Assistant to the, then, General, later Field Marshall, Sir Geoffrey Baker,

GCB, MC, earlier in his career.[67] Sir Geoffrey, known as 'George' Baker, died in May 1980, but Ian Baker passed the enquiry letter to his namesake's widow and to Sir Maurice. Sir Maurice's equally prompt response is worth quoting verbatim for his contribution to colourful tales of cannibalism, despite his erroneous understanding of Wesleyan Baker's descendants:

> In 1969 we made a world trip, which included a memorable three days in Fiji. General Baker was indeed the grandson of Rev. Thomas Baker. We flew into Nandi (sic) in our Comet, and were met by the then Minister of Defence, Rata Panaya (sic). Since it was lunchtime, and we were due then to change into a smaller aeroplane and fly east to the capital, the Minister gave us lunch in the airport restaurant. He handed Lady Baker the vast a la carte menu; she ran her finger down the menu and said: 'I cannot see boiled Grandfather on the menu' at which Rata Panaya cried with laughter so much that he was unable to speak for a full five minutes!'[68]

Sir Maurice kindly passed his letter to George Baker's widow, Lady Valerie, who had a shoulder injury at the time which restricted her correspondence. She delegated her daughter Alix Baker, FRSA, the family archivist and a leading military artist, to respond. Alix Baker regretted, however, that Sir Maurice was mistaken and advised: 'The Rev. Dr Thomas Baker has no connection whatsoever with our family. My father's grandfather did indeed finally settle in Fiji and die there, but his name was Dr John Haller Hutchinson and he died from illness, not as the haute cuisine of cannibals!'[69]

As CEO of the Family Planning Association of Fiji, Lasarusa attended international conferences on AIDS in Australia in 1990 and Thailand in 1991, when the impact of AIDS in that country made a big impression. By the mid-nineties, however, Lasarusa and Debra had returned to Liverpool. Twenty years later he was recovering well from a replacement knee joint ordained by so many years on the rugby field.

---

67 Maj Gen Ian Baker letter to author, 12 May 1993.

68 Sir Maurice Johnston's letter of 31 May 1993 to author.

69 Alix Baker's letter of 4 June 1993 to author.

The King's Shropshire Light infantry

Kuata Vamarasi (Fred) MARAFONO, MBE

Fred's family came from the Pepjei district of Fiji's northernmost (and Polynesian) island of Rotuma. According to *The Telegraph's* obituary of Fred, his father was a farmer who had served in the British Army in Burma during WWII. It is more likely that Fred's father served with the Fiji Defence Forces of the day in the Solomons campaign. In 1961 Fred was a student at Navuso Agricultural College and hoped to become a veterinarian, but was attracted by the opportunities in the army. Fred was keen to be involved in this project in late 2012, but died early the following year without sharing any of his experience in KSLI, or what attracted him to become the first of the '212' to pass selection in April 1964 for 22 SAS, where he remained for the rest of his service, finishing as a WO1. The rest of his remarkable life is dealt with in Appendix F.

Lasaro TEKULEKA

Lasaro was listed as a teacher from Navua in 1961. In 2014 Apakuki Nanovo recalled that Lasaro was allocated to the KSLI, which merged with other regiments in 1968 to form the Light Infantry. Other former comrades recall he served six years before returning to Fiji, where he joined the Fire Brigade at Nausori.

King's Royal Rifle Corps - Royal Green Jackets

The historical link between the WWI Fijian Defence Force and the King's Royal Rifle Corps attracted several '212' and a couple of pioneers before them, one of whom was Mike Netzler. Mike was born in Samoa, but lived in Fiji from the age of nine. He was a police constable before moving to the UK a couple of years ahead of the '212' recruitment. His grandfather left Sweden after WWI and arrived in Samoa via the USA. Mike, who was serving with 1RGJ in 1961, was despatched to Heathrow to escort to Winchester the four young fellow-Fijians allocated to the Green Jackets.

Voate RAKANACE

Voate, also known as Wati and nicknamed 'Pepe', served as a police constable in Lautoka before enlisting but had his roots in Bau. Pepe was an extroverted joker, charismatic and entertaining. However, he almost went too far with his teasing while serving in Berlin with 1RGJ when he deliberately crossed onto the Soviet side of the barrier fence twice, knowing that he was watched by the Soviet guards. On the second occasion, they arrested him and the incident was headlined by the BBC and local (if not British) newspapers.

He first married Gertrude, an East German, with whom he had a daughter. Pepe left the Army after twelve years and then married Anna Marie, another German from Hanover, with whom he had two further daughters. One daughter died tragically on a German autobahn with her husband, a Fijian who had followed the '212' into the British Army in 1999-2000.

Pepe always wanted to be a success, and joined an international hotel chain serving in various places around the world in managerial roles, finally ending up in the USA where he left the company. He enrolled in a private flying school, obtaining a pilot's licence.

Pepe returned to Germany with Anna Marie and occupied a large house in Hanover that Anna Marie had been left by her parents. Pramod Tikaram visited him there on many occasions and noticed that he was putting on lot of weight. The combination of the weight and heavy smoking may have contributed to his death back in Fiji where he was undertaking selection tests with Fiji Airways, and died of a massive heart attack in 1981.

Amani RATINI

When he enlisted, Amani gave his occupation and address as 'farmer, Suva'. Former comrades remembered him in 1992 as probably born in Suvavou on the city's outskirts. He is identified in a photograph of the four newly-arrived Green Jackets as 'S. Ratini' and is remembered by Mike Yasa and Tom Morell as 'Samuela'. Tom also recalls that Ratini was the last of the dozen '212', apart from those who joined 22 SAS, to qualify as a parachutist in 1966, apparently after transferring from 1RGJ to 2 Para.

Samuela VUETIBAU

Sam was another noted by the *Fiji Times* as unemployed, then living at Navua west of Suva. He served for nine years with 1RGJ and was remembered by former comrades in 1992 as living in the UK at that time.

Mikaele Mataika Kolinio YASA

M. M. K. Yasa, known as Mick in the army and Mike in later life, was born in the village of Kereira, Moala, in the Lau group on Christmas Eve 1937, making him the eldest of the '212' who did not lie about their age in order to be accepted. He was also the only one of the '212' with tertiary qualifications, and one of only six who had done any prior foreign travel.

Mike's father was a farmer and a steward of the village church. Mike, the second of eleven children, described his early life on the island at some length in his 2009 memoir *Of Baluka and Nibong Palm*. He has vivid memories of collecting tins of canned food in the flotsam and jetsam on Moala's beaches as a result of WWII naval engagements in the surrounding waters of the Pacific Ocean. His Sunday-school teacher impressed on him that those who had faith in Christ could achieve whatever they wanted, and Mike dreamed of becoming Governor of Fiji. He was despatched to RKS in 1950 where he became Dux in 1955, and a senior prefect. Lasarusa Turaga was a year or so below him.

From 1956-57 Mike attended the Koronivia Farm Institute, Nausori, now known as the Fiji College of Agriculture, where the Principal, R.L. Hartley, was an Englishman who had a speed boat to commute to his home in Lami. This was Mike's first substantive contact with Indo-Fijians. Fifty years later he recalled the 'childish and racist' banter and antics between the two groups, which he thinks reflected the way British administrators 'divided and ruled' the colony, deliberately advising leaders of the two groups to have nothing to do with each other. The Fijians referred to the Indians as 'curry eaters'. One evening Mike returned to Koronivia from a rugby match to find many of the Indian boys excitedly completing application forms for a scholarship to study in India. Mike was told he could apply too, and was delighted when he won.

He believes that K. D. Bhasia, the Indian High Commissioner at the time, may have had a big influence on the decision.

Mike departed Fiji for Poona/Pune without the opportunity to say goodbye to his parents. 1958-60 was spent at Poona University on an Indian Government scholarship before returning to Fiji to work for the NLTB. Mike was the first Fijian to study at Poona. Most Fijian students who were sent to study agriculture in other countries went to Australia or New Zealand. A cousin studied at the University of Queensland's School of Agriculture at its Gatton campus outside Brisbane. Mike graduated with a Diploma in Agricultural Studies.

At Poona Mike won medals for boxing and the javelin. In his first heavyweight match, facing a rather large Parsee opponent, Mike thought he would test the Parsee's strength by letting his opponent land a punch to the side of his head. Unimpressed with the outcome, the future Reverend Yasa chose not to turn the other cheek, flattening his opponent with his next punch. He used the same test, with the same outcome, when fighting another large Parsee named Saldana in a subsequent tournament at Madras (contemporary Chennai).

Mike enlisted for the adventure, 'to see (more of) the world'. He chose 60th Rifles, KRRC for its historical affiliation with the FDF/RFMF. After coping with his first British winter in 1961-62 during basic training, Mike elected to serve with 2RGJ. His choice was based on the regiment's projected posting to Germany and his reading of WWII and of Hitler—he wanted to see Berlin and the Fuhrerbunker. His three Fijian comrades chose the First Battalion of the Regiment, as it was scheduled for Malaya where the climate had more appeal than the Fuhrerbunker. In 2013 Mike recalled that their decision was also influenced by curiosity to see the country where a Fijian battalion had been deployed a decade earlier, as much as its warm climate and food that was more like that of Fiji.

2RGJ proved a fortuitous choice for Mike. The Battalion's second in command was a Major (Brevet Lt Col) named Dwin Bramall. Bramall later became CO 2RGJ when it deployed to Borneo in 1965. The future Field Marshall, Chief of the Defence Staff and Knight of the Garter became a mentor and life-long friend.

An Australian officer who instructed at Camberley and occasionally hunted with the then CDS described Bramall as 'a big bastard, a bit of a bullshitter, but very very smart'.

2RGJ were redeployed from Berlin to the then colony of British Guiana for several months in 1962 to help contain law and order, in a fractious multi-racial community with many parallels to Fiji in 1987. Mike identified with all parties to the political turmoil and could see the possibility of similar problems in future for Fiji.

One of his most vivid memories, however, was the uncertainty and fear of nuclear war generated during the Cuban missile crisis in October of 1962.

His other vivid memory of his Guiana service, not mentioned in his autobiography, is that of his Platoon Commander, Lt Richard Hill, quelling a riotous assembly with a well-rehearsed platoon drill. Hill ordered his bugler to attract the crowd's attention. He then ordered his designated tape man to 'roll the tape', much like a fire fighter unrolling a hose, in a straight line across the crowd's front, announcing: 'Anyone crossing the line will be shot'. The technique was effective, largely because the young officer and others like him were clearly resolute in projecting their authority. Many years later, in response to a question, Mike agreed that Lt Col Rabuka and others in authority in May 1987 might have used this approach rather than default to the easy option of a military coup as a device for stabilising a volatile situation in Suva.

As the battalion returned to the UK, Mike was advised that on the CO's recommendation, supported by Bramall, he was to attend the Officer Cadet School, Mons.

At Mons, Mike was in Kohima Company and, according to Tom Morell, that was when he developed a taste for Dubonnet. Officer cadets were in demand as 'young gentlemen escorts' during the debutante 'season' in England at that time and Dubonnet was the debs' preferred tipple. This resulted in much 'taking the piss' when Mike drank with other '212' in pubs around Aldershot. Fifty years later, when Tom and Mike renewed their acquaintance in New Zealand, Tom presented Mike with a bottle of Dubonnet.

Mike was commissioned a 2Lt on 17 October 1964 and was very proud to be the first Fijian to be commissioned at a British Army officer training school. In his autobiography however, Mike's modesty prevails and he does not mention that he topped the course. Laurel Bentley, another '212', was posted to Mons at the same time. Mike's return to Fiji and subsequent developments are dealt with in Chapters 4, 6 and 7.

The Royal Ulster Rifles

Seven of the Fijians were allocated to the North Irish Brigade by the War Office, and all served their first few years with the First Battalion of the Royal Ulster Rifles (1RUR) based in St Patrick's Barracks, Ballymena, County Down, Northern Ireland. In 1968 the RUR amalgamated with the Royal Inniskilling Fusiliers and the Royal Irish Fusiliers to form The Royal Irish Rangers.

Talaiasi LABALABA, BEM

Laba (pron. 'Lamba' in Fijian), as he became known in the army, is the best known of the '212' for his heroism in the battle of Mirbat in 1972 where he was killed in action. Laba served four years with the RUR, including an operational tour in Borneo during 'Confrontation' with Indonesia. He became the fifth of the '212' to pass selection for 22 SAS and is dealt with at length in Appendix F.

Peni LEVACI, now known as Ben TEMO

Ben changed his name by deed poll while living in the UK. He was born on Taveuni and has always considered Cakaudrove as home. His father, from Vanuabalavu, was multi-skilled, as skipper of a local passenger boat, manager of a copra estate, and as an engineer building the Buca Bay road.

Ben was educated at the Vatuvonu School Buca Bay on Vanua Levu, and left school early to help operate a ferry across a local river but returned to school after a bridge was built. Ben was interviewed in Savusavu by the recruiting team, which he understands had extended their interviews to Vanua Levu at the insistence of Ratu Penaia Ganilau, then Deputy Secretary for Fijian Affairs in the colonial government who later became *Tui Cakau* (high chief) of Cakaudrove. Ratu Penaia later served as Governor General after Independence and was Fiji's first President from 1987-93.

Ben was born on 14 November 1943 and was not yet eighteen when he departed with the first contingent of '212'. He was unprepared for the weather when transiting New York, dressed in his school uniform and plastic sandals! His travel experience was very limited—he had never been to Viti Levu nor even Labasa, and Ben wanted to see the world and experience adventure. He had uncles who had served in Malaya. Two 'cousins' from Taveuni, Epeli Matata and Kasiano Qaduadua, also enlisted and served with Ben in 1RUR.

Those in the RUR did their basic training in Londonderry. Ben served six years as a regular soldier as a L/Cpl with Talaiasi Labalaba in the RUR followed by another six years in the reserves. Ben did not enjoy his active service in Borneo 'fighting Chinese and Indonesians, and now the buggers are here building roads' he recalled in 2013, erroneously referring to Chinese combatants. That said, he has no regrets. He trained in Australia en route to Borneo, and later served in Hong Kong, Libya and Cyprus. In Australia he recalls being at Eglinton, near Newcastle, twinned with Eglinton, Londonderry, Northern Ireland. He has fond memories of a 'Captain Wheeler' who was captain of the RUR rugby sevens team and became a Major General—R.N. Wheeler. This was the officer who, as Colonel of the Royal Irish Rangers, issued the amalgamation order of the day on 30 June 1992, to form the Royal Irish Regiment.

Forty-three years later, General Wheeler recorded on the Royal Irish website an account of a pilgrimage he made to the site of the B Company camp in Sarawak and their forward platoon base at Nibong. The General illustrated his article with a photograph of the then-named Peni Levaci, who was described as 'an all-round sportsman who played rugby and was an army heavy-weight boxer'. When Ben was subsequently queried on his army boxing career, he admitted to having been the BAOR heavy-weight champion during his service.

After his army service, Ben worked as a farm manager at Maiden Bradley, near Warminster in Wiltshire, for twenty years. He met his future employer at an agricultural show in Salisbury, and when asked whether he knew anything about farming, denied knowing anything about sheep. The farmer offered to teach him, and Ben boasts of being 'England's first black shepherd'! When the farmer died, the farm was bought by a developer who built a hotel near Stonehenge.

Ben spent the next twenty years driving trucks throughout Europe as far as Istanbul, and in the UK, where he claims to be familiar with every little by-road and lane. He returned to Fiji to retire in 2009, after taking regular holidays there since 1983.

Ben's wife Barbara is a nurse from London who he met after he broke a leg playing rugby. Two sons remain in England, one of whom served in the army, including service in Bosnia, but left after five years. Barbara has been a vegan since her first visit to a farm as a school-girl. Ben and Barbara should give advice on how to maintain a successful marriage, as they must have had many interesting exchanges over diet in their kitchens over the years.

Asiveni LUTUMAILAGI

Asiveni was born in Namotmoto village outside Nadi and finished his schooling at QVS, where he was well-versed in army life through the school cadet corps with whom he attended camps with the Royal Fiji Military Forces in the school holidays. He was appointed CSM of Bau House in his final year, 1958.

Asiveni's parents were devout Methodists, his father a school teacher and his mother a nurse. Asuveni was the eldest of eight children (six of whom were boys). In 2013 his younger brother Joeli recalled that most opportunities for young men leaving school in the early sixties went to the sons of Fijian chiefs. In 1961 Asiveni was employed as a clerk in the District Officer's office in Nadi, and when the recruiting team arrived he was given the task of listing more than one hundred applicants who presented for interviews and IQ tests in Nadi. He was also tasked with manning the *tanoa* (kava bowl) for the traditional welcoming ceremony for the recruiting team, and was very impressed by the smart uniforms they wore, particularly Captain S. H. Hardcastle with his kilt and all the paraphernalia of a Scottish regiment.

Unlike many of the recruits, Asiveni had no problem with Hardcastle's accent as one of his teachers at QVS was a Scot named McGarry. The British DO had answered Asiveni's many questions in previous weeks, and was not surprised when Asiveni added his own name to the bottom of the list he had prepared.

Asiveni's civilian experience may have influenced his early selection for a posting as a clerk in the battalion HQ where he served on his first overseas deployments to Hong Kong, Libya and Australia for training. He was then sent to Borneo on operations countering Indonesian President Sukarno's 'Konfrontasi' with the new Malaysian state. The close attention to detail and staff duties he developed over twenty-two years service was evident in his correspondence with his biographer in 1993.

Asiveni subsequently served in Germany several times (including Berlin from 1981-83) then Gibraltar and Bahrain. In 1969 he was a Lance Corporal and a member of the battalion's hockey team. Throughout his army service Asiveni kept in close contact with Kitione Uluinayau who served with 1SWB before settling in Germany. He and Kit were members of the School of Infantry's 1972 seven-a-side rugby team.

By coincidence, Asiveni and his 1RUR comrade Kasiano Qaduadua married sisters during their service in Northern Ireland. Asiveni returned to Fiji in 1984 to a six-acre (2.4 ha) cane farm and married a second time to Miriame. He died in 2010.

Epeli MATATA

Epeli was shown as 'teacher, Taveuni' when he enlisted, and served eighteen years before accepting a redundancy and returning to Taveuni. He appears in a photograph in Corran Purdon's *List the Bugle* as a Corporal leading a patrol with the RUR in Sarawak.

Kasiono QADUADUA

Kasiano was unemployed and living on Taveuni when he enlisted. He married Shirley, an Irish woman, and eventually returned to Fiji, settling on the island of Qamea, off Taveuni. He is remembered by colleagues as having boxed for RUR.

Watisoni ROGOSE

Watisoni was a cane farmer's son born near Sigatoka in Nadroga. He stayed with an uncle at Namoli village near Nadi for his last years at a Muslim high school in Lautoka. He was a student at Fulton Missionary College in 1961 and the recruiting officers seemed to stimulate his urge to travel.

Watisoni found himself in the RUR with two other Nadi blokes, Asiveni Lutumailagi and Talaiasi Labalaba, with whom he had his portrait taken on leave in Fiji in 1963. Watisoni became known as 'Sonny' to the British squaddies but Apakuki Nanovo and other '212' also came to refer to him, predictably, as 'Dr. Watson'. In Borneo Sonny served under Lt Roger Wheeler in the same platoon of B Company as Peni Levaci and Epeli Matata.

Sonny had enlisted for the minimum six years and had had enough of world travel and army life in 1967. He was staying at the Union Jack Club in London with Tom Taleua when they met Jone Kucuvu of 1SWB, who persuaded them to come to Rochdale with him for a long weekend of watching rugby. Sonny met his Freda that weekend and decide to stay. Fifty years later he likes to joke that 'its been a very long weekend'!

Mateo ROKOVESA

Mateo was born the sixth of thirteen children of a subsistence farmer at the coastal village of Naweni on the Hibiscus Highway on the southern side of Vanua Levu, an hour's bus ride from Savusavu. After local schooling, Mateo was sent to RKS from 1955-60 but returned to Naweni as an auxiliary teacher awaiting admission to the Teacher Training College at Lautoka, when he heard the recruiting team's siren song. A younger brother, Iliesa Kadavu, also enlisted directly from RKS. The seven Fijians did their twelve weeks' basic training at Eglinton Training Depot, Londonderry. Fifty years later, Mateo recalled that Kasiano Qaduadua and Labalaba excelled at this training, while he and Watisoni Rogose contracted influenza!

Peni Levaci, who also enlisted in Savusavu, recalls that the Naweni rugby team was noted for playing hard in the fifties and sixties. Mateo became known as 'Rocky', representing the RUR as a middle-weight boxer and in both seven and fifteen-a-side rugby. During 2RUR's tour in Borneo, Rocky served in the intelligence section and taught English in local schools as part of the Regiment's 'hearts and minds' campaign during Confrontation.

Rocky's pugilism outside the ring eventually cut short his army service and he returned to Naweni after four years. He was unable to resume his teaching career, and from a modest start as a *yaqona* grower he has now included livestock on his small farm. He married in 1975 and has adopted a niece and nephew. In 1978 he declined a suggestion from a cousin serving with the RFMF that he return to the colours with Fiji's first UN peace-keeping deployment in Lebanon. He regrets that he was unable to become a teacher and earn a good pension with Fiji's National Provident Fund.

In 2010, Hurricane Thomas caused significant damage to Naweni and the village is being moved to higher ground. In his later years Rocky has become a lay preacher and manages the village shop.

APPENDIX F: 'THE GENTLEMEN FROM HEREFORD'

After serving the required minimum of two years with the first corps or regiment to which they had been allocated, at least fifteen of the two hundred men presented themselves for selection into the British Army's elite special forces unit, the 22nd Special Air Service (22 SAS) Regiment based at Hereford. Seven of the '212' passed selection; all served with distinction, with all but one being awarded medals for bravery or distinguished service.

Two of the seven were in the assault teams that resolved a terrorist seizure of the Iranian embassy in London in 1980, and one of them received the highest of five gallantry awards from the Queen the following year, when the Lord High Chamberlain at Buckingham Palace greeted them as '...the gentlemen from Hereford: how nice to see you without your masks!'[70].

Innumerable books have been written on 22 SAS operations, and the individuals who served with Britain's SAS regiments since the first was formed by David Stirling in the Western Desert in WWII. Those who have served with 22 SAS as the regular army's unit (since it was so designated in the 1950s) are subject to secrecy undertakings. Those who breach these undertakings, not least those of general rank, by publishing a memoir or engaging a journalist 'ghost writer', are excommunicated from the society of the Regiment.

---

70 Recollection of Tom Morell in 2013.

Those who sin thus have no further access to the Regiment's home base at Hereford, or the 'Pal-U-Drin' club enjoyed by all ranks serving there.

An entertaining book could be written on the exploits of the seven '212' who served with 22 SAS, but others including former commanding officers and the likes of 'Andy McNab' and 'Soldier I' have already covered much of that ground with frequent positive, often humourous, references to the Fijians with whom they served. At different times between 1992 and 2013, Talaiasi Labalaba's mother and aunt spoke with pride of their recollections of a man who died heroically at Mirbat in 1972. Laba's son and daughter grew up without ever knowing their father.

Five of the surviving six Fijians who served with Laba were happy to discuss to varying degrees their memories of him, their childhood memories of Fiji, reasons for enlisting, early years in the army and subsequent careers. They were not questioned on details of their operational deployments, given the extensive published revelations by others, and out of respect for their secrecy undertakings. The wife of a sixth was kind enough to assist with some of these details on her husband. They appear hereunder in the order in which they passed selection.

A disproportionate number of Fijians in B Sqn, 22 SAS, RAF Sharja, February 1970. Rear, L to R, Laba, 'Valdez' (Vakatalai) and Takavesi.
Photo: The late Mrs Torika Canano, Laba's mother

WO1 Kuata (Fred) MARAFONO, MBE

After two years with the King's Shropshire Light Infantry, Fred was the first of the '212' to pass selection for 22 SAS in April 1964. He was one of only six out of ninety volunteers with this ambition at the time. Seconaia Takavesi and Jim Vakatalai believe that the seven '212' were the first 'coloureds' selected into 22 SAS, apart from a couple of trail-blazers named Yip from Hong Kong and 'Darkie' Davidson, an Anglo-Burmese who was something of a legend in the Regiment and had served in Malaya.

In late 2012, shortly after the publication of *From SAS to Blood Diamond Wars*, Fred agreed to assist with this project, but the limited email exchanges had not progressed far before his death in March 2013. This is why accounts of Fred's early life, his service with the Regiment and his equally colourful second career are based on second-hand accounts from his former colleagues and the limited revelations in his book, co-written with Hamish Ross. The latter offers little on anything beyond Fred's employment in Sierra Leone. In an exchange with Jim Vakatalai in June 1998, Jim referred to an article on the conflict in Sierra Leone in *The Times* a month earlier mentioning a 'mercenary' (which Fred did not consider himself to be) known as 'Fiji Fred'. Fred may have been unimpressed if he could have heard the opening words of Jim's eulogy for Fred:

> Long before the Union Jack came to the Fiji Islands the Rotumans were famous for two things: sailors and mercenaries!

Fred was not keen on the 'snail mail' of the early nineteen-nineties, and his second son Wilson kindly responded to two letters sent to Fred at the time seeking assistance with documenting a record of the '212' 's service. Wilson was at Keele University at the time and later followed Fred into the Regiment, so that correspondence faded.

George Chute remembered Kuata Marafono as 'a nice, quiet Rotuman boy' at the time of their enlistment. There was little indication of the future hell-raiser mentioned in the *Blood Diamonds* memoir and elsewhere. In 1983 Peter Dickens described Fred as 'a gentle and intrepid warrior from Fiji' who had been allocated to the Regiment's B Squadron based on the assumption that he had 'grown up in canoes'.

Fred's early responsibilities as a medic involved a month's attachment to the casualty department of Paddington Hospital. Many years later, in the context of Fred's subsequent service in Northern Ireland, Dickens asked Fred what motivated him to accept extreme hardship and danger 'in aid of a people so far from his home'. Fred's initial answer was 'the cause', which he quickly clarified as 'the Regiment.'[71]

In November 1961, Fred was a student at the Navuso Agricultural College and hoped to go on to study veterinary science in Australia or New Zealand. In 1967 Jim Vakatalai and Fred returned to Fiji on DOMCOL, and Jim accompanied Fred to Navuso where Fred thanked his tutors for their encouragement in his last school years.

Jim served with Fred in B Squadron in 'the jungles of Borneo, the moonscape of the Radfan and the back streets and alleys of Aden' in the early years of their service. This included what might have been a 'career limiting experience' when Fred refused an order from the camp RSM at Waterloo Lines, Aden. The RSM had Fred jailed for insubordination, but Major Viscount John Slim, serving with HQ Middle East Land Forces, persuaded the RSM and others to drop the charges. Slim's father was the lauded British military commander Field Marshal William ('Bill') Slim (1st Viscount Slim) who in WWII led the so-called 'forgotten army', the 14th Army, in the Burma campaign. John Slim had served with 22 SAS in Malaya. Fred never forgot this intervention.

Fred's early orientation to agriculture was revived during his tours of duty in Oman, where he spent a lot of time living and working with Dhofari villagers on 'heart and mind' projects and engaging the 'adoo' (enemy) of the day. Fraternising with the villagers involved convivial serves of unpasteurised camel's milk, which was later identified as the cause of the brucellosis Fred developed. Brucellosis infection remains a threat to veterinarians working with cattle in many parts of the world.

---

71 Peter Dickens, *SAS–The Jungle Frontier*, 1983 p. 102-103.

In 1969, Fred married an Englishwoman, Angie, who was the bedrock for his three sons while Fred pursued 'SAS and Foreign Office commitments all over the world', according to Jim Vakatalai. Talaiasi Labalaba was Fred's best man.

Four of the '212' served in the Falklands conflict of 1982, close to the end of the service of those who served the usual maximum time of twenty-two years in the British army. Hoss Ligairi understood that 'someone senior in the MOD' had directed that none of the original 200 Fijians still serving should be involved in the conflict so close to their eligibility for the maximum pension—the logic, apparently, being that these men had already 'done their bit' for 'Queen and country'.

If there was such a directive, it must have arrived at Hereford after a decision had been taken to deploy elements of 22 SAS to staging areas in Ascension Island or Chile. Hoss was serving with 21 SAS, the Territorial Regiment, at the time. Dave Rosa, however, arrived in Port Stanley after the cessation of hostilities with a detachment of EOD specialists tasked with cleaning up the minefields the Argentinian occupiers had laid around the town and elsewhere. In one of his many letters home to his wife Ann, Dave relayed an account of a discussion he had with a farmer in an isolated location who had answered a knock in the middle of the night and found his visitor was a Rotuman requiring assistance for his SAS patrol!

Shortly after his army discharge, Fred began a second career with a company controlled by SAS founder Sir David Stirling. Fred's work involved protecting the interests of mining companies in unstable countries including, eventually, Sierra Leone with Executive Outcomes, a South African company best known for its provision of mercenary forces to countries and companies 'in need'.

Jim Vakatalai concluded his eulogy to Fred noting that in September 2000, three months short of Fred's 69th birthday, an SAS officer involved in a rescue operation in Sierra Leone was surprised and delighted when he boarded a Sierra Leone helicopter gunship to be greeted by Fred as the door gunner!

Fred's obituary in *The Telegraph* of 29 March 2013, referred to his father's WWII service 'in Burma', which is almost certainly an error as it is far more likely that his father served with the Fiji Battalion in the Solomon Islands. The obituary also included the citation from the MBE awarded to Fred in the New Year Honours list for 1983, and in accord with *The Telegraph* we agree that the citation bears quoting at length:

> 'It is doubtful whether any officer or NCO can equal the number of operations which WO1 Marafono has volunteered for and taken part in. On all, his standards of leadership and gallantry have been a positive inspiration to subordinates and superiors who have come into contact with him. Many anti-terrorist techniques currently in use in Northern Ireland and in the UK are the result of his unstinting work and clear vision. Perhaps his greatest contribution to the Regiment has been in the jungle where he has evolved many methods of operating which will form the basis of Special Operations for many years to come. His abilities as a visual tracker are legendary, and he is conceivably the leading expert in this field in the Service. Over many years he has consistently put the Service's need before his own and has been a key figure in influencing many matters of Regimental and National importance.'

WO1 Jim VAKATALAI, MM

Jim also wasted no time presenting for selection to the Regiment, and passed in May 1964. James Vuli Vakatalai was born in Suva but like Takavesi identifies the village of Lomaloma, Vanua Balavu, as his family's roots. He was a student at MBHS with Bob Dass and others when the recruiting team arrived.

Fifty years later, Dass had vivid memories of his school-days with Jim, who Dass says was an avid reader of everything he could get his hands on, from Shakespeare to *Time* magazine. Dass recalls that Jim knew all about the recruiting team and was keen to be considered, persuading Dass to skip a Latin class and attend the recruiting centre in Suva. Jim later took the initiative on behalf of others who had been selected but had not completed their schooling, and asked Captain Hardcastle to give them permission to delay their departure for the UK so they could complete their Senior Cambridge exams.

For his part, Jim says he never had any doubt what he wanted for a career, and that was to join the British Army and earn selection into 22 SAS Regiment. His inspiration for this ambition was *The Winged Dagger*, Roy Farran's account of his WWII experience of operations in the early SAS units with David Stirling and others. The last of these 'originals', Jimmy Jock Storie, died in 2012 and is remembered on a plaque in the Stirling Lines Chapel in Hereford.

Farran was a daring and highly decorated soldier. His first book was an entertaining account of his service in the Western Desert as a POW, and his later service with the early SAS regiments, written in the 'Boy's Own' style favoured by some at the time. Farran made no reference to his disastrous post-war experience in the Palestine police force beyond a droll reference to himself as 'a notorious anti-Semite'. Jim was unaware for many years that his model soldier had proved to be a very poor under-cover police officer who was responsible for the death and disappearance of a sixteen-year- old Jewish boy he had detained. Farran was acquitted of murder charges in controversial circumstances and needed a best-selling book to pay for his legal expenses.

Farran's brother Rex died opening a parcel bomb addressed to 'R. Farran' at the family home in England, by those who believed in 'an eye for an eye'. Ben Macintyre's 2016 account of Farran in *SAS: Rogue Heroes* further glamourises Farran, without dwelling on the latter's accountability for the death of Alexander Rubowitz. Neither does Barry Davies in his *Heroes of the SAS* published in 2000. Jim also had several uncles who served with the FIR in Malaya, one of whom spoke highly of the 22 SAS troopers he had encountered.

Jim was allocated to the REME and diligently served his mandatory two years servicing armoured vehicles, before he was eligible to apply for selection for 22 SAS. He does not pretend that his selection course was anything other than arduous, but says that at the time he was determined that nothing would stop him qualifying. He exemplifies the claims of others who passed selection that while physical fitness is important, it is mental toughness that is critical.

Jim is an agreeable raconteur with a well-developed sense of humour, and it is easy to spend hours in his company discussing his life in the SAS without realising that he has not really discussed anything remotely sensitive. He entertains, but gives nothing away that is in breach of the secrecy undertakings he and others of his ilk made to the MOD and HMTQ. The Italian mafiosi and their code of 'omerta' (silence) has nothing on these blokes. The corollary of this code is that anyone who boasts loudly of their association with such Special Forces units has invariably either failed selection for such units, or been a fringe dweller of some sort.

Jim realised that his dreams had come true and that he was following Farran's example in relation to the WWII SAS operations when, a few short months after passing selection and qualifying as a basic parachutist, he found himself on the Indonesian side of the border in Borneo in September 1964.

Jim retired from the army after twenty-four years. One of his last jobs, and one he enjoyed more than most, was as the WO1 Training Officer for the Regiment. In this capacity he had a light helicopter at his disposal and he delighted in liaising with senior police officers throughout the UK on training matters. He enjoyed arranging to meet them near a suitable landing area for his helicopter and seeing their faces when a largish Fijian in plain clothes emerged from the cockpit. Not quite what many expected, but the name should have been a clue!

Apart from developing superior basic infantry skills and qualifying as a parachutist, Jim specialised as a medic and acquired several languages, including French and good Arabic. He found Malay very similar to Fijian, with many common words with the same meaning. Spanish came easily as the vowel sounds were very similar to Fijian.

Jim enjoyed 'working in mufti' with Laba and others in the souks and wadis of Aden. In Dhofar in 1971 he had his right femur shattered by 'adoo' (enemy) fire. On Operation Dharab in 1975, he was awarded the MM in circumstances 'where even John Wayne would have been digging a foxhole with his elbows'. He admits that serving in Northern Ireland was not easy for Fijians in the SAS, and that their roles were largely limited to airborne surveillance and night operations.

Jim married late in his service, to Sue, a local Hereford girl, who was relieved when his employer for his first job after his discharge called her at home to advise Jim had arrived safely in Peru. It was a revelation to both Jim and Sue at the time that after many years of being together this was the first time that she had any idea where he was when he went away. Jim volunteers that the wives and partners of SAS personnel 'also serve', and that this service is rarely recognised or understood by the public or many in authority in the army/MOD.

After more than two decades of seeing off the Queen's enemies, Jim was disinclined to consider a quiet life back in Fiji, or further service with the RFMF. Instead, he decided to build his own house around a small barn in a village outside Hereford. Fortunately, he had retained essential building skills learned from his carpenter father. He also established his own security consultancy and found that protecting Japanese bankers from kidnapping in Zurich or elsewhere could be particularly lucrative, returning between UK£5-10,000 per month, depending on the threat. Columbia was a frequent temporary place of residence.

Jim was most animated and open on the subject of his good friend Laba's premonition of his own death at Mirbat. Laba revealed this to Jim in Singapore in the first instance, later specifying Mirbat as the place he would die whilst he and Jim were on a flight from Masira (an offshore island of Oman) to Salala in a Skyvan aircraft.

Talking to Jim one cannot avoid noticing some deformation of fingers on both hands. Questioned whether this resulted from some action by the Queen's enemies over the years, he laughs and explains that he was first afflicted by sarcoidosis, a rare condition more commonly found in

Scandanavians than Fijians, in 2001. He jokes that 'one of my ancestors must have eaten a Scandanavian'! References to the Fijians in 22 SAS joking about cannibalism litter the various accounts of former members of the Regiment, usually in the context of complaints about the meagre contents of their ration packs and threats to supplement their rations with other members of their patrol. 'Soldier 'I' SAS' gives a distorted account of Laba claiming a family link to John Wesley through a cannibal forebear[72]. At the time of this particular leg-pulling, Laba was probably referring to the fate of the Rev. Thomas Baker in the hinterland on Viti Levu (not too far from Laba's birthplace) in July 1867. Ann Rosa recalls her late Sapper husband warning her that if his plate was not full, she might find herself on it. The best account of such jests, however, comes from an Australian SAS officer who attended a Close Quarter Battle course during an exchange at Hereford in the nineteen seventies. The Australian and a 22 SAS Trooper course mate were having a quiet beer at the Pal-U-Drin Club one evening when a Fijian, somewhat the worse for drink, stumbled toward the bar. The young woman behind the bar took an involuntary step backward, possibly concerned by a leering, scarred face. The Trooper reassured her by calmly noting 'It's alright loov, he only wants to fook you, not eat you'![73]

S/Sgt Sekonaia TAKAVESI, DCM

Ilisoni Ligairi and Sekonaia Takavesi served together in the King's Own Royal Border Regiment for two years before passing selection in April 1964. Tak recalled his first three years in the KORBR. He admitted extreme difficulty coming to terms with the way NCOs addressed recruits on the parade ground, and was often unsure whether he would shout back, laugh, cry or punch the NCO. Hoss was the best shot in their platoon, having the benefit of previous service with RFMF.

---

72 Kennedy, pps. 63-64.

73 Governor Maddocks recorded in his memoir (p.139) that Ratu Epeli Nailatikau's father, Ratu Sir Edward Cakobau, liked to answer questions about Fijian prowess at Rugby with 'I don't know about the others but Rugby is in my blood; my grandmother ate a Cambridge Blue'.

On first acquaintance, Tak wastes no time in advising that he/we (meaning anyone with 22 SAS service) is/are very private person (s) with reason to be sceptical, if not deeply suspicious, of any interlocutor who admits to an interest in recording any aspect of his life. He then spends some time expanding on his bitter experience of past exchanges, either with those who advertised his autobiography or with another writer, who betrayed his 'off the record' comments and failed to show Tak an account of their exchanges before publication. He regrets his past naivety in trusting that someone he did not know would adhere to an old fashioned 'gentleman's agreement'. One is left in no doubt that this is a man who does not suffer fools or forgive or forget a breach of trust.

He takes his time to relax and discuss those aspects of his life with which he is most comfortable—his childhood, adolescence and early years in the British Army. Seventy years after his birth, Tak still identifies closely with his birthplace of Lomaloma on Vanuabalavu in the Lau group. He was 'in the middle' of eight children of a school teacher who was transferred to the largest island, Viti Levu, when Tak was five years old. He identifies closely with Laisenia Qarase, a cousin from Vanuabalavu, who became PM and was overthrown in (then) Commodore Bainimarama's 2006 coup.

Tak's father later became headmaster of the village school at Nairaukarauka, near the administrative centre of Vunidawa in Naitasiri province. Tak thinks it possible that his family originated in Naitasiri. He later went to school in Nabua and to Nausori secondary school. When the recruiting team arrived in Suva, Tak had been accepted as a junior clerk in the colonial government at a time when a white-collar job was something young Fijians considered special and a sign of starting out on a significant career, despite the low wages.

Tak has iconoclastic views on some subjects, one of which is the role played by his late high chief of the Lau islands, the long-serving PM of Fiji, Ratu Sir Kamisese Mara. Tak is not alone in arguing that good copra prices and a regular shipping service to the Lau group were key elements in the education of island children on the main island of Viti Levu, in or near Suva. Ratu Mara established his own business to control this trade but failed to service it properly, and the island shipping services failed through what Tak claims was Ratu Mara's greed.

Tak does not recall precisely why the army recruiting officer's spiel appealed to him, and volunteers again that he was a naive young man with little idea of what to expect from army life. Unlike his childhood friend from Lomaloma, Jim Vakatalai, Tak had not read much about the British Army or specialist units like 22 SAS. He was surprised to see his name among those listed in the *Fiji Times* of 6 November 1961 and was afraid to tell his father of his enlistment.

He recalled little of his time in the KORBR (Appendix E) and in 2014 volunteered even less on his time in Hereford and warmer climates during his service with 22 SAS. Others, however, have recorded the detail[74] of his courage at Mirbat where he was awarded the DCM for his assistance to Laba, and his service in Aden, Borneo, Princes Gate and the Falkland Islands. Australian SASR personnel who trained at Hereford in the seventies were impressed by Tak's physical toughness and his off-duty antics in the watering holes of the town.

After being discharged from the army, Tak became a security consultant, working in Columbia first, in 1985, countering kidnapping. Later employment took him to Pakistan and Iraq. A newspaper article written on 11 November 2003 by Alastair McQueen noted that Tak was wounded in a vehicle ambush in Iraq when working as a contractor. His experience in Iraq left Tak with a scathing view of the sorts of companies and individuals who tried to capitalise on the unstable situation in that country after the second Gulf War: 'Too many amateurs and wannabes promising conditions and equipment they did not have'.

---

74 *Storm Front*, by Rowland White and *Soldier I SAS* by Michael Paul Kennedy to cite two examples.

In his later years, Tak has been affected by gout which seems to cause him more grief than have enemies of the Queen and others over several decades. Tak notes that the Regiment attracted a number of Barnado boys who were orphans, abandoned by their families, or came from broken homes. Tak recalled Philip Tagimuri, David Kado and others who attempted selection for 22 SAS but failed.

S/Sgt 'Hoss' LIGAIRI, BEM

Ilisoni Vaniqi ('Hoss') Ligairi is perhaps the best known and recorded of the '212', including those who joined 22 SAS, with whom Hoss served from 1964-83. He is a quietly-spoken and modest man who did not seek any of the publicity he has attracted. He is certainly undeserving of the derogatory press reporting he has received from those whose main agenda is usually to portray anyone with SAS experience as a thug or a mercenary.

MGen Tony Jeapes in his 1996 text *SAS Secret War* (first published in 1980 immediately after his posting as CO 22 SAS) refers obliquely to service in Dhofar with a Fijian corporal named 'Mule Gilairi', so nicknamed because of his immense strength. Hoss denies the immense strength, and says he acquired the nickname 'Hoss' after the character of that name played by Dan Blocker in the *Bonanza* TV series that was popular from 1959-73. He adds with a grin that Jeapes, an unusually elongated fellow, was given a Swahili nickname for giraffe when they served together in Kenya.

Hoss first came to Fleet Street attention in 1976 when a small, suitably armed, 22 SAS patrol in civilian clothes and unmarked cars strayed across the Northern Ireland border and was intercepted by the Garda in Eire, creating a diplomatic incident of the worst sort. He and his colleagues were arrested but released after intense pressure from Whitehall, and later fined for possession of unlicensed firearms. Hoss's background continued to be a source of speculation to the media and other observers during his subsequent service in the Fiji Military Forces from 1987-2000 and thereafter, as recorded in Chapters 7 and 8.

Hoss was born in February 1938 in Wailevu, near Savusavu on Vanua Levu, Fiji's second largest island. He was the youngest of nine children of a Methodist minister. His eldest brother, Epi Ligairi, became well known as a heavy-weight boxer. Hoss attended LMS from 1951-55, followed by a year at DAV Indian School where Sam Tamata was also a pupil. Hoss returned to study at LMS from 1957-59.

In 2013, Hoss recalled the few options available to school leavers in the late fifties; there were limited positions for teachers and doctors. He was not interested in teaching, and joined PWD briefly as a tradesman after leaving school. He had been in the RFMF for six months before the recruiting team arrived. As one of the older recruits, and with his FMF orientation, Hoss was designated OIC of the second contingent of ninety-five men.

From 1961-64 Hoss served in the King's Own Royal Border Regiment with Seconaia Takavesi in Borneo and Aden before passing selection for SAS.

In 1968 Hoss was involved in training US Special Forces after General Westmoreland ordered that all SF officers had to qualify at a US Ranger course.

Hoss was discharged in 1983 after completing his last posting as a PSI with 21 SAS. Hoss was forty when he married Unaisi (Eunice) from Qamea and their son Taniela and daughter Raijeli were quite young when they returned to his village near Savusavu in 1984. He had never lost his love for Fiji and his province of Cakaudrove. His father died in 1985 and the church his father had consecrated was completed in 1994.

Shortly after 14 May 1987, Hoss received a call from RFMF headquarters at Queen Elizabeth Barracks (QEB), advising that his country needed his experience and Colonel Rabuka wanted some advice. He is adamant that he was in his village at the time of the first coup, and while he was aware of the unrest in Suva following the election of a FLP/NFP coalition government, he had nothing whatsoever to do with planning the coup. Because of Hoss's close and open relationship with Rabuka in the years that followed, many, including his biographer and some of his Fijian former comrades in 22 SAS, assumed he was involved. When asked who planned the training of those led into the parliament by Captain Isireli Dugu ('Captain X' in the books about Rabuka), Hoss said 'I think Rabuka trained them himself'. When asked whether Dugu had any involvement in the training, Hoss observed: 'Dugu is a doer, not a thinker'. He was not sure whether Rabuka deliberately chose 14 May as the date for the coup based on the anniversary of the date the Girmit indenture arrangement was initiated for Indian labourers. It would appear to have been a coincidence.

Eunice died in 1990 and in the Fijian village tradition, is buried close to the family home next to the church built by Hoss's father. Regardless of his actual involvement in Rabuka's first coup, Hoss remained a strong supporter of Fijian nationalism. In October 1990, former *taukei* activist (and former RSM, 1DWR) Ratu Meli Vesikula told his biographer that Hoss, and other '212' whom Ratu Meli did not identify, attempted to persuade him to give up his support for the NFP/FLP coalition after Ratu Meli changed sides. According to Ratu Meli, Hoss vigorously defended the RFMF role after May 1987, claiming it had the support of Fijians.

Throughout his FMF service Hoss maintained a very low profile. He was the grey man in the background, rarely in uniform and usually in the short-sleeved white shirt and mid-grey sulu preferred by Fiji's male civil servants. Either he or his staff adopted pseudonyms for referring to him, and even his former '212' comrades referred to him in 1992 as 'Mr Vaniqi' or 'Major Whiting'. He played golf occasionally.

Hoss left the FMF in 2000 with no pension after thirteen years, and insists he had no involvement in planning or carrying out George Speight's coup. He was asked by the CRW unit for advice and gave it, noting that the CRW seemed unsure of themselves. He appears earlier in this narrative in the 'Aftermath' Chapter which briefly covers Fiji's coups of 2000 and 2006, and the CRW mutiny against then FMF commander Commodore Frank Bainimarama, now Fiji's elected Prime Minister. In November 2013, Hoss was very much the respected village elder. He was closely involved in lobbying for a new high school for the district, a village 'Dream Centre' with library, games and internet facilities for the local youth, and in building a village bus shelter on the Savusavu-Labasa road with funding from the Rotary Club of Geelong.

Sgt Talaiasi LABALABA, BEM

Known to his family as Talai, but throughout his army service and since to others as Laba (pron. 'Lamba'), a boy of humble village origins grew to a heroic figure in the ten years of his army service. Laba's father was killed fighting the Japanese in the Solomon Islands but his mother, Torika Canano, remarried after WWII and the future hero of Mirbat grew up the eldest of eight children in the village of Vatutu on the Nawaka river, several kilometres from Nadi.

Laba's mother recalled in 1992 that he attended Nawaka District School, and then RKS up to Class 8. He subsequently attended Nadi Muslim High School until Form 4, and Sri Vivekananda High School for Form 5. Unfortunately, Mrs Canano was not asked why he attended so many schools. It is tempting to speculate that going to Indian schools in his formative years probably contributed to the ease with which Laba adapted to life in nineteen-sixties England, and mixing with other races in Borneo, Aden and Dhofar during his army service.

Twenty years later, his mother's younger sister Vilimaina Seirua recalled Laba walking six miles to school and swimming across the river if necessary, even when it flooded. Vilimaina said Laba liked soccer, rugby and athletics at school. Laba was still at school in Nadi when the recruiting team arrived and was one of the twelve young men who travelled to the UK as a third detachment after they had completed their exams. His mother said that she and Laba's stepfather were very proud of Laba when he was accepted for the British Army. He joined the army with relatives Asiveni Lutlmailagi and Kalioni Ratunabuabua. His mother said Laba had always wanted to travel, and returned on leave three times to his homeland, first in 1965.

Laba and his cousin Asiveni Lutumailagi were allocated to the Royal Ulster Regiment, and saw service together in Borneo after training in Libya and Australia between 1962 and 1965 when Laba passed selection for 22 SAS. He soon found himself back in Borneo, often as lead scout on cross border patrols under Operation Claret, details of which remained secret until many years later. He spent three years with B Squadron (including undercover operations against terrorists in Aden on Operation Nina) by which time Trooper Labalaba had been promoted to Lance Corporal. Laba's bravery and leadership in Borneo and Aden were acknowledged with the award of a BEM. The last paragraph of the citation signed by the then CO 22 SAS, Lt Colonel John Slim reads:

> LCpl Labalaba's conduct and exceptional high personal standards of leadership and courage since joining the Special Air Service in 1965 have not only been an example to his Fijian countrymen and land of his birth, but an inspiration to his fellow British comrades within the Special Air Service Regiment.

High praise indeed from one who had served with 22 SAS on operations during the Malayan Emergency.

Laba returned to RUR from 1968-71, during which time the Irish Brigade was restructured, Laba was promoted to Sergeant, and served in the reconnaissance platoon of the Royal Irish Rangers. He was discharged in 1970-71 and intended to return to the Pacific to offer his services to the New Zealand SAS squadron then on active service in South Vietnam. He re-enlisted under unusual circumstances when he encountered his old squadron passing through RAF, Bahrain, en route to Dhofar in support of Sultan Qaboos. The Sultan's attempts to modernise Oman were frustrated by Marxist terrorists based in neighbouring Yemen. The strategic importance of the Sultanate at the time, and the importance of the SAS success at Mirbat, have been explained at length by others and do not need repeating here. And it would be superfluous to do more than outline Laba's super-human effort operating a 25-pounder howitzer, largely alone and unassisted, until Takavesi and later Captain Kealy managed to join him in the gun pit after he was wounded. What is known only to a few of Laba's surviving colleagues in the Regiment is the story of Laba's unusual, perhaps paranormal, premonition of his death. Jim Vakatalai was very keen to ensure that their biographer recounted the story, as many Fijians in particular would find it intriguing.

Jim recalls Laba's stepfather died in 1971, and Laba being depressed in Singapore when he learned of the death of a close friend, Eunice Hibbert, in a car accident on 24 June 1972. Laba said: 'I'll be next'. Jim dismissed this premonition, but soon afterwards when they were on a flight from their offshore island base at Masira to Salala in Oman, as the Skyvan passed over Mirbat Laba looked out the window and said: 'That is where I will die!'. Over forty years later, Jim noted:

> 'The scene is still vivid in my mind's eye—the fort, the Omani flag and the gunpit.' Unusually, the following morning the SSM had to change the orders for allocating troops to tasks for the forthcoming week. Jim had been designated to the troop destined for rotation at Mirbat, but Laba was tasked to replace him. The reason for the change was the need for another soldier to return to Hereford for urgent personal reasons. The returning soldier had been allocated to his task because of his (Dhofari) Arabic language skills, and Jim was assessed as the better linguist to replace him. Laba was thus not originally destined to be at Mirbat and 'the rest is history'.

The Regiment organised Laba's burial party at St Martin's Church in Hereford, where those who 'failed to beat the clock' in 22 SAS are buried. When it was Jim's turn to salute the coffin, he was astonished to see that the grave prepared to receive Laba was next to that of Laba's friend Eunice. There is no doubt that Laba's heroism was deserving of a Victoria Cross had the Battle of Mirbat occurred in a conventional conflict, regardless of whether a formal state of war had been declared between the protagonists. The rotation of 22 SAS squadrons was a critical element of British Army Training Teams (BATT) deployed to Dhofar, but it was not a commitment the British Conservative government of the day wanted to acknowledge publicly. They certainly didn't want the publicity the award of a VC would generate. At the time, only two military awards could be made posthumously for gallantry—the VC and a Mention in Despatches, or MID.

It is thus interesting to compare the citation for the MID awarded to Laba with that of his BEM:

There can be no doubt that the leadership and determination displayed by Labalaba was an inspiration to every man in the garrison, equally it provided a bulwark which the enemy found impossible to breach. Had the enemy taken the 25pdr there is no doubt they would have captured the city by directing it onto all the substantive defensive positions. To a large extent Labalaba's leadership, his incredible bravery and his determination in the face of overwhelming odds have contributed disproportionately to the defeat of the enemy and to the retention of the city of Mirbat in government hands.

This citation was signed by the then CO 22 SAS Lt Col Peter de la Billiere on 16 August 1972. De la Billiere's Brigade commander endorsed the recommendation thus: 'Very strongly recommended as Corporal Labalaba showed the most outstanding devotion to duty and heroism.'

The matter of whether Laba deserves a retrospective VC award continues to stir debate whenever soldiers and others familiar with Mirbat meet. In an article for *The Spectator* of 3 January 2015, Bruce Anderson claimed that 'Charles Guthrie, Field Marshal, who served in the SAS and was later its Colonel-Commandant, believes that no soldier ever did more to earn the Victoria Cross than Sergeant Labalaba.'

Anderson may not have been aware that as a young officer, Guthrie passed selection for SAS with Laba. Anderson's article concluded with the observation that eleven VCs were awarded to those defending Rorke's Drift, a place of no strategic importance, in 1879. Mirbat was more important and thus 'Mirbat deserves a VC.'

Laba's heroism will never be forgotten in Hereford or Vatutu. The Regiment erected a statue to Laba outside the Sergeant's Mess in Stirling Lines and thus, as Anderson said in his article, 'the brave salute the bravest.'

The Vatutu village elders prepared a simple memorial with the following inscription:

Nai Vakananumi (In Memory)
Cpl Talaiyasi Labalaba
Born 13.7.42
Died Shella (sic), Middle East, 1972.

In February-March 1983, one of Fiji's periodic category 5 cyclones, named 'Oscar', devastated much of Western Viti Levu, including Vatutu and nearby villages. When the then Defence Adviser at the British High Commission in Wellington, Group Captain Mason, included reference to the damage to Laba's mother's house in his report, members of 22 SAS, the Royal Irish Rangers Association and the Army Benevolent Fund dug deep to send money to Mrs Canano to assist with rebuilding her house. The Regiment has dug even deeper over the years to meet most of the cost of building a substantial and cyclone-resistant home in neighbouring Nawaka for the mother of Laba's son, Isaia Derenalagi. Torika Canano died in 2002 but Isaia lives in the house with other relatives. Isaia's mother has also passed away.

Many who served with Laba in RUR/RIR or 22 SAS have visited Vatutu and Nawaka since 1972 and members of B Squadron erected a second memorial to Laba outside the village church on 29 July 1998. In November 2013, Laba's biographer's visit to the village was brokered by Hoss Ligairi's great nephew, Pastor Epi Ligairi. When the young chief gave his blessing to the visit he had but one question: 'Why did Laba not receive the VC'?

Laba's headstone at St Martin's bears the inscription: 'Greater love hath no man than that he should lay down his life for his friends (John 13:15)', which is apt. The grave is accompanied by two small embellishments in stone. The first reads:

'Laba Mirbat
A flower
Born to blush
Unseen'.

It is intriguing to speculate on the source of the above, taken from Thomas Gray's (1716-71) *Eulogy Written in a Country Church-Yard*. Perhaps it is a memorial from the mother of Laba's daughter, Sarah, who was an infant when Laba left Hereford. Sarah has also visited Vatutu. The following line of Gray's poem reads: 'And waste its sweetness on the desert air'. Given the circumstances of Laba's death, this omission is perhaps not surprising, regardless of the identity of the source of this memorial, whether a poetry-loving former comrade or a bereft lover.

Another stone accompanying the headstone has the following inscription:

> This stone was retrieved from the gun pit at Mirbat, Dhofar, Oman. To honour the fallen on the 40th anniversary of the battle of Mirbat, 19th July 2012.

To commemorate Queen Elizabeth's Diamond Jubilee in 2012, a panel of historians nominated sixty 'New Elizabethans' as subjects for the BBC's James Naughtie to describe in individual twelve-minute broadcasts. Laba was chosen as one of those who had either changed Britain over the previous sixty years or influenced change. While a large part of Naughtie's presentation covered the increasing profile of the SAS over the period, and the changing demands on Britain's army in particular, Laba was the only soldier listed in company with poets and pop stars, artists, writers, politicians like Thatcher, Blair and Powell, and figures such as Germaine Greer, Rupert Murdoch and Norman Foster. Not bad for a boy from Vatutu.

Laba is also well-remembered in Buckingham Palace. HRH the Duke of Cambridge unveiled the statue outside the Sergeant's Mess in 2009 when

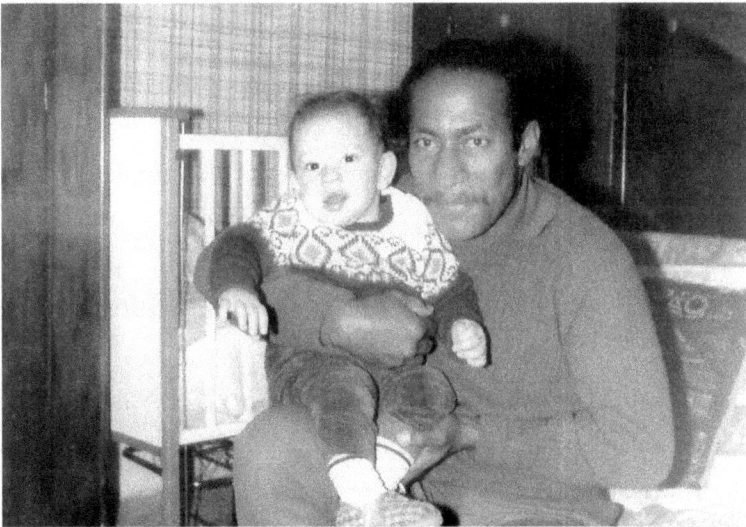

Talaiasi Labalaba with Kasiano and Shirley Qaduadua's eldest child, Josefa, circa 1970
Photo: Shirley Qaduadua

the Regiment ensured that Laba's son Isaia and daughter Sarah, together with Sarah's mother Lynne, were present. At the unpublicised 1981 investiture of five awards for bravery following the rescue of hostages at the Iranian Embassy, among the first words Queen Elizabeth had for Tom Morell in presenting his George Medal were: 'Tell me Colour Sergeant, how is Laba's mother faring in Fiji'?

L/Cpl Sotia PONIJASI

L/Cpl Sotia ('soldier') Ponijasi, whose name was juxtaposed by either the recruiting team or the *Fiji Times*, was a student at Lelean Memorial School in 1961 but was born at Naroi, Moala where he received his early education in the same class as Lote Kaitani and Semesa Naivalu.

Sotia spent his first few years in the DWR before passing selection for 22 SAS in 1966 with a reduction in rank. His three years in D squadron included operational service in Aden, but by 1972 Sotia sought discharge and transferred to the New Zealand army with the hope of serving with the New Zealand SAS squadron in Vietnam. A change of government in New Zealand at this time resulted in the New Zealand forces being withdrawn from Vietnam and Sotia's (usually known as 'Poni') service appears to have been uneventful. Nic Naico, who earlier tried to join Australia's Pacific Island Regiment in Papua New Guinea, recalls asking Hoss Ligairi about Poni's service at this time and was told: 'He spends most of the time planting flowers'.

This may have been an exaggeration on someone's part, but it has been a long time since a New Zealand government felt its position at the bottom of the world sufficiently threatened to invest substantially in defence infrastructure.

Poni rose to become a Warrant Officer in the NZ SAS and met his wife Mere, from Fulaga in the Lau group, in the early 1970s. Their two sons were born in New Zealand and acquired New Zealand citizenship.

Ponijasi quickly found himself 'the meat in the sandwich' in 1987 when the NZ government and Rabuka's military government sought to assess his loyalties. His RFMF service from 1988-92 was dealt with in Chapter 7.

His subsequent service is not known, and efforts to contact him through former colleagues have been unsuccessful. Some believed that he found employment in California or Hawaii and became a lay preacher.

WO2 Tom MORELL, GM

Tom's background and his first few years of service with Royal Signals is dealt with in Appendix D and elsewhere in this book. Though unnamed at the time, Tom achieved a degree of celebrity during the successful resolution of the Iranian Embassy incident at Prince's Gate in April-May 1980. The rope which Tom used to descend from the roof of the building snagged in his karabiner, suspending him several feet above a balcony; as a result, he was badly burned by the fire ignited by the flash grenades used to disorient the terrorists. As soon as he was cut loose, he led his team into the building to deal with the terrorists and the siege was resolved within minutes. The Regiment had an emergency aid post established in the street, cleverly concealed in a horse float. When Tom presented himself for initial treatment the medic responsible for the aid post said: 'Laba would be proud of you'.

Tom had met his second wife, Rosalind, a midwife and hospital administrator, when he was attached to the casualty department of St Thomas' Hospital in central London earlier in 1980. Two more sons and a daughter resulted in the years that followed.

In 1983, Tom accepted a five-year extension to his enlistment which he took to retain army support for his younger boys attending public schools. When he was discharged in 1985 as a WO2, he made a vow never to carry a gun again and has stayed true to that promise.

Tom's first contract employment involved providing CT advice to the Sri Lankan Government on counter-hijacking. Such 'specialist interests' were the main reason why he did not return to Fiji after his army service. From 1988-91 he found contracted employment through 'Control Risks' to Mohammed Al Fayed. The initial agreement for six months morphed into three years protecting al Fayed's wife (Miss Finland, 1978) and children. Later contracts from 1991-2003 involved working for oil and mining companies, including British Petroleum, in Colombia, Venezuela and Ecuador. He quickly became fluent in Spanish and flew 1.3 million miles (2.09 million km) as a 'fly in-fly out' security adviser. In 1997 he moved to New Zealand but continued commuting to work in South America for another six years. One of his older sons has since followed his father into a security consultancy career. Others may follow.

Since 2003 Tom has worked for himself as a property investor/ developer in Hamilton, with a successful business model. Rugby, parachuting and defenestration from a seized embassy eventually took their toll on Tom's knees, both of which now pivot on titanium. For the first of these operations, Tom was asked by the anaesthetist whether he was allergic to anything. 'Only land mines' was his answer, referring to some unpleasantness in Dhofar in the 1970s.

A fitting memorial to a very brave soldier. Laba's son in Fiji and daughter in Hereford were hosted by 22 SAS for the unveiling by the Duke of Cambridge in 2009.
Photo: author

APPENDIX G: ROYAL ARMY SERVICE CORPS,
LATER ROYAL CORPS OF TRANSPORT

War Office records indicate thirty-two of the 200 men were allocated to the RASC of the day, in the first instance. Twenty-nine of them are accounted for hereunder. Some were transferred to the RAOC (which later became the Royal Logistics Corps), where they used the specialist skills they had acquired in their earlier service.

Daniel AITCHESON

Daniel did not appear in the *Fiji Times* list of 1961, and thus there is no record of his occupation or where he enlisted. He attended St Columba's Primary School in Suva with Mo Beg, passed away before the fiftieth anniversary of his enlistment, and left no other memory with those who survived him.

Ram ANAND

Ram, who later became known as Ashok Anand, was noted by the *Fiji Times* as 'Sharma, Rama Nand, student, Suva' when he enlisted. He was educated at the then Shri Vivekananda High School in Nadi, and contributed articles to *Jagriti* (*The Awakening*), a Hindi language newspaper published by the Sangam Sarada Printing Press to give Fiji's Indian community a voice.

Ram served in the RASC for only four years before seeking a discharge on compassionate grounds. He recalls the highlight of his service was winning the BAOR featherweight boxing title for his battalion.

Ram joined the UK civil service and worked at Heathrow Airport before becoming a prison officer, spending the last years of his working life with young offenders. He returned to Fiji in 1972 where he married his first wife.

He then married again, to a Gujarati woman born in Kenya, and they had five children. He has remained living in Middlesex and last visited Fiji in 2010.

Semisi BAROKEI

Semisi was another for whom the army appealed more than his apprenticeship. He was a classmate of Isikeli Maravu in Verata House at QVS. After serving six years in the BAOR and the UK, he settled in London before securing employment with a 'sultan or prince' in Qatar, according to the late Apakuki Nanovo. He eventually returned to Fiji and settled in Cautata, Tailevu.

Tom Thomas BENNETT

Tom was another apprentice in Lautoka whose service was cut short when he was killed in an accident while on leave. He is remembered by Sam Tamata as a very good runner.

Rajendra BIKRAM

Rajendra was possibly the only one of the '212' who described himself as 'self-employed' when he enlisted, giving his address as Nausori. He enlisted as Rajendra Prasad s/o (son of) Bikram but became known as Rajendra Bikram in the army, probably due to the army's preference for patronyms. He served nine years as a plant operator, initially in the RASC and later in RAOC/RLC, acquiring the nickname Reggie. Rajend was born a Hindu but was buried a Roman Catholic by his fourth wife, a former nun from Assam whom he met in India. She had him baptised as Reginald, the name by which he was known later in his life. Reg spent his final years living in the south of England.

The Rev Sam Tamata, who enlisted with Reg in the RASC, recalled him being settled in Poole and studying law when last contacted in the late eighties or early nineties.

Lawrence John BILLINGS

Lawrence was born in Labasa, but the family home was the village of Dogotuki on Vanua Levu. The family name has German origins and his mother's brother, Gus Billings, was the Divisional Engineer (Northern). Together with George Chute and Keith Zoing, Laurence attended Labasa European Primary School.

Lawrence was an apprentice motor mechanic in Labasa and wanted to see the world. An uncle had 'been to sea' but none of his family had served in the World Wars or Malaya. He was not related to any of the other '212'. Lawrence's army service and decision to settle in Germany is dealt with in Chapter 4.

Joseph HENRY

Joe Henry grew up in Nadi, where he was completing an apprenticeship as a fitter and turner in 1961. He was keen to enlist, perhaps influenced by his father Tom, a building supervisor at Nadi Airport who had served in the Solomons in WWII. His mother, Elizabeth Lelo, was related to David Lelo who served with Royal Signals. A brother, Louis, became a Catholic priest and a sister became a nun.

Joe's army service was probably the shortest of the '212', as he was found to be deaf in one ear and was discharged from the RASC in 1962 after six months. He declined an offer of repatriation to Fiji, deciding to take his chances in England. Joe had mastered the practical operation of lathes and other machine tools as a fitter and turner, but not the theoretical aspects of the trade, and could not read technical drawings.

The first few months in England were hard, but he eventually found work as a cleaner in a factory. Joe worked his way up via a correspondence course, completing his qualifications. He married an English girl in 1964 and they moved to Germany, where his wife was killed in a car accident. Joe decided to stay in Germany, settling near Frankfurt with a German partner and raising a son.

David KADO

David Kado and his cousin Jioji Areki shared a common Japanese grandfather who had settled in the Lau group of Fiji, but was detained as an 'enemy alien' in WWII and repatriated to Japan via New Zealand. David was employed as an electrician when he enlisted and is recalled by others from that time as having an engineer father and attempting selection for 22 SAS during his army service.

He served with Sam Tamata in a petroleum supply unit before returning to live in Suva, but did not wish to become involved with this project.

Noa LARUA

Noa was not listed in the *Fiji Times* but is remembered by Joe Tuwai as having Labasa, Macuata, origins and by Tom Morell as serving with 63 Para Company RASC in the late nineteen-sixties. He served twenty-four years, acquiring the nickname 'Lash', and was a Sergeant with the Junior Leaders Regiment, RCT in 1983.

He settled in Nottinghamshire, and Joe Tuwai recalled that Noa was a guest on Cilla Black's popular *Surprise Surprise* program around 1985 when Noa's 'surprise' was to be reunited with his parents on camera. Joe also advised that Noa participated in experimental treatments for cancer before passing away in April 2016. Noa's pallbearers included his cousin S/Sgt Louie Turagavou, and grandsons Pte Kane-Larua-Brooks, Pte Niall Larua-Brooks, Pte Jordan Larua-Brooks and Marine Lee Brooks.

Pita LIVALIVA

Pita was also not among those listed in the *Fiji Times* but is remembered by former comrades as having served in the RASC and later emigrating to Australia. He had moved from a Melbourne address in 1993 and later lived in the nearby Mt Macedon area, but has since evaded further detection.

Tomasi MATAKITOGA

Tomasi was the younger brother of Sunia Matakitoga, who also served twenty- two years, but in the RAOC/RLC. Tom was discharged as a S/Sgt with 42 Sqn, RCT.

Frederick J. MAYBIR

Fred was born in Navua, educated at MBHS and was unemployed in November 1961. He recalls Captain Paul Manueli as OIC training at the RFMF in 1961. Fred appears to have been influenced by his father Louis Maybir's WWII service in the RNZAF, and his grandfather's service in the RAN in both World Wars. His Christian great-grandfather, Bon Mahabir, was born in India and his grandfather Charles anglicised the family name to Maybir before moving to Fiji from Australia shortly after Federation in 1901.

Among the first pieces of legislation passed by the newly-independent nation were Acts restricting non-European immigration. These became known as the 'White Australia Policy'. Geoffrey Blainey has described the effects of the deportation of Pacific Islanders and others, including indentured Indian labourers, on the infant sugar industry which then required subsidies to survive without cheap labour.[75]

Fred completed an initial six years, mainly in Germany, but also including six months in Thailand on Operation Crown, 'driving' during the construction of an airfield in Ubon Ratchathani Province bordering Laos and Cambodia. Fred was one of those who said of themselves 'I was not a good soldier' but he re-enlisted shortly after being discharged; his cousin Mo Beg recalls Fred was assessed best recruit on his second basic training course, but shortly afterwards Fred was found to have a hearing deficiency which appeared to have gone undetected during his previous service. He was subsequently given a medical discharge.

Fred married a Yorkshire girl and they had one daughter before the marriage failed. In 1968 he applied to join the Australian Army and emigrate to Australia but was unsuccessful with both ventures. Fred returned to Fiji for DOMCOL in 1967, and has since been back only once for a four-day visit. He has since 'done everything' including working for the British Post Office, in a glass factory in Yorkshire, as a bus conductor and as a security officer. He has settled in London.

---

75 72 *A Shorter History of Australia*, Geoffrey Blainey, 1994.

Ramkrishna MUDALIER

Ramkrishna was listed in the *Fiji Times* as 'farmer, Nadi' and was almost certainly the son of a cane farmer. He appeared in a War Office file as allocated to the RASC, but is not recalled by former comrades interviewed for this book and appears not to have kept in contact with many others.

Filimone NAVUSO

Filimone's parents were from the villages of Rukua and Raviravi on the Western side of Beqa Island, south of Viti Levu. Apakuki Nanovo recalled in 2013 that Filimone attended RKS and the Koroniva Farm Institute a couple of years behind Mike Yasa. In 1961 Filimone was working with Sam Pillay as a field assistant with the Department of Agriculture at Nadroga. Filimoni served with the RASC in the UK, Borneo and Singapore. His younger brother, Mika Vuidravuwalu, also enlisted. Filimoni died back in Fiji.

Benjamin Bal RAJ

Ben was listed in the newspaper as 'unemployed, Navua' and later in War Office records as serving with RASC. Azam Ali recalled in 2016 that Ben served nine years, spending the last few as a medical orderly, and returned to Navua and employment in the radiography department of Suva's Colonial War Memorial Hospital. It appears that Ben never married and did not live long after his return to Fiji.

Subhas SINGH

Subhas attended DAV College in Suva and was a clerk with the Treasury Department in 1961. He served six years before settling in London and resuming a career in banking.

Alex SANERIVE

Alex was listed in the *Fiji Times* as 'student, Levuka' and is variously remembered by other '212' as of part-European and Rotuman extraction, and the son of a doctor. Some knew him as 'Severini' and the War Office recruitment file noted him as 'Samoan'. Little else could be gleaned beyond the fact that he was last recorded in the Sydney suburb of Ashfield in 1992.

He apparently died a few years later. His army service included a posting to Bracht in Germany with Vosa Cama.

Thomas Allan SWANSON

Allan was born in Suva, the eldest of six children whose parents were both part-European Fijians. Allan's mother was a first cousin of Doreen Petersen, one of the twelve women. His paternal grandmother's village was Vadravadra, near Ba. Allan's father was a rigger for CSR and his mother found work with a dry-cleaning company in Suva after his father was accidentally killed in 1953. Somehow the family found the resources to send Allan to Suva Grammar School where he joined the school cadet unit. He finished his schooling at Mount Roskill Grammar School in Auckland, making him one of only six of the '212' to have travelled outside Fiji before Christmas 1961, and thus to have his own passport.

Allan's father and two uncles had served during WWII, but the incentive to enlist in 1961 related more to finances than an enthusiasm to serve. Allan began his working life as an apprentice fitter with the PWD in Suva, earning the princely sum of one pound and eight shillings per week. On a visit to Ba however, Allan found that CSR paid their apprentices more than double the government wage, and in 1961 he became an apprentice carpenter at the CSR Mill in Ba. The company funded a five-year technical drawing correspondence course administered from Brisbane. Allan was interviewed by the recruiting team at St Teresa's School in Ba and expressed a preference for serving in the infantry. His basic training course with RASC at Aldershot included ten or twelve other Fijians, including Sam Tamata who was awarded the distinction of top recruit. Allan was then posted to 1 Petroleum Reserve Depot at West Moors, near Wimborne Minster in Dorset. During his basic truck-driving course, Allan broke his ankle vaulting out of the rear of the truck and was given a medical discharge after eighteen months of service.

Allan returned to Fiji in 1963, was offered the opportunity to return to his apprenticeship and considered returning to the UK, but finally opted for New Zealand where he had relatives. He settled in the forestry town of

Tokorua which attracted many Pacific Islanders, married Sophie in 1965 and stayed for twenty-three years working as a leading hand fitter in sawmills and pulp/paper mills. By 1988, however, Tokorua had downsized and much of the heavy equipment from failing industries was sold to Indonesia and China. Allan accepted an offer of redundancy and found work as a fitter in Sydney, settling finally in King's Park to the west of the city.

Mosese TACINA

Mosese was remembered by another '212' as the *Tui Toga*, Rewa, and by others who advised that he served nine years before returning to Fiji and a job with the Patterson Brothers transport company.

Tomasi TALEAUA

Tomasi was a student at LMS in 1961, and one of the twelve whose departure was delayed by the army until they had the opportunity to sit their Senior Cambridge examination. He is remembered by former comrades as having Kadavu origins, and serving nine years with RASC/RCT before working on oil rigs based in Barrow-in-Furness, eventually settling in Rochdale.

Sauyawa (Sam) TAMATA

Sam was born in Lawaki village in Nakasaleka District, northern Kadavu, the eldest of seven children. He attended Kavala Bay Primary School and Vunisea Provincial Boarding School, together with Kiniviliame Navusolo and DAV College in Nabua, Suva.

In 1961 Sam was an apprentice in the PWD mechanical engineering branch, where Tom Morell's uncle George Morell was the chief mechanical engineer. Sam had concerns about a limited future for him and others from modest backgrounds in Fiji:

> For me it was a sense of adventure. The possibility of going to Britain and seeing the world. Even then I sensed there was not much scope for advancement or improvement for me. Fiji at that time I felt, was strongly nepotistic, that to move forward and to improve your lot was not what you know rather who you know. I suppose this is the failing of human nature.

He expressed a preference for the RE but found himself allocated to the RASC of the day. Elements of the RASC, however, were reorganised into the RAOC in the Macleod restructure of 1965. Sam adapted well to the army, and Allan Swanson remembers Sam being nominated best recruit in their basic training course. Sam served nine years and was discharged as a Corporal. Sam's unit was involved in the supply of petroleum products. Their war role would have involved the construction of petroleum depots. He served on UN peace-keeping duty in Cyprus during the EOKA troubles, and in Germany. Sam's recognition of his true calling is dealt with in Chapters 4 and 9.

Solomone TAROGI

Solomone was born on the tiny island of Ono-i-Lau, but enlisted as a carpenter from Nausori. His cousin Panipasa Luva also enlisted and served with the RAC. Solo served twenty-two years with RASC/RCT and was discharged as a Sergeant from 27 LSG Regiment. Joe Tuwai recalled in July 2014 that Solo had attended LMS and DAV College, and married a Norwegian woman who he met while on adventure training in Norway. Solo died in Norway around 1999. Panipasa's widow Liz recalled that the couple had no children.

Wame TAWAKE

Wame enlisted from school, initially serving with RASC and qualifying as a parachutist in 1965 for 63 Para Logistics Company. He later transferred into REME, serving with 16 Para Workshop. Former '212' colleagues recalled Wame had family links to Kadavu, but he chose to settle near Nabua outside Suva on his return to Fiji after his discharge in 1983.

Sekove TUNI

Sekove was not listed in the *Fiji Times* but served twenty-two years, and was discharged as a Corporal with 2 armoured division headquarters and signals squadron. He died before 2011; efforts to learn more about him were unsuccessful.

Tomasi TUNIDAU

Tom was a student in 1961, but enlisted with older brother Jona who became a sapper and also served twenty-two years. Tom finished his service with 52 Port Sqn, RCT and returned to Fiji where he drove trucks on inter-island ferries for many years. He spent the last four years of his working life with the Reserve Bank of Fiji as a security officer and died in 2000.

Sikeli VAKALALA

Sikeli had family origins in Rewa but was noted as 'labourer, Savusavu' when he enlisted. He appeared to find his niche in the army, discharging as a S/Sgt with 250 Field Ambulance Unit in 1983. He qualified as a parachutist, serving with 63 Para Logistics Company early in his service, and was a formidable rugby player, featuring in the front row of a team of Fijians which played the BAOR fifteen on Fiji Day 1976 at Wildenrath, Germany. In 1973 he was awarded a MID for his service in Northern Ireland

Isikeli returned to Fiji and joined the Fijian Affairs Department, and finished his service as *Roko Tui*, Ra. He was a director of the ill-fated Bolatagone Motors venture and was closely associated with the *taukei* movement in 1987. Isikeli's daughter followed him into the army and was still serving in the Logistics Corps in 2015.

Mosese VAKATALE

Mosese attended RKS and joined from school. Mosese's parents were teachers, but by the time Mosese was born his father had become a Methodist minister and was stationed at Naviti in the Yasawa group. Mosese later identified with Batiki in the Lomaiviti group as his home; this was where his father originated and eventually retired.

None of Mosese's family had served with the Fiji Military Forces in Malaya or earlier conflicts. His elder sister Taufa, who was at university in Auckland in 1961, believes that peer pressure from Mosese's classmates at RKS was probably the main reason for his enlistment, together with the lust for adventure, a desire to see the Queen again and see the England he had heard so much about. Taufa was disappointed that her only brother chose the army ahead of the opportunity for further education in Fiji or elsewhere, and would have tried to dissuade him had she been in Fiji at the time.

Taufa returned to a distinguished career in Fiji, as the first Fijian Headmistress of her alma mater, the Adi Cakabau School. She later became the first Fijian woman to be appointed Permanent Head of a government department, the first to be a Cabinet Minister, and then the country's first female Deputy Prime Minister. Vaciseva Tabua, who also had Batiki origins, was the only '212' to whom Mosese was closely related.

Mosese was very pleased that he had the opportunity to travel further than his older siblings, and sent Taufa a postcard from Hawaii en route to England and another of a snow-covered English landscape after his arrival. Following his basic training and driving course with the RASC, Mosese was based near Yeovil and became involved in supporting a youth group through which he met and became engaged to an English girl. Mosese died in Germany on the night of 5 May 1965, killed instantly in a head-on collision shortly after driving his unit Chaplain home. He is buried in the Hanover Military Cemetery.

Laurel Bentley, later Harper, with Vaciseva Tabua's cousin Mosese Vakatale, circa 1962.
Mosese was killed in a head on collision in Germany in May, 1965.
Photo: Laurel Harper

Wainikiti VOSABALAVU

Wainikiti was the eldest of nine children and was born on Ono-i-Lau. His father served in the Solomons in WWII. He attended Draiba Fijian School and DAV College, and in 1961 was an apprentice motor mechanic in the Government Workshop at Walu Bay.

He served 15 years in the RASC/RCT and was promoted to Sergeant, but was later reduced in rank for some misdemeanour. He was a Corporal in Borneo and met his first wife, Shelley, 'from Malaysia' at the time; they married in Singapore. He later married twice more, for the last time after his second wife died.

Wainikiti returned to Fiji in 1978 for a year but then returned to the UK. He mentioned a son who died in London at age 29, but not the circumstances of his death. He had no regrets whatsoever about his British Army service. Nic Naico, whose first wife was Shelley's sister, recalls Vosa was 'a good boxer in the ring representing RCT, but a bad boxer out of it.'

Mosese WAQAIRADOVU

Mosese appeared in the *Fiji Times* as 'labourer, Suva'. He was recalled by former comrades in 1992 as serving for eighteen years with the RCT before he returned to Fiji where he died.

Appendix H: Ordnance/ RAOC/RLC

War Office records indicate fifteen of the men were allocated to the RAOC of the day in the first instance, but a total of seventeen spent all or part of their service with the Corps.

Azam ALI

Azam appeared in the *Fiji Times* as Abdul Azam Ali s/o (son of) Rehmat Ali. He later became known as Azam Ali but was known as Pedro in the army. He was born in Suva but grew up in Lautoka, which he considers home. He enlisted while still a student at Shri Vivekananda College, Nadi, joining the army 'to seek adventure and travel the world'. And because he got badly sunburned the day before the recruitment interview, and did not have the courage to ask his father to write a letter to the teacher! Azam does not recall being offered his preferences for regiment or corps—individuals were chosen for their IQ, education and physique. Azam was enlisted into RAOC and transferred to RAMC in July 1963, the only Fijian to serve with them at the time. He later qualified as a combat medical technician and an NBC instructor.

Azam served for twenty-four years, in BAOR, Malaya, Singapore, Brunei, Borneo and Northern Ireland and was discharged as a Sergeant. In 1994 Azam was employed as a security officer with British Airways. He was qualified to run a casualty department (accident/emergency centre) without doctors supervising every admission, but found his qualifications were not recognised outside the army in the UK.

Akuila Vaniqi BALEISUVA

The *Fiji Times* recorded Akuila as 'clerk, Nausori', but some of his comrades recall he came from Bua in Vanua Levu. He was educated at Lelean Memorial School, became known as 'Balei' in the army and was discharged after twenty-two years as 'Sgt Vaniqi, RAOC 22 Air Despatch Regiment Workshop'. Akuila was last noted back in Suva in March 1984, as company director of Bolatagane Motors Ltd, the joint venture proposal by several '212' returnees to establish a Volkswagen franchise in Fiji. He died before the 50th anniversary of the '212''s enlistment in 2011.

Vosa CAMA

Vosa was born in Udu village on Kabara in the Lau group, noted for its boat builders and navigators.

In the army, his family name was pronounced 'Kama'. He was named Vosa after his mother's brother. Cama (pron. 'thama') is the clan name for the artisans of Udu village who make the outriggers for sea-going *drua* canoes from native *vesi* hardwood, also used to make the best *tanoas*.

Vosa was the second of four children. His younger brother was named after their father's family so did not share the same surname. Vosa's mother's village was Tokolau, and through his mother Vosa is a cousin of Filimone Jitoko who became a High Court Judge and was Fiji's High Commissioner to London in 1987. Many understood that Jitoko was disappointed by Rabuka's coup and the subsequent coup-induced changes to Fiji's constitution.

Nat Ledua was another 'cousin' because his mother is from the same village as Vosa's mother. Vosa left Kabara at age eleven or twelve to attend Lelean Memorial School at Nausori. The school commemorates Reverend Thomas Baker, who was killed and eaten by cannibals whose appetites could not manage the missionary's boots—one of which survives in the Fiji Museum. Vosa was in the same class as Tom Waqabaca, and Jimmy Naivalu also attended LMS.

Vosa was an apprentice book-binder when the recruiting team arrived in October 1961. The recruiting office was very close to a window of Vosa's work area, and when he expressed interest in applying his supervisor encouraged him to enlist because 'there is nothing for you here'. Vosa left Fiji in the second chartered aircraft with Hoss Ligairi as the designated OIC.

He was allocated to the RAOC and is pictured in the March 1962 photograph of the course for which Sunia Matakitoga was judged the best recruit. Vosa served from 1961 until he was medically discharged as a Corporal in the late sixties. He volunteers that he 'was not a good soldier' and was frequently in strife for his pugilism, often after drinking too much, on postings as diverse as Singapore, Kluang (with David Whey) and Bracht (with Mike Vuli and Alex Sanerive).

He served several months in Colchester Correctional Centre (or, 'The Glasshouse') for assaulting his platoon sergeant, but avoided a dishonourable discharge when the circumstances were reviewed by his CO. Vosa's repeated offences lead to treatment at Netley Hospital, established for WWI 'shell shock'/PTSD cases where he was visited by Dave Rosa. It is arguable that Vosa may have avoided some of the incidents which got him into trouble if he had had other Fijians working with him.

Despite his repeat offences, Vosa did well to qualify as a B1 Technical Storeman– the highest grade—within 3-4 years, specialising in aircraft and MT spares. He was active in regimental rugby and athletics (discus) teams and played rugby for the Johore State team when posted to Malaysia and Singapore. In Brunei Vosa was attached to a REME unit supporting the RAF with spares from the RAF base in Changi. In Bracht he served with an RAOC Ammunition depot. Vosa returned to Kabara on DOMCOL in 1966 but his only attempt to get back again in 1983 was frustrated by a hurricane. He had returned to see his mother who was seriously ill in Suva. He was disinclined to return to Fiji permanently because of the circumstances of his discharge, had no further military service, and did not attend the 1983 Dortmund Parade. His only regret regarding his army service is his errant behaviour.

After leaving the army, Vosa first found employment in a series of storeman jobs, including at the Rover car factory. He was later employed in a number of security jobs, the last of which was with the British Legion Security Co. In 1969 Vosa met Lily in a pub in London. Lily was born in Israel of Yemeni extraction. After completing her military service, Lily came to London on a discharge fare and stayed. They married in 1998 after Vosa had a stroke in 1996, but had no children. Vosa and Lily had the option of living in Israel but chose to stay in England, where he retired in 2004. In 2014 Lily had to be hospitalised with Alzheimer's Disease as Vosa could no longer care for her at home. Lily died in 2018 and Vosa accompanied her body back to Israel for burial.

Sunia Mateiwai MATAKITOGA

Sunia was recorded as a clerk in Suva when he enlisted. Vishnu Sharma recalls that Sunia was assessed as the best recruit on their basic training course with 1 Training Battalion, RAOC. Sunia served for twenty-two years and was a WO1 when discharged from 22 Engineer Regiment Workshop, RAOC. His brother Tomasi Matakitoga also served twenty-two years with the RASC/RCT. Sunia had married an English woman and, according to *Soldier* magazine in early 1983, had decided to stay in the UK. After his discharge Sunia served with the Sultan's Armed Forces in Oman, where he was killed in a road accident.

Subramani NAIDU

Subramani was born in Labasa and educated at, St Augustine's College, Wailevu followed by Natabua High School in Lauktoka. When he enlisted he was noted as 'Planter, Labasa'. None of his relatives had served with the FMF but he found through his first marriage that he was related to Vicki Grant, one of the twelve '212' women who enlisted. He has fond memories of this early service with two of the other women from Fiji, Emma Heffernan (who taught him to play squash) and Lou Peckham (who used to cut his hair).

Subramani was known as 'Luke' in the RAOC where he specialised as an ammunition technician, qualified as a parachutist and served in the heavy drop unit. He discharged as a Sergeant after nine years' service in Germany, Kenya, Aden, Sarawak, Dubai, Kuwait, Djibouti, Somalia and Guiana. He later qualified as a Warrant Officer in the TA. He met his second wife from Fiji in the UK, and initially worked for the Pinkerton security company before settling in Australia in 1996.

Subramani, or 'Babu' as he is now known, prefers the climate at Caloundra in Queensland and regards Australia as 'the most tolerant country in the world'. He has no regrets about his army service, but bridles when he recalls some racial slurs during that time, including at the Union Jack Club, and notes that he 'could never become an Englishman'.

Apakuki NANOVO

Apakuki was born at Ekubu in Vatulele, Nadroga and attended Nausori Tutorial College. In 1961 he was listed as 'office boy, Suva'. An uncle served in the Solomons and Apakuki enlisted to see the world. Apakuki was known as 'Happy' to RAOC colleagues throughout his army service from 1961-92, and as 'Kuki' to other '212'. He retired as a Captain, commissioned at the same time as Manasa Talakuli. Only Joe Tuwai served longer. Apakuki saw operational service in Aden and Northern Ireland, and other service in Hong Kong, BAOR, UK, Kenya and Brunei. While serving in Hong Kong in 1969, Kuki played rugby with the OC Mule Company, RCT. He enjoyed his service and was very proud to have served.

Kuki was the second longest-serving of the '212' and one of only two of them to be promoted WO1 Conductors RAOC, the most senior NCO rank. The other '212' to reach that rank was Manasa Talakuli, Kuki married Kalisi in Suva in 1969 and they chose to stay in the UK for their children's education. Their son Viliame followed Kuki into the army and in 2017 was a serving Colonel. Their daughter works at Leeds University.

The authority of the rank of Conductor did not lapse with his retirement from the army. When Conductor Nanovo 'called a parade' of several aging comrades to RV at the White Horse Hotel in Worcester to meet their biographer, one pleaded absence due to an appointment for admission to hospital for some surgery. The plaintiff was advised 'forget the hospital, come to the parade'!

Kuki was a popular and respected figure in the army, in his second career with an automotive engineering company in the West Midlands and in retirement. In his later years he helped many young men from Fiji join the army. When he succumbed to illness in 2015 his former comrade and close friend of over fifty years, Pramod Tikaram, remembered him in his eulogy as 'sweet tempered, sober, kind, humorous, thoroughly good and thoroughly beloved'.

RAOC Training Battalion, Blackdown Barracks, Surrey, February, 1962.
L to R: Apakuki Nanovo, Vosa Cama, Sunia Matakitoga, Sakiusa Vocetaki.
Photo A. Nanovo

John NARAIN

John's mother was a Rotuman and his father Nepalese. He was born at Nabukavesi, baptised and confirmed into the Roman Catholic Church, and educated at St Columba's and Marist Brothers' High School. The *Fiji Times* listed him as 'Narain Jayendra, Clerk, Navua'.

John was training to be a school teacher in 1961. He was another wanting adventure and to see the world. He claims 'a few relatives (Fijians) served in both World Wars' but did not explain whether these relatives were on his father's or his mother's side of the family.

John served in RAOC (later the Royal Logistics Corps) for nine years in the UK, Germany, Singapore, Borneo, Aden and Cyprus, leaving as a Corporal ammunition technician. John was the RAOC bantam-weight boxing champion for four years, and held the army championship in that grade for two of them. During this time, he claims he lost only one bout in 38 and scored knockouts in 28 of them. John decided to settle in the UK, 'married locally' but had no children. He had various jobs after his army service, at one point managing a wine bar in London owned by an Australian woman, ending 'with the railways in a managerial capacity'.

James PETER

James is one of a handful of the '212' who apparently did not serve very long and of whom not much is known. There is little memory or other record of his service beyond the *Fiji Times* record of 'clerk, Suva' and a War Office file reference to him being allocated to RAOC. In 1992 several '212' advised their biographer that they thought he had remained in the UK.

Vishnu SHARMA

In 1961, Vishnu was a clerk with a printing company which produced *Fiji Samarchar*, a Hindi newspaper. Vishnu was born in Yalalevu, Ba. His grandfather was a 'Girmitiya' and a Hindu priest. His father tackled several occupations throughout his life, successively becoming a watchmaker, photographer, truck and taxi driver and farmer, before also becoming a priest in his later years.

Vishnu appeared in the *Fiji Times* as 'Vishnu-Deo s/o (son of) Shiu Shankar Sharma, clerk, Suva.' He served for nine years, primarily in UK, apart from FARELF in Singapore, followed by BAOR. He had three children with his Danish wife who died in 2009. Vishnu is one of the few '212' to have a Facebook page, on which he notes he 'only ever had three employers.' The last of these was London Transport (now called Transport for London) from which he retired in September 2005.

Chandra Kaur SINGH s/o (son of) Ram Kaur Singh

The *Fiji Times* recorded Chandra as 'former Police Constable, Suva' and the War Office recruitment file noted him as allocated to RAOC. He is remembered by Vishnu Sharma as C. K. Singh who trained with him, but other memories and records have faded.

Ratu Manasa TALAKULI

Born in Nakelo in 1940, Ratu Manasa was another clerk in the Fiji Civil Service when he enlisted. He was known as 'Sam' during his basic and trade training at the RAOC Depot & Training Battalion at Blackdown Barracks, Deepcut, Surrey. His first posting took him to Central Ordnance Depot Bicester as an Orderly Room Clerk.

Ratu Manasa served in many overseas postings including Hong Kong, Singapore, Germany and Brunei. He returned to UK from Hong Kong in 1965 and volunteered for the Royal Marine Commando Logistic Regiment and trained at the Royal Marines training centre, Plymouth. His unit exercised for months at a time in Norway, Malta, Cyprus, and Singapore.

Ratu Manasa married Adi Samanunu Cakobau in October 1969 at the Garrison Church, Rheindahlen. In the same year he was promoted to Sergeant, working at Ordnance Branch at the British Army's Headquarters on the Rhine. Adi Samanunu was the eldest child of Fiji's first Governor General, Ratu Sir George Cakobau, the last *Vunivalu*, or High Chief, of Bau. As such, she was the most senior Chief of Fiji's Kubuna Confederacy, but chiefly and other politics worked against her succession to her father's title in her lifetime. Adi Samanunu served as Fiji's Minister for Fijian Affairs in 1994-95, and later as High Commissioner to Malaysia and Ambassador to Thailand in 1999. She died in June 2012.

In 1979 Ratu Manasa was promoted to Warrant Officer 1 and was seconded to the Royal Brunei Malay Regiment, Brunei. Whilst still serving in Brunei in 1983, he was appointed to WO1 Conductor RAOC, the most senior Warrant

Officer appointment in the Army. Adi Samanunu worked at the British High Commission Brunei when Manasa was posted there. In December 1983, Ratu Manasa was commissioned and promoted to Captain. He then served in Germany, Warminster and Northern Ireland. He was promoted Major whilst serving in Bicester in 1991 and retired from the army in 1992.

Ratu Manasa's lifelong ambition was to become a lawyer, and Apakuki Nanovo recalled his early studies with the Open University at Southampton. Immediately after leaving the Army, Ratu Manasa studied at Oxford Brookes University, where he earned a Bachelor's Degree in Political Science in 1995. He was later awarded a degree in Law from Hull University in 1996.

He lived and worked in the Warminster area from 1996 to 2006, when the death of his eldest brother in Fiji changed all his plans. He was required to return to Fiji to rejoin Adi Samanunu and assume his duties and responsibilities to the *vanua* of Nakelo. Ratu Manasa suffered ill health in his later years and died in Suva's Colonial War Memorial Hospital in January 2014. He rests in the chiefly burial ground at Nauluvatu, Nakelo, survived by his only son.

Pramod Singh TIKARAM

In 1961 Pramod was a part time clerk at Suva Motors and enlisted to escape family pressure to attend university. He came from a family of high achievers. His grandfather came from Alrgar in Utar Pradesh, near the border with Nepal and was recorded only as 'Tikaram' when he arrived in Fiji in 1912 under the Girmit ('agreement') scheme of indentured labour for the colonial sugar industry. Grandad saw opportunities to make more money than the weekly gold sovereign paid to labourers, and went into the transport business with a bullock cart.

Grandfather Tikaram prospered and diversified into trucks, buses and taxis. Tikaram and his wife Singari had eleven children. Like immigrants everywhere Pramod's grandparents put a premium on education for their children. Madho Singh Tikaram, the second of seven sons, was Pramod's father. The third son became Sir Moti Tikaram who studied law at

Victoria University of Wellington, New Zealand, and became the first 'local person' (his term) to fill a succession of legal appointments in Fiji, including acting as Chief Justice in 1971.

Pramod's father expanded the family business interests, based in Lami on the outskirts of Suva, to include the installation of telephone systems. Pramod followed his father and uncles to MBHS, knew nothing about the British Army but in 1961 it provided an escape from the pressure to attend university. He developed pneumonia shortly after arriving in England and was separated from his cohort while recovering for three weeks in Cambridge Military Hospital, Aldershot. He enjoyed his early years when he was known as 'Tiki' and was judged best recruit in the platoon on his basic training course.

During 'Confrontation' with Indonesia, Pramod served with 152 Air Maintenance Platoon based at Kuching airport, Sarawak, Malaysia. He remembers that supplies that were air-dropped to Commonwealth forces frequently landed in Indonesian territory. In Kuching Pramod met and married Rohani, a Malay Muslim. Their son Ramon was born in Singapore, and their daughter Tanita in Germany. The family became frequent return visitors to Kuching, but their first visit to Fiji was not until 1980.

In his subsequent army career Pramod saw service in Belize, Northern Ireland, the UK and Germany. He developed a passion for golf and was discharged a WO1. Returning to Fiji in 1984 with a foreign wife and teenage children did not appeal, so the family decided to stay in England. Pramod's initial employment for the first eighteen months after the army did not inspire him, but his RAOC/RLC experience and studies in management secured his appointment with Racal Vodapage Ltd which was building a new business. He was soon promoted to a senior management position and evolved with Vodafone as it grew.

Pramod accepted a redundancy package after his sixtieth birthday and now concentrates on his golf. Ramon became a successful actor, and Tanita's success as a British pop/folk singer-songwriter is reflected in the awards for her record sales decorating the family dining room in Basingstoke. Pramod's younger brother Pravin Tikaram was the first Indo-Fijian to teach at QVS in the 1970s, specialising in Maths and Science. After the 1987 coups Pravin moved to New Zealand and taught at Lake Taupo until retiring.

Timoci TUPOU

Tim was not listed in the *Fiji Times*, but was one of four applicants who were attending bible school together. A Lauan, Tim was the first '212' to qualify for the Parachute Regiment after basic RAOC training in 1962, and later served with 16 Para Heavy Drop Company. Tom Morell and David Whey encountered Tim in Singapore in 1965 when Tim's unit was attached to 2 Para for jungle warfare training at Johore Baharu.

Sakiusa VOCETAKI

Sakiusa was another employed as a clerk in Suva when he enlisted. In 1992 several '212' recalled Sakiusa completed eighteen years' service before he returned to Fiji to work for Courts in Samabula. Apakuki Nanovo recalled in 2014 that Sakiusa failed his basic parachute course, but was allowed to stay in the airborne unit because he always volunteered to carry the Bren gun in his section!

Tomasi VOSAMACALA

Like James Peter above, Tomasi appeared only in the *Fiji Times* and thereafter was not recorded or recalled by those who enlisted with him. War Office records indicate that he was allocated to RAOC.

Maikeli VULI

Mike was born in 1938 in Lomati, one of only five villages on the tiny (34 sq km) volcanic island of Cicia in the north of the Lau group. He was educated at RKS and QVS. In November 1961 Mike was a clerk at the Vehicle and Plant Records Office of the PWD at Walu Bay. He enlisted because he wanted to offer his services to Britain, the Queen and Fiji. He had another incentive, as his grandfather's nephew Sefanaia Sukanaivalu, from the neighbouring village of Yacata, was posthumously awarded Fiji's only Victoria Cross in Bougainville in WWII. Sukanaivalu's name means 'returning from war' or 'end of war', suggesting that either he was born soon after the Armistice in 1918 or that his name commemorated the recent return of a relative from the conflict.

Mike, however, has no recollection of a common great-grandfather serving with the Fiji Labour Battalion or the New Zealand Army, as some Fijians did. In 1999 Marsali Mackinnon, a journalist and former public affairs officer with the Australian Embassy in Suva (1989-93), interviewed the late Sir Len Usher about his life for an oral history project, the *Fiji Oral History Part 1: Part-Europeans and Europeans*.[76] Sir Len recalled accompanying Ratu Sir Lala Sukuna to Yacata in 1944:

> The people of Yacata didn't know that Corporal Sukanaivalu had won the VC, and the VC didn't mean very much to them— they didn't know anything very much about the Victoria Cross. And so Ratu Sukuna decided he would go himself to Yacata to tell them about it, and as was customary he invited me to go with him—I was then in the Public Relations Office, and we were able to take a portable cinema projector and show films of the War, both in Europe and in the Solomons. And we projected these films on the side of the church. Then Ratu Sukuna told the people of Yacata about the VC, and about its record, and about how few people, how few men had ever won the VC, and in what honour they were held, and then he told them about how Sukanaivalu had won the VC.

Sir Len also told Marsali his recollection of the actual presentation of Sukanaivalu's VC to his parents at a subsequent ceremony in Suva:

> The parents were a very modest couple, and—it was one of the biggest parades, military parades, on Albert Park that I've ever seen. And the Governor Sir Alexander Grantham inspected the parade, and came back to the dais, and then Suka's mother and father came and sat on the dais in front of him. Ratu Sukuna read the citation in English and in Fijian, and then the Governor stepped forward with the VC in his hand, and Suka's father

---

76 This oral history audio media project comprises 28 taped interviews with 26 senior members of Fiji's mixed-race and European communities, living in Fiji and Australia. The interviews were conducted by Marsali Mackinnon from 1998 to 1999. They trace the history of a number of Part-European and European families in Fiji through the 19th and 20th centuries, beginning with the first arrival of their European ancestors. It includes many previously un-recorded personal memoirs, as well as family stories passed down the generations—a significant contribution to the social history and intangible heritage of Fiji—and the South Pacific region.

cupped his hands, and the Governor placed the medal in his hands, straightened up, looked at them, and then saluted—this very humble couple that were seated in front of him. And that was a salute, I think, a tribute from the people of Fiji and more—to a very brave man, to the parents of a very brave man.

Ratu Sukuna was no ordinary soldier himself, and knew all about bravery under fire. Rejected by his British mentors when he interrupted his studies at Oxford to offer his services to the British Army in WWI, Ratu Sukuna enlisted in the French Foreign Legion and was awarded both the *Croix de Guerre* and the *Medaille Militaire* for his bravery[77]. His biographer, Deryck Scarr, has noted that he 'showed every inclination to leave his bones in France.'

The *Medaille Militaire* is France's highest award for bravery in battle, but Ratu Sukuna joked with his wife and others that he won the award 'for cleaning out latrines.'[78] Ratu Sukuna's younger brother Ratu Tiali Vuiyasawa was at school in Melbourne and frustrated in his attempts to enlist until he crossed the Tasman and was able to enlist in the New Zealand forces by passing himself off as a Maori.[79] Ratu Tiali served with the NZ Pioneer Battalion in France from September, 1916 to January, 1918 but appears to have missed his brother's opportunities to show his mettle. He re-enlisted in WWII, serving with the Fiji Labour Corps.[80]

Yacata remembers Sukanaivulu every year on the anniversary of his death on 23rd June—Sukanaivalu Day—but it was not until that day in 2012 that a memorial was built on Yacata for the VC winner by a private company, Vatuvara Limited.[81]

---

77 Scarr, *Ratu Sukuna - Soldier, Statesman, Man of Two Worlds*, p 37.

78 Ibid p. 84.

79 Ibid p. 39.

80 Howard Weddell, *Soldiers from the Pacific*, p. 228.

81 Page 141 of Scarr's biography focusses rather oddly on the MCs awarded to a couple of Bauan chiefs in WWII, and omits to mention Sukanaivalu by name, referring only to 'a man of no rank'. Chiefly status has nothing to do with bravery under fire, as Talaiasi Labalaba showed in 1972.

The headstone on Sefanaia Sukanaivalu's grave at Bita Paka Commonwealth War Graves Cemetery, Rabaul, PNG. The VC was awarded posthoumously for Sukanaivalu's attempts to rescue wounded comrades and sacrificing himself so that others would not risk their lives for him in Bougainville in June 1944. Sukanaivalu was Mike Vuli's grandfather's nephew and had served as a stretcher bearer for Mo Beg's father.

Photo: Author

Mike spent nine years in RAOC, leaving as a Corporal Storeman Class 1, specialising as an ammunition technician. His service included British Guiana, Bahrain and Bracht, BAOR. He married Rose, a Yorkshire girl with two daughters from a previous marriage, and they soon added Alison to the family. Rose's father and brothers were coal miners, but it was not so much their influence as simple economics that attracted Mike 'down t' pit' and into unusual employment for a young man from Cicia. Mike was earning twenty-eight pounds a week as a security guard, but miners earned a basic income of thirty-five pounds a week after six weeks of basic training.

Mike spent ten years until 1984 down the Broadsworth mine before moving to the Markham Main Mine in time for the miner's strike led by Arthur Scargill which was 'expected to be over in a week'. The strike in fact lasted a year, with the miners eventually forced back to work by the Thatcher Government with no gains and an industry crippled and destined for eventual demise. Mike has vivid memories from that time of depending on weekly community food parcels, and feeling the loss of the free coal for heating that came as each miner's entitlement along with his wages. Mike and his neighbours were driven to scrounging coal from a nearby reserve pile which the Hatfield Mine Manager had bulldozed and buried. Mike specialised in development work underground, shoring up the walls and roofs of the shafts as they extended behind the advancing coal face, and extending the attendant rail lines and conveyor belts. In seventeen years he came close to a serious accident only once, when a wall collapsed and briefly buried a colleague who survived without serious injury.

He spent his last five years as 'the first Fijian coal miner' down the Hatfield Mine before accepting a redundancy in 1992. Mike was not sorry to leave the industry and having to protect his 'snap' (lunch) from the mice and rats. But he enjoyed the mining fraternity of Yorkshiremen, Frenchmen and others such as Russians, Poles and Yugoslavs, many of whom were from families of displaced persons ('DPs') from WWII. In passing, he mentions the fact that throughout his time in the mines he was the only 'coloured' miner. A well-grassed tailings hill opposite his comfortable home outside Doncaster is a constant reminder of his time underground.

Mike undertook retraining, and worked at odd jobs until retiring at sixty, staying in the UK for the sake of his family and their employment opportunities. He tried to steer his daughter Alison into university, perhaps to study science, but Ali was a talented dancer and at seventeen went to Spain to develop her routines, later winning a Doncaster Council Scholarship to NIDA. This began her first career as an actor. For several years, most notably as Polly Stevens in the *Peak Practice* series with the stage name Ludmilla Vuli, Ali proved to her father that it was possible to make a good living without a university degree! Both parties were satisfied, however, after Ali had a daughter of her own, acquired a degree, then became a teacher and eventually a psychotherapist.

Mike managed to return to Cicia on DOMCOL in 1966-67, but another forty-eight years would pass before he returned again with his extended family in July, 2015. That was his chance to spend many long nights around the *tanoa*, catching up with relatives and answering questions about life in *Bolatagone*, the army and 'down t'pit'. Back in Doncaster he remains a night owl, maintaining contact with friends around the globe on Facebook and listening to Fijian radio programmes online.

In more recent years Mike Vuli has sponsored a number of young Fijian men aspiring to join the British army, including his great nephew, Josefa Tukana in 2000. Mike is pictured above with Josefa's bride, Adi Unaisi Tukana, at a wedding in 2013.
Photo: Mike Vuli

APPENDIX I: REME

I n 1961 the British Army's biggest recruitment shortfalls lay in finding those suitable for skilled trades. Probably unexpectedly, they found a rich source of those they needed most among the Fijians. Royal Signals and REME required the best and brightest for maintaining systems increasingly dependent on the latest technology. Forty-seven of the two hundred men were allocated to these corps, with fifteen for REME. Cyril Browne recalls that after sixteen weeks of basic training at Hazlewood Barracks, he and three other REME recruits were sent to the Army Aviation/Air Corps base at Middle Wallop for specialist training in aviation electronics: Ashok Dutta, Adama Rokotini and Meli Basu. In later years, Joe Mae Cagilaba and John Riley from Royal Signals, together with Wame Tawake from RASC/RCT, transferred to REME.

Ratu Meli (Sam) BASU, MBE

Ratu Meli Basukunavanua Vesikula was at Lelean Memorial School when the recruiting team arrived, and one assumes the clerk recording names of the candidates found it more convenient to record 'Meli Basu'. The War Office file on the recruiting in Fiji recorded Ratu Meli with the highest overall score for aptitude and suitability out of the two hundred men selected. 'Tu Meli', as

Basic REME training course at the School of Electronic Engineering, Baillieu Barracks,
Arborfield, Berkshire, UK, early 1962.
L to R: Moazzam Beg, Albert Simpson, Ashok Dutta, Isireli Raibosa, Josese Tokainaqele,
Manindra Mohan, Samuela Seruidakuwaqa, Jone Kama, Jim Vakatalai, Joe Colata
Kamanalgi, Adama Rokotuni, Maciu Vatu, Cyril Browne, Meli Basu. Photo: Mo Beg

he is known to close friends, completed[82] the sixteen weeks of basic training
and was then posted to the Army Aviation/Air Corps base at Middle Wallop
for specialist training in aviation electronics. Meli's preference, however, was
for a regiment of the line. After two years in REME he transferred to the
First Battalion of the Duke of Wellington's Regiment (DWR, or 'the Dukes')
where he was known as 'Sam Basu' and became the only '212' to be appointed a
Regimental Sergeant Major. This element of his career is covered in Appendix
E and other developments in Chapters 3, 5 and 7.

Mirza Moazzam BEG

Mirza Moazzam Beg, or Mo to his mates, has an interesting family
background. Mo's paternal grandfather was an indentured Muslim labourer,
but his father Manzoor attended Suva's Central Medical School, qualifying

---

82 The War Office file on the recruitment of Fijians did not include an 'RO Test Score'
    for every recruit but the scores varied from the minimum of 17 for the infantry to the
    43 scored by Ratu Meli. Five others allocated to REME scored between 34 and 37. We
    could not locate scores for those allocated to Royal Signals.

as an 'Assistant Medical Practitioner' and was eventually recognised as a 'Medical Officer'. Mo is the second of five sons, all named after Mughal emperors by his father, who was one of the few Fijians of Indian extraction to serve with the Fiji Battalion in the Solomons in WWII.

Mo's father retained his faith, but married a Methodist who had all five boys baptised as Methodists; however, the boys were educated at Catholic schools run by the Marist Brothers. This is a multicultural family. Dr Manzoor Beg served as a Medical Officer with the 3rd Bn Fiji Infantry Regiment in the Solomons in 1944 and was Mentioned in Despatches for the same action in which one of his stretcher-bearers, Sefania Sukanaivalu, was awarded the Victoria Cross.

He was a qualified doctor, but the British government did not recognise qualified 'coloured' doctors with commissioned rank at the time. Warrant Officer Beg attended the Victory Parade in London in 1946 and then stayed for a year to study tuberculosis. He was photographed at the parade flanked by two of his country's highest chiefs, Ratu Sir Lala Sakuna and Ratu George (later Sir George) Cakobau. Mo had other relatives with WWII service. An uncle, Vincent Giblin, also served as a Sergeant in 2nd Bn Fiji Infantry Regiment in the Solomons in 1944. Another Uncle, Louis Maybir, served as a Sergeant in the Malayan Emergency. Mo's cousins Charles Giblin and Fred Maybir also enlisted in November 1961.

Mo's maternal grandfather Charles Andrew Maybir served as an Engineer on the ship MV Maureen which serviced the Gilbert Islands (now Kiribati) from Fiji during the WWII years. In 1961, Mo was employed as a clerk in the Treasury Department and saw the army offer as a chance to travel and see whether the grass really was greener in England. He hoped to join an infantry regiment but was allocated to REME. After his basic training he began specialist training as an Electronics Technician to work on fire control equipment on tanks and other armoured fighting vehicles. He volunteers that he later failed a trade test and was redeployed on clerical and other general duties within REME but had no complaints about the less demanding duties.

Mo served with the BAOR, in Malaysia (Sarawak, Johore, Kelantan), and Singapore. He saw operational service in Sarawak at the tail end of the 1963-66 Indonesian 'Confrontation' with 78 Aircraft Workshop REME, servicing helicopters (Wasp, Bell and Alouette) and fixed-wing De Havilland Beavers, and the last of the Austers. He was stationed 7 miles outside Kuching, on the road to the Indonesia-Kalimantan Border.

Mo was discharged after six years and hoped to further his education in the UK. He was eventually minded to move back to West Germany to work as a civilian for the BAOR. Fate intervened when he met his future wife in 'Kangaroo Valley' (Earls Court, London) and his whole life changed for the better: 'Alicia was the best thing that happened to me and she certainly put me right—I owe her a great deal'. Mo joined BOAC, studied and acquired a qualification from the Chartered Institute of Transport. BOAC became British Airways and he stayed with them for thirty-two years, becoming a middle manager in BA's cargo division, travelling extensively in relation to IATA and other matters. Mo lost Alicia in 1998 and retired in 2000 to focus on their son, daughter and grandchildren. He still travels extensively.

In June 2014, police raided the adjoining terrace house next to Mo's house in response to his complaints about an unusual and irritating noise. The noise turned out to be caused by a worn pump bearing servicing a hydroponic marijuana plantation of 200-300 plants, grown under artificial lighting in four rooms!

Cyril Francis BROWNE

Cyril was born in Suva, but considers his mother's family copra estate at Waimotu, Natewa Bay on Vanua Levu, to be 'home'. When the recruiting team arrived in 1961 he was employed in the Motor Spares Dept of Millers Ltd in Suva. Harry Powell and Charles Giblin also worked for Millers. Harry, Charlie and David Lelo were in his graduating class at Suva Grammar School. Keith Zoing and Sefton Erasito were a couple of years ahead. Don Dunstan, the future Premier of South Australia, was at Suva Grammar with Cyril's brother-in-law, Bob Dods.

Early hovercraft operational trials in Sarawak 1964-66.
Photo: Cyril Browne

Cyril served nine years, qualifying as an Aircraft Technician Class 1 in electrical instruments and radio, and was a Sergeant when he discharged. His service included Germany in 1964, Sabah and Sarawak, and Malaysia from 1964-66 when he was involved in the first operational trials of hovercraft in the region. He also served in Brunei and Singapore where he met Loretta; they married in December 1968.

Before Cyril got married, he thought he might return to Fiji and join Fiji Airways, but in 1970 he emigrated to Australia and settled in Sydney's northern beach suburbs working for Telecom Australia.

Ashok Chandra DUTTA (see also p321)

Ashok was born in Suva in 1938 and attended Marist Brothers High School with Mo Beg. He was a cadet surveyor with the Public Works Department in 1961. His six years in REME took him to Borneo and Labuan with Army Aviation and colleagues remember him as a keen photographer.

Jone KAMA

Jone, from Mokani near Bau, enlisted while at school. He would like to have had a scholarship for further study, but complained 'these were largely given to the Ratus and Adis'. The British Army recruiting team offered the best possible opportunity for the '212' enlistees to improve themselves.

Jone qualified as a parachutist in 1964, served with 16 Para Brigade workshop, and finished his twenty-two years as a S/Sgt with 28 Amphibious Engineer Workshop, REME. He returned to Fiji and contemplated attending the Methodist Theological College but decided against it.

Jone has three sons and a daughter, all of whom were born in Aldershot and followed their father into the British Army. Charles Kama served with Royal Signals in the early nineties after initial service with the RFMF, including peace-keeping with UNDOF in Syria. He played rugby for the BAOR team. His sister Litia served with the British Army in Afghanistan and returned there as a civilian manager. Jone is proud to call himself 'an old squaddie', is proud of his children's service, and has no regrets about his own enlistment and service.

Joe Colata KAMANALAGI

Joe's enlistment was recorded under his middle name 'Colata' in the *Fiji Times* as 'clerk, Suva', but Mo Beg recalls him as a cadet surveyor in the Public Works Department. He was known throughout his army service as Joe Kamanalagi. He had Kadavu origins and was a prefect at MBHS a year ahead of Beg and Tom Morell. Joe is variously remembered as serving for 9-12 years, being married to an English woman, living and working after his service in the Barrow-on-Furness area, and retiring in Salford.

Mahendra (Manindra) Prasad MOHAN

Manindra attended Dayandra Anglo Vedic (DAV) college in Suva and was another listed as 'clerk, Suva' by the *Fiji Times* in 1961. He enlisted with his nephew Pramod Tikaram and served six years. He initially returned to Fiji and became a mechanical instructor at the Government Training Centre in Suva (then known as the Derrick Technical Institute). A few years later he emigrated to Vancouver.

Isireli RAIBOSA

Isireli was a clerk from Rewa working in the Registrar General's Office in Suva when he enlisted. He did not serve the full period of his initial enlistment, and after a medical discharge he remained in England working for the General Post Office, and later with the British Library. Maciu Vatu remembers him as 'a clever lad' who died of a heart attack in 1970.

Adama ROKOTUNI

When the recruiting team arrived in Suva, Adama, from Tailevu, was an engineering apprentice with the Public Works Department. He was another graduate of MBHS but preferred the infantry to REME and transferred to the SWB. Adama was a keen athlete at school, represented the BAOR as a sprinter and was a member of a trophy winning SWB rugby sevens team in Hong Kong in 1966.

Adama's son Philip also joined the Army (Royal Logistics Corps) at 17, served the full twenty-two years, retiring as a WO2 after serving in BAOR, Northern Ireland, Bosnia, Iraq and Afghanistan. On his retirement he worked in schools as a mentor for young people..

Ted Albert SIMPSON

Albert enlisted from MBHS in Suva but gave his occupation as 'farmer, Savusavu' where his family owned plantation land. He spent nine years in the army, attached to 16 Para Brigade. Bob Dass remembers that Ted's first posting was to Libya for several months and he did not particularly enjoy the experience.

After his army service, Albert worked as a postman and union official, married an English woman, had two children and spent most of his later years living in Salisbury. Two of Albert's siblings also moved to the UK and a brother established a legal practice in Sydney. Albert's wife Carol suffered badly from asthma in her later years. Carol died in 2014 and Albert is now rediscovering his siblings and children. His daughter Carmen became a successful events organiser, married a geologist, and now lives in Perth, Western Australia.

Samuela SERUIDAKUWAQA

Sam was a radio technician working with the RNZAF Squadron based at Laucala Bay in 1961. He is remembered by Maciu Vatu as changing his name to 'Tony Bennett' before his death in Germany. Mat and Sam served together from January 1963, maintaining Military Transport (MT) stores for the Royal Malta Artillery at Dortmund, Germany. Both Fijians enjoyed working with the Maltese.

Filipe TAGIMURI

Filipe, a Lauan, was another who enlisted while at school and may have been among those who lied about their age to be accepted. He served nine years, which included an early unsuccessful attempt at selection for 22 SAS. After leaving the army, Filipe lived in Barrow, Cumbria, and worked as a welder on offshore oil rigs. He succumbed to cancer around 2000.

Josese TOKAIGALE

Josese completed basic training with REME but opted for a transfer to R Sigs whilst doing his trade training. He was the first of the '212' to die accidentally in 1964 and is also recorded in Appendix D on signallers.

James Vuli VAKATALAI, MM

Like Meli Vesikula, Jim also had a clear idea of what he wanted from his army service. At the first opportunity, he sought selection for 22 SAS and was successful. His career is dealt with in Appendix F.

Maciu VATU

Maciu's full name is Maciu Vatu Navulatamata Dovoivoi, but he was enlisted under only his first two names and the chief clerk at Popering Barracks saw the wisdom of this convenience. The literal translation of these first names is 'Matthew Stone' and Mat was usually referred to by other '212' as 'Mr Stone' and by other squaddies as Stoney.

Mat was born on 28 December 1940, in Navuatu village on Kadavu. Despite rare visits to Navuatu since 1961, Mat still considers the village home and some of his relatives are employed at the nearby Dive Kadavu resort. Mat's first memory of schooling was in the village church hall after WWII, where he learned to write with a slate and chalk in the absence of pencils and paper. A school was built in the village in the 1950s staffed with qualified teachers, and Mat was fortunate to be accepted at Kadavu Provincial School, a boarding school for boys. An alternative was the Richmond Methodist School, named after the town in Yorkshire.

Mat subsequently passed the entrance examination for Queen Victoria School (QVS). His classmates included Laisenia Qarase, who was deposed as Prime Minister of Fiji by the Bainimarama coup of 2006, and Ratu Epeli Nailatikau, deposed as RFMF commander by Sitiveni Rabuka's coup in 1987, who later served as Fiji's High Commissioner in London and as the country's President.

Mat was sixteen when he left Kadavu for QVS at Tailevu for four years, where his antics earned him the nickname 'Spy 13' after a popular comic book character of the time. From QVS's early years until after Mat left, the principal was always an Englishman and most teachers were Australians or New Zealanders. Mat recalls one of the latter, Graham Leggett, as an enthusiastic teacher of English.

During Mat's time at QVS, his physics teacher was a young graduate named Filipe Bole who later served as Education Minister. (Bole was also the successful candidate in the Lauan seat contested by another '212', Jioji Areki, in the 1987 election). Mat regrets that he did not make better use of his time at 'Quvee' and left after completing his Fiji Junior Certificate of Education in 1960. Another senior QVS teacher at the time was Semesa Sikivou, a Rewan who was keen to erase Fiji's chiefly/class system. At Independence in 1970, Sikivou was appointed Fiji's first Ambassador to the United Nations. He later served in a succession of senior government positions, including as Minister of Education (1977-82) and Minister of Foreign Affairs (1985-86) before accepting a CBE award from a grateful government.

A family member and hero of Fiji's military and sporting communities influenced Mat's decision to join the RFMF TA after leaving school and eventually enlist with the British Army. In 1939, Mat's cousin Isireli Korovulavula was a member of the first Fiji rugby team to tour New Zealand. The team was undefeated but, as Mat notes: 'They did not play the mighty All Blacks.'

The following year Isireli was commissioned into the RFMF Battalion which subsequently served in the Solomons campaign, where Isireli won a Military Cross and was promoted. Isireli was part of the Fiji contingent to the Victory Parade in London in 1946. In the 1950s, Isireli served with the Fiji Battalion in the Malayan Emergency, with two of his sons, Manu and Nacani, also serving.

It is no surprise that as a young school leaver, Mat was encouraged to join the RFMF reserves/TA by his cousin Isireli who, by 1960, had become Governor of the Korovulavula Correctional Establishment at Walu Bay. Mat was inclined to serve in an infantry regiment, having just completed his basic infantry training at QEB, but was foiled by his own guile. Mat recalls completing the aptitude tests and being advised that he did not meet the minimum standard, so he rejoined the queue and repeated the test after checking the correct answers to the questions with others in the queue. His subterfuge backfired, however, when his high assessment resulted in him being allocated to REME with Mo Beg, Jim Vakatalai and Meli Vesikula on basic training at Popering Barracks, Aborfield Cross, near Reading.

Mat's orientation to electronic engineering was short-lived. He spent most of the next six years as a technical storeman, maintaining WWII-vintage military transport stores and thinking 'God help us' if the Soviet forces of the Cold War moved westward. In January 1963 he was posted in support of the Royal Malta Artillery (RMA) based at Dortmund, West Germany, where he worked with Cpl Sam Seruidakuwaqa. He later transferred to Wrexham Barracks at Mulheim/Ruhr with RMA in 1965. Mat's final posting was to Fallingbostel, near Hanover, for 1966-67, during which time he utilised his

DOMCOL to visit his parents back in Fiji. In June 1967, Mat found the Germans 'absolutely polite and friendly towards the many foreign nationals who worked there rebuilding their country after the devastation of WWII'.

Mat took every opportunity to visit neighbouring countries on leave and enjoyed them all. He also learned to ski on an army exercise in Scandanavia.

Mat was posted to Catterick Camp for his resettlement course prior to his discharge on 10 October 1967. He was retained as a reservist for the next ten years, receiving the princely sum of £20 a year!

Mat cheerfully admits that he never managed to settle, avoided marriage after the army, and had varied employment opportunities throughout the UK in subsequent decades. He worked in the oil and ship building industries, with British Airways, factories and local government agencies until he retired. Like his other '212' peers, he has no regrets about his decision to join the British Army. While Mat had no children, his more recent connection to the British Army is through his brother's eldest daughter, Dovoivoi Iva, of whom he is very proud for her five years' service which included tours of duty in Iraq and Afghanistan. Dovoivoi was also born on Kadavu, schooled in Suva and enlisted in 2000. She now lives in California.

Ashok Chandra DUTTA (addendum)

Ashok's eldest son, Tom, contacted the author via Echo Books to offer the following supplement to the brief reference to Ashok in the 2018 publication.

Ashok was born in Suva in 1938, the grandson of Bhagwan Ram (known in Fiji as Lalli Maharaj), who arrived from India in 1904 as part of the Girmit indentured labor system and later became a candy store owner serving twenty families in his community. Ashok attended Marist Brothers High School with Mo Beg and worked as a cadet surveyor with the Public Works Department in 1961.

His six years of service with REME took him to Borneo and Labuan with Army Aviation, where colleagues remember him as a keen photographer. After meeting Anitra Myrene Rose Amputch in Suva, Ashok enlisted in the British Army and was stationed at Tidworth Garrison, where they married and their first two sons, Thomas and Robert, were born. After Ashok's discharge the family traveled through Singapore and Malaysia before settling in Vancouver, BC, Canada in the late 1960s, where their third son Glen was born.

In Canada, Ashok maintained his military interests with a Canadian regiment and served for years as President of the Fiji Canada Association, maintaining strong ties to his heritage and community. After completing his service as a journeyman electrician, Ashok transitioned to education, becoming an instructor at BCIT (British Columbia Institute of Technology), where he taught the electrical profession to young tradespeople. During his tenure at BCIT, he authored a training manual for electricians in collaboration with WJETS (Western Joint Electrical Training Society), contributing significantly to electrical education in British Columbia.

In his later years, Ashok became deeply involved in community service work, including AA men's groups and prison outreach focused on recovery and second chances. He drew from his own experiences with recovery, having overcome personal struggles with alcohol to become a mentor and educator. Within the Indo-Fijian community, Ashok was revered as a pillar of the community, particularly known for making time for young people enduring life's struggles and providing guidance during difficult periods.

Ashok died of natural causes in New Westminster, BC, in January 2018, leaving three sons; Thomas (Tom), Glen and Robert and a granddaughter, Kalinda Dutta, Tom's daughter. His legacy continues through Thomas, who has followed in his footsteps in service work, conducting a prison ministry and parental reading programs while pursuing doctoral studies in leadership, graduating from Middlesex University in London—notably, just seven miles from the Tidworth garrison where Ashok had served.

APPENDIX J: PIONEER WOMEN
-'THE SUNSHINE SQUAD'.

'Sunshine Squad' was a term coined by London's *Daily Mirror* to refer to the twelve adventurous young women who enlisted 'from the Pacific islands' without mentioning Fiji, when reporting the arrival of the women recruited in Fiji. The use of the term may have reflected a perceived need for uplifting stories in a winter of severe discontent, or it may have been influenced by the relatively recent (1958) success of the movie *South Pacific*, based on the novel by James A. Michener, whose texts made frequent references to exotic women throughout Melanesia and Polynesia.

Almost 50 years later, the influence of Rodgers and Hammerstein's classic film sound track persisted on the UK media's reporting of events in the real-life South Pacific. The 21 March 2015 edition of *The Economist* headlined an article on the devastation Cyclone Pam had wreaked on Vanuatu the previous week as 'No enchanted evening'.

The initial proposal to consider women volunteers in Fiji was opposed by then Director WRAC, Brigadier Dame Jean Rivett-Drake, who objected to the proposal in a confidential memorandum to the Director of Recruiting, MajGen J.E.L Morris, on 28 August 1961:

> '3. I am under the impression that they will be jet black and woolly-haired and I feel most strongly these women will present considerably more problems to us than the coffee coloured Seychellois.[83]

---

83 War Office file WO32/19455 folio 27B.

4. If the worst happens and we are told at the highest level we must consider women from FIJI I feel we must insist that the numbers be very restricted. I consider it would be essential to have a senior WRAC officer present who would have the last word on their acceptance, regardless of their suitability on paper.

5. In my opinion it is of utmost importance that before we are asked to consider any further such enlistments we should be told the position and status of women in the Country concerned and in particular their customs with regard to marriage.'

Initial drill training for WRAC recruits, Lingfield Surrey, 1962. Second file from left: Vaciseva Tabua at rear, Louisa Peckham in middle rank and Betty Foster in front.
Photo: Betty Foster/Hansen

The twelve women travelled separately to the men via Sydney and Singapore, with their arrival diverted to Stansted because Heathrow was closed due to some of the worst winter weather in a century. Shortly after their arrival, the Fijian girls were bussed to Southampton for a TV appearance. Their Cockney driver had great difficulty recognising the address in Union Street because he read the street sign as 'Onion'!

All the women did their basic WRAC training at Lingfield Barracks in Surrey, before proceeding to Houndston Camp, also in Surrey. The WRAC basic training camp at Guildford was being rebuilt at the time. Three of the women were selected for training with Royal Signals at Catterick in

Yorkshire, and the remainder attended an eight-week clerks' course at Yeovil in Somerset. There were no overseas postings for WRAC at that time.

Munivai Taukave AISAKE, later McGoon and Brooks

Munivai, from Fapufa which is one of the smallest and most isolated villages on Rotuma, was the eldest daughter in the family. She was a stenographer working in Suva in 1961. After completing her army service, Munivai remained in England and married another Fiji expatriate named Charles McGoon, the son of a Vagadace, Levuka boat-builder. Charles came to England in 1961 to study electrical engineering. The marriage did not last very long; Munivai remarried to Alan Brooks and settled in London.

Alan and Munivai had two daughters, Tessa and Laura, but Munivai tragically died of a brain haemorrhage in 1993. In 2012, Laura was a torchbearer for the opening of the London Olympics and participated in the opening ceremony.

Laurel Roberta BENTLEY, later Harper

Laurel is the only child of a Rotuman-born woman and a father of Scottish-Samoan descent. She was born in Suva and does not identify with any other part of Fiji. Laurel's father died when she was twelve years old. She was educated at Suva Grammar School and Auckland Business College. In 1961 she was a junior stenographer in the Fiji Government's Public Relations Office. It was her first job.

Like so many of her peers at the time, Laurel longed for the opportunity to travel—her year in Auckland had given her the taste for it, and she wanted to do something different, beyond the limited possibilities in Fiji at the time. She applied to the recruiting team out of curiosity but became concerned and reluctant when selected. Her mother encouraged her to go.

Laurel recalls men and women who served with her from the Seychelles, Malta, British Guiana, Southern Rhodesia, Mauritius, and Trinidad and Tobago. After her basic training at Lingfield, Surrey, Laurel's first posting with Munivai Aisake (the twelve women were posted in pairs, wherever possible) was to Dreghorn Barracks outside Edinburgh where she worked in the Orderly Room of Scottish Command in Craigiehall, built in 1699.

Laurel asked for a transfer back to London/Aldershot and was posted to OCS, Mons, to work in the orderly room. One of her duties was to interview the officer cadets for NOK and religion details for their PPFs (Personal Particulars Forms) and some cadets were inclined to object. Her S/Sgt supervisor told her to ask such candidates to sit down until he could sort them out.

Laurel served three years, acquiring no new specialist skills, and was discharged as a Corporal. She married in August 1964 to Alex Harper, a soldier she met while serving at Mons, when his Platoon of the Black Watch was the demonstration platoon. Laurel was discharged in December 1964 and joined Alex in Germany. Laurel returned to Fiji with Alex in 1966. Alex worked for Carpenters and Laurel had a succession of jobs with Hunts Travel, Burns Philp, Suva City Council, the Central Monetary Authority (later the Reserve Bank of Fiji) and FSC/CSR Marketing where she worked with 'a very nice field officer at the time' named Rasheed Ali, who later became the CEO.

Laurel and Alex had four children, the eldest born in London, the others in Fiji. The family migrated to Australia in 1981 and settled in Melbourne. They returned for a holiday in 1983. Alex died in 2008. Their son Andrew served in the Australian Army. Laurel's only other visit to her homeland was in 2011.

Tausia CAKAUYAWA, later Savu

Tausia was born in her mother's village of Motusa on Rotuma, but her father was from Kadavu. She attended Ballantine Memorial School and Dudley High School in Suva. She qualified as a stenographer and in 1961 was employed as the personal assistant to the Police Commissioner. Tausia had no close relatives who had served with the RFMF, but was attracted by the prospect of being one of the first women from Fiji to serve in the

British Army and by the opportunity to travel abroad. Her daughter, Asinate Korocawiri, recalls that her mother often spoke of her friendships with fellow Rotuman Munivai Aisake, and with Vaciseva Tabua who was in the same marching girls' team.

Tausia first encountered chronic health problems during her army service and may not have completed the three-year enlistment. She returned to Fiji and her former employment with the civil service, later marrying Viliame Savu, a Lauan former post office radio technician with an electronics and hardware business, with whom she had four children. In 1990 Savu was Treasurer of Sakeasi Butadroka's Fijian Nationalist Party and was an unsuccessful FNP candidate in the elections of 1977, 1982 and 1987. Tausia succumbed to leukaemia in New Zealand in 1970.

Edwina Caroline EYRE, later Jameson

Edwina is a descendant of the explorer and colonial governor Edward John Eyre. Eyre was the first European to traverse Australia's Nullabor Plain and Great Australian Bight with the help of an Aboriginal companion known as Wylie. Eyre later served as Lieutenant Governor of New Zealand and Governor of Jamaica. He was twice charged with murder, but never convicted, over his brutal suppression of a peasants' revolt in Jamaica, the Morant Bay Rebellion of 1865. In southern Australia and in New Zealand there are villages, hills, a peninsula, a lake and a highway named after him.

His third son, Charles Ormond Eyre (1856-1924) was disowned by his family for marrying a Fijian woman, Silovati Ranadi. Charles was Edwina's great-grandfather. Edwina was born in Lautoka and educated at Suva Girls Grammar School. The *Fiji Times* of 27 September 1961 included a photograph of Edwina as a contestant in the 'Miss Hibiscus' competition, sponsored by Burns Philp, Lautoka, where she worked as a clerk-typist. The 5 October edition of the newspaper also featured Edwina as a contestant for the 'Miss Sugar' title.

Whilst working at the Burns Philp office, Edwina became curious about the activities of the recruitment team, as so many of her friends seemed to be applying after women were invited to apply. She applied out of curiosity and attended an interview, but was surprised and a little alarmed when advised she was successful.

Edwina enlisted for three years and was not offered a second tour. She married her first husband, Len Downing (another soldier) after three years and stayed in England for another four, before returning to Fiji with their first two children. Her daughter is now a solicitor in London and one of her two sons is an air traffic controller in Auckland.

Edwina served in the WRAC with signals units, and hoped for a posting to Hong Kong or Singapore but spent most of her time in the less exotic area around Aldershot, together with Betty Foster and Doreen Petersen. Emma Heffernan, Lily Pirie and Laurel Bentley were employed near Bicester as clerks. Edwina was promoted to Corporal, then briefly lost her rank for allowing her future husband and a couple of others to visit the Communications Centre when she was the duty NCO. Her rank was restored shortly afterwards.

Edwina has no regrets about her army service, but did not like being ordered to do tasks and objected to the treatment of the colonial WRACs, including those from the Seychelles. The British Army saw them as 'exotic' and needing special food (assuming they were not familiar with Western food), and made the unfounded assumption they all liked to perform the hula. In subsequent employment, Edwina worked for CSR, Pan American, BA/BOAC and Air New Zealand before moving to New Zealand in 1982, eventually settling in Hamilton.

Betty Rosaline FOSTER, later Hansen

Betty was born in Levuka in 1942 of Rotuman parents. Her parents returned to Rotuma during WWII and she and her younger sister Jane were raised by their grandmother Lavinia Mamao, a Rotuman who had married a Scot named Charles Gibson. Betty's father died very young of unknown causes on Rotuma in 1945. Her mother Rene stayed on Rotuma, but many years later followed her daughters to Sydney where she died. Jane was a stenographer who finished her working life as a court reporter.

Betty attended Levuka Primary School and Suva Grammar before becoming a machine operator in the accounting section of the Burns Philp store in Suva. She had no relatives who had served in Fiji's military in the World Wars or Malaya. She and her good friend Lulu Peckham applied out of curiosity, and the first indication that they were successful came from Lulu's boyfriend of the time who worked at the *Fiji Times,* had seen the list of those accepted, and asked them whether they thought they were 'too good for Fiji', or words to that effect. Other '212' experienced similar expressions of envy when they were accepted by the recruiting team and resentment on their return from their service. Many of the Fiji WRACs were given no credit for the skills and experience they had gained in the army.

Betty underwent basic training at Lingfield in Surrey, before being posted to Catterick in Yorkshire with two others for Signals training and later service at Aldershot. Betty and Doreen were teleprinter operators. Edwina was a switchboard operator. Betty served the three years for which

'Sunshine Squad' preparing for meke in Catterick, 1962. Betty Foster seated left, Vaciseva Tabua standing and Louisa Peckham on right.
Photo: Betty Foster/Hansen

she enlisted and was the only woman to be promoted to Sergeant. Part of the enlistment conditions involved three tickets for free travel anywhere in the UK, and Betty made the most of these. She also spent a week in Germany and her photograph album today is a tooled leather souvenir of that visit.

On her return to Suva Betty considered joining the Australian Army. From 1964-69 she operated accounting machines for Armstrong and Springhall, who sent her to Wellington for six months' training. After emigrating to Sydney in 1969, Betty met and married Peter Hansen, a Rotuman who had entered Australia by 'jumping ship' in Sydney. Hansen later died in Canberra after working for twenty years installing sewage systems for the ACT Government.

Betty raised her daughter Leah by herself, and worked for sixteen years as a cook in an old folks' home. She has no regrets about her army service and has few recollections of racism or discrimination in colonial Fiji, apart from the 'coloured' and the separate European and part-European ends of the Suva swimming pool recalled by Doreen Petersen hereunder. Betty died in Sydney in May 2018. Leah became a senior producer with Australia's multicultural Special Broadcasting Service.

Victoria Teena Regina GRANT, later Partridge

In 1992 Vicki recalled that she had 'enlisted by default', having taken the recruitment examinations to get time off from her job as a clerk/typist in colonial Fiji's Immigration Department. She later processed the British passports for each of the '212'.

The Grant family were prominent Catholics who owned cinemas in many towns throughout Fiji. Vicki's mother was an immigrant from the Gilbert and Ellis Islands (today's separate nations of Kiribati and Tuvalu). Her brother Martin became a Marist Brother who served the Church in Glasgow, and a sister became a nun in the Order of St Joseph, served in Haiti, became very ill and died in France.

Vicki enjoyed her time in the army, particularly England's pub culture which she later blamed for her feeling 'maladjusted' on return to Fiji. She felt that the overall experience had much to do with the eventual emigration of most of the twelve women, like her good friend Laurel Bentley/Harper with whom she remained in contact in Melbourne.

Vicki's first marriage to a RNZAF serviceman ended in divorce, and her two children remained in New Zealand. With her second husband Maurice Partridge, Vicki established a cleaning business in Sydney's south western suburbs. In 2011 she lost a sixteen-year battle with cancer.

Emma Olive HEFFERNAN, later Grant

Emma was another stenographer attracted by the opportunities offered by the recruiting team, and served three years including a posting to Aldershot with close friend Laurel Bentley. Emma found requests for the 'Sunshine Squad' performances of Fijian dancing tedious, and refused to participate.

She returned to Fiji after her service, but soon moved to Australia where she became a model, appearing in glossy magazines, including *Vogue Australia*. She returned to Fiji married to a senior manager of the Carpenters group of companies, before settling in Greenwich, Sydney, on the Parramatta River, once known as 'the Thames of the Antipodes'. Emma's brother Edward Heffernan joined the RFMF, serving as company Commander in UNIFIL, Lebanon, and later as Sitiveni Rabuka's ADC after May 1987.

Louisa PECKHAM, later Baldwin

When the recruiting team arrived, Lou (or Lulu to her close friends) was employed as a stenographer at Burns Philp in Suva with Betty Foster. Va Seruitanoa recalls her as a fellow marching girl in 1960-61. At the completion of her army service, Lou returned to Fiji and married a European named Baldwin, but by 1995 had settled in Brisbane. She was later diagnosed with cancer and spent her last years in Melbourne with her daughter before losing her battle with the disease in December 2011.

Lou's nephew (or great nephew) Ron Peckham is married to the daughter of Timoci Ulaiasi's brother in Levuka, Vanua Levu. A grave beside the road opposite Taveuni Airport marks the last resting-place of a William Peckham, who died at Mate in October 1901.

Louisa Peckham in a personalised postcard, circa 1962.
Original card provided by Betty Foster/Hansen

Doreen PETERSEN, later Wilkes

Doreen was born in Suva, but identifies with the Petersen family home at Naselesele, Taveuni. Her parents had a plantation at Navakabua, Natewa Bay, Vanua Levu. Doreen attended Suva Grammar School and in 1961 was working for Hunt's Travel Agency in Suva. Curiosity took her to the interview, and she was carried along by a 'tide of excitement' after selection.

Doreen married a soldier named Duffel whom she met in Aldershot, and served only 12 months. She lived in Germany and Malaysia with her first husband and emigrated to Australia in 1964. Doreen is a descendant of Gustav Petersen, a Swedish trader who had been in Vanuatu and married Cordelia Valentine who was born in Fiji of an American father and Fijian mother from Verata. This couple's son, Edward Petersen (Doreen's grandfather) whom Doreen suspects may have been a 'blackbirder', married Sarah Bruce whose father was a Scot and whose mother was from Drekenewai.

Doreen's father, also named Edward Petersen, married Annette O'Connor, whose sister Sophia (Ruddock) served as Fiji's representative on the International Olympic Committee. Doreen's family spoke Fijian at home because her grandparents could not speak English. Doreen, the eldest of ten children, was the first of her family to attend Suva Grammar School which was reserved for children of expatriates and 'Kai Loma'[84] children.

---

84 Literally 'in between'—a term used for part European Fijians

Fifty years later, Doreen recalled that 'coloured' applicants were not employed as staff of the Fiji branches of the Bank of New South Wales and Bank of New Zealand. She also retains a vivid memory of an incident in which two younger sisters were directed to opposite ends of the Suva swimming pool because one had a very fair complexion and the other was quite dark. She is also related to the Pickering family, through whom Doreen is related to Prime Minister Frank Bainimarama's grand-mother Louisa Pickering.

Doreen eventually settled on the Central Coast of New South Wales with her second husband.

Lillian Asenaca PIRIE, later Millar

Lily was born in her mother's village of Vakabuli near Lautoka in Vuda/Ba province. Her birth was registered as Asenaca Naicika, but she changed it to Lillian Asenaca Pirie when she started school. Her father came from Sydney to work for CSR in the sugar mills, and never returned.

Lily grew up in Naidovi, Cuvu, and considers it her 'home'. She was educated at St Joan of Arc School Sigatoka and Loreto High School, Levuka before spending her last year of school at St Joseph's, Suva. In 1961 Lily was employed as a clerk for Burns Philp. She worked in the office and Edwina Eyre was in the motor department. Lily recalls between two and three hundred men and women being interviewed in Lautoka.

None of her relatives had served in WWII or Malaya, and she applied for enlistment on impulse, not expecting to be chosen from so many applicants. Lily was not related to any other '212'. She was known in the army/WRAC as Lily Pirie. Lily recalls the six-day weeks in the army, but says she was never homesick. The biggest initial transition was to accommodate the cold, arriving in England's winter from Fiji via Sydney and Singapore. Fortunately, the army provided coats for the women on arrival.

Lily served for three years, was elevated to L/Cpl, and has no regrets about her army experience. She returned to Fiji for family reasons, to secretarial work with the Fiji Police Force in the first instance. She met and married Captain Claude Millar, the initial developer of Blue Lagoon Cruises, in Lautoka, and they had three children—two boys and a girl. In September 1978, Claude and Lily moved to New Zealand for the sake of the children's education and developed a business at Opononi, north of Auckland.

At one time, Lily worked for the Union Steamship Company and Claude and Lily returned to Fiji in 1994 to develop the leasehold Nanuya Island Resort in the Yasawa group, west of Viti Levu. Her two sons also returned to Fiji and the family continued to operate Nanuya until selling their interest in 2014.

Fane SIVOKI, later Morell and Ubitau

Fane was born in Lakeba but left around 1956 to attend Adi Cakabau School (ACS) for girls at Sawani, outside Suva. One of Fane's classmates was Vaciseva Tabua who recalls the girls got their early training as stenographers at ACS. The school was founded in 1948 by the colonial government as a boarding school to provide a 'refined' intermediate education for Fijian 'girls of rank' and has since produced many distinguished graduands.

In 1960 Fane started work as a stenographer for Peter Westwood, a former District Commissioner, at the Government Buildings Secretariat Department. She lived at Nawela Hostel for Women, located at the top end of the Botanical Gardens. The hostel was new and mainly for single women who worked in the Fiji civil service.

Fane and Tom Morell had been 'an item', in today's parlance, for some months before the recruiting team arrived, and some of their friends joked that Fane enlisted primarily to keep track of Tom. She was very good at the latter, and was discharged shortly after completing her basic training and married Tom.

Tom remembers a wonderful wife and mother who did a marvellous job raising their four boys during his frequent deployments overseas with 16 Para Signals Squadron and later 22 SAS.

Their home was often the focal point and bivouac site for those '212' who were based in or transiting Aldershot in the early years. Tom earned the title of 'Mayor of Aldershot' over the period of his years there. Hoss Ligairi recalls Fane fondly for her support to his wife Eunice when their children were young, and Hoss was frequently away from Hereford.

The marriage lasted until the late seventies, producing four fine sons, three of whom followed their parents into the army via the Green Jackets (2RGJ), with one emulating Tom's lengthy service, including most of his career with 22 SAS.

Hoss recalls Fane returned to Fiji in 1985. She found employment as the manager/house keeper of Borron House, a colonial mansion built in 1927 for plantation owner James Borron. In WWII it was the divisional HQ for American armed forces in the Pacific Theatre, and was later bequeathed to the Fiji Government and used as the State Guest House. Fane appears to have still been its manager when Prince Andrew was a guest in 1995. In the early nineties Borron House boasted a Taiwanese chef, courtesy of the Republic of China's representative in Fiji at the time, who was always looking for ways to ingratiate himself with the leaders of Pacific island nations who might be prepared to recognise his government officially.

Fane's second husband, Nemani Donu Ubitau, was a widower from her home village of Yadrana, Lakeba. Donu was a supervisor with the Public Works Department at the time. His nephew Inoke Ubitau and Teresa Maravu attest that Fane's last years were very happy, but she died after major surgery in 2000. Donu died in 2013 and the couple are interred in the same grave at Vakuwaqa Cemetery on Suva Point.

Vaciseva TABUA, later Seruitanoa

Va was born in Suva, but her family origins are in Batiki in the Lomaiviti group. She was educated at Draiba Primary School, Suva, Adi Cakabau School, and LMS, Nausori. At LMS she was in the same form as Tom Waqabaca and Freddy Mua. After leaving school, Va attended the government stenographic school for a year before her first civil service employment in the Inland Revenue Department and the Registrar General's Office. At the time Va's best friend was Tausia Cakauyawa.

In Fiji in the late fifties, many teenage girls were attracted to teams of marching girls. Several of the twelve women who enlisted in 1961 were marching girls, including Va, Doreen, Betty, Louisa and Tausia.

The *Fiji Times* of 16 September 1961 included a photograph of Va as a contestant in the Miss Hibiscus competition, sponsored by the Civil Service.

At her enlistment, Va recalled undertaking a IQ test followed by an interview. She was interested in the opportunity to see England, possible adventure in the army, and the chance of improving her secretarial skills.

Her father Sitiveni Tabua served in the Solomons. LtCol Navunisaravi, an uncle by marriage, served in Malaya from 1953-56 as a Corporal, later becoming CO of Fiji's Territorial Battalion. The *Daily Mirror* encouraged the women in what it dubbed 'The Sunshine Squad' to perform hula dances in the snow during one of the coldest winters in a century—especially Betty and Lou. But never Emma, who would have nothing to do with the *Mirror's* 'Sunshine Squad' publicity.

After completing her basic training, Va served as PA to the OC Huron Camp (for training WRAC officers) in Somerset. She served only a year before returning to Fiji because her father was terminally ill, and she was an only daughter. She was known in the army as Tabua, or Private Tabua. When discharged her shorthand was 120 wpm and her typing 70 wpm.

Va rejoined the Registrar General's Office on her return and found subsequent employment with CSR, the Native Lands Trust Board (NLTB), Air Pacific and the Ports Authority of Fiji. Va's only regret is that she did not serve longer in the army. Va's association with the Taukei movement in 1987 is dealt with in Chapter 7.

By 1992, Va still vaguely hoped for an entirely Fijian government but had come to realise that there were limitations to such an ideal after returning to live in Taveuni and Labasa.

Va met her first husband, an RFMF soldier, in Suva. They had seven children, but divorced after eighteen years. She had another four children with her second spouse, Ratu Samisoni Seruitanoa, with whom she settled on an old plantation at Kasavu settlement, near Nakobo village on Vanua Levu. By 2013 Va had forty grandchildren and six great grandchildren.

APPENDIX K:
MAJOR WORSLEY'S REPORT

Report by OC Recruiting Team, Fiji

Introduction

1. Recruiting in Fiji is conditioned by politics and is likely to be so in the future. On arrival, I saw the Governor, who laid down in general terms the limits within which the recruiting team could operate; he stressed, first of all, that the number of recruits to be taken away should not exceed 100 men, secondly, that recruiting should be multi-racial, and here laid down a broad ratio of about 60% Fijian, 30% Indian and 10% part European, and, thirdly, that the main administrative centres of the Colony should be visited by the team in order not to give people cause for grievances arriving from not having reasonable opportunities to present themselves for recruitment. At this stage the Governor felt it was too early to talk about potential recruiting beyond the agreed hundred.

2. Implementing the Governor's policy took some days to arrange because the Government secretariat had been awaiting the arrival of the team before thinking in detail about the ramifications of recruitment in the Colony for the British Army. In addition, the secretariat, already hard pressed by the prevailing delicate political situation had, I suspect, misgivings that recruitment would significantly add to their political difficulties. All departments of the Government, however, went out of their way to be helpful

and without this help it would have been impossible to proceed far with the job. The press and radio also gave much assistance although at times it seemed misguided. The Fijian Military forces were extremely helpful over all administrative matters whether they concerned the team or they concerned the recruits. They also made their officers' mess available for an official cocktail party I gave towards the end of the team's visit.

Political situation

3. From a bit of hurried reading I had been able to do before going to Fiji I was aware that there were racial problems there, but I was not aware of the involved and difficult political problems the Government faces. This is not the place to describe them in any detail, but it is worth mentioning them in outline so as to provide an idea of the atmosphere in which the recruiting team worked.

4. In very general terms the Government has two problems: first to prevent a deterioration in the poor relationships between the Indians, who number about 200,000, and the Fijians who number about 170,000, and, second, to prevent situations arising that would give the Fijian people as a whole, ie Fijians, Indians and others, grounds for militantly expressing dissatisfaction with Europeans, whether in the Government or in commercial and industrial organisations. The sugar riots of 1960 were manifestations of the former and the Suva riots of 1959 of the latter. The recruiting team's work was conditioned to a greater or less degree by both fundamental problems: as regards the first, it was important not only to give the impression but also to demonstrate clearly that recruiting was on a multi-racial basis; as regards the second, it was important to make sure that everybody who wished to apply to join the British Army was given a definite chance to prove himself although the importance of doing this did not become apparent until after we had been recruiting in Suva for a few days.

5. Some examples may help to illustrate how the team's work was conditioned by the political situation. After I had made a detailed press release, given a press conference and made a broadcast on the Fiji Broadcasting Corporation, all, of course cleared by the PRO, describing the way in which

the team was going to carry out its work, which I stressed was limited to dealing with 40 applicants a day, recruiting started in Suva on Monday 2nd October. On the first, second and third days something in the region of 200 applicants presented themselves daily, a figure far in excess of that which the team could handle. I therefore made arrangements with the Secretary for Fijian Affairs for a form of pre-selection by the Fijian Administration to be carried out so that the recruiting office was not besieged by large numbers of Fijian men who had to be turned away. On the fourth day it was reported by a Fijian member of the Legislative Council (MLC) to the Government that there was a large number of dissatisfied Fijians in the Suva area who had applied to join the British Army but who had been given no kind of test or interview. This Fijian was also the District Officer for Suva and his views were supported by his superior, the Commissioner for the central Division, who said that the situation was developing not unlike that which existed immediately before the Suva riots of 1959, when an apparently trivial dispute between the management of the Shell Oil Company and its employees, both Fijian and Indian, resulted in riots. An emergency conference was held, with the Secretary for Fijian Affairs in the Chair, attended by the Assistant Colonial Secretary, Commissioner of Police, Commander of the Fijian Military Forces and various other representatives of departments that would be directly and adversely affected if a serious internal security situation arose. Severe criticism, much of which was emotional and specious, was levelled at the way the Government Secretariat was handling the recruiting. I pointed out that the Secretariat and Fijian Affairs were merely trying to help the recruiting team by arranging for a method of pre-selection and offered to extend widely the amount of testing the team was doing; this offer appeared to satisfy the main critics and, as was subsequently borne out by events, although it gave a certain amount of extra work to the team, resulted in no further complaints of this kind.

6. A second example occurred when, as a result of discussions between myself and the Government, an Indian and a Fijian were attached to the team

during its tour of Viti Levu to work, among other things, as advisers in matters concerning their respective races. The Fijian is a District Education Officer and also an MLC. From the first, he had seemed reluctant to join the team and, after two days with it, urged me to release him and return to his district because of considerable pressure of work in his department; realising that this was not the true reason for his wanting to leave the team, I pressed him for further grounds. After some time, he admitted that as a Fijian politician he feared that the ratio of Fijians to Indians in the successful applicants would favour the Indians too much and that, if so, he could not be associated with the work of the team. In the circumstances, I was compelled to agree to his release and from this time onwards a racial adviser was attached from each administrative district for the duration of our stay in the district.

7. A third example concerned the agreed right of the Governor to veto from the list of successful applicants those people considered to be essential to the future development of the Colony. It was at first felt within the Government Secretariat that it would be unwise to make it known that some applicants might be prevented from joining the British Army for fear that it would give cause for dissatisfaction among those vetoed. When I submitted my original list to the Government of 200 names, the Governor, acting, of course, on the heads of Government departments, removed 22 names from the list whose places were taken by those on a reserve list; the final agreed list was published in the press and over the radio. Some few days later I was approached by a reporter from the Fiji Broadcasting Corporation who stated that he had heard on good authority that the Governor had vetoed 22 names and that it was a flagrant abuse of individual rights and that the press was investigating it further. As a result of consultations with the secretariat, we agreed to make an immediate press release frankly declaring that the Governor had reserved the right of veto and the purpose of the veto. The release was made but the day after the leading article in the *Fiji Times*, the English-speaking newspaper in the Colony, condemned the idea of the veto and criticised the Government for reserving special powers to

retain government servants without extending similar rights to commercial firms. As is obvious, the argument was fallacious, but its presentation in the form of a leading article was not best calculated to keep emotions about the recruiting campaign in check.

Educational standards of applicants

8. The educational standard of applicants was surprisingly high. At the outset I agreed with the Government that I would try to select people with educational standards that would satisfy Army requirements but, at the same time, not remove from the Colony people with fairly high educational qualifications and who, therefore, had a definite potential within the Colony. The Government accepted my argument that the modern Army, being a good deal more technical than it was even a few years ago, requires a higher standard of recruits than it used to and that, because men recruited in Fiji had to be able to speak good English, it was necessary to make a final selection from relatively well-educated men. A satisfactory compromise was reached when it was agreed that 75% of those accepted should have educational qualifications not exceeding those of the Fiji Junior Certificate and that the remaining 25% could be better qualified and include university entrants. It was ultimately possible to select many perfectly adequate recruits from among men without educational certificates but who had reached a certificate level of education. The results of the RO tests show the high standard of intelligence of the recruits as compared with that obtained in other parts of the world. All but three obtained scores between 20 and 43.

Increase of number of recruits
from 100 to 200

9. After a few days recruiting it was clear to me that the response was going to be considerable and that a high proportion of the applicants would be suitable as recruits. I felt that as the team would be testing some hundreds of men and interviewing about 400 (the final figures were 803 tested and 424 interviewed) it would be possible, without extending the stay of the team and providing the Governor agreed, to enlist about 200 men.

I discussed this matter with the Government simultaneously with that of the educational standard of recruits and was pleased when the Governor agreed that the figure could be accordingly increased, although he stressed that it would not be possible to go beyond this figure because he considered it necessary to prevent too large a proportion of well educated youth leaving the Colony, especially Fijians, for if too large an exodus occurred it would adversely affect recruitment into the Civil Service, the Police Force and the Fiji Military forces and jeopardise attempts to bring the Fijians forward into more responsible positions.

Potential for further recruitment

10. Although at the outset of the campaign the Governor wished the number of recruits to be restricted to 100 and considered it too early to talk about future potential, as will be gathered from the foregoing, he showed increasing sympathy for the view of exploiting further the apparently good material available. On 14th November, the day before I left Suva for FARELF, I had a final interview with the Governor, who helpfully agreed with some qualifications, that if a requirement continued to exist for recruits he would not object to a recruiting team visiting there in about a year's time to take away a number similar to the one we have taken on this occasion. His qualifications are that it would be important to see how the present batch of recruits reported on life in the British Army and that the requirements of the Colony would have to be reviewed before another recruiting team visited it. Nevertheless, his agreement in principle is clear.

Handling of recruits

11. The bulk of the recruits (about 70%) are Fijians and it is important that the units these men go to understand that Fijians cannot be regarded in the same light as men from other Colonies. The Fijians are a proud people and are very conscious of the fact that Fiji was ceded to and not conquered by Britain; they are intensely loyal to the British Crown and consider that their satisfactory preservation as a race depends on the maintenance of Crown

Colony rule in Fiji. Fijians lead a community life where the Chiefs have considerable authority; the young Fijians accept this social order without question. I have been advised both by the Government and by leading Fijians that against this background the Fijian will be deeply offended if he is regarded as an inferior to the white man in any way at all but that, at the same time, he must be carefully controlled and that he will respond to discipline and clear orders rather than to an easy-going informal atmosphere.

12. The Fijian is traditionally a warrior and a sportsman and, thus, should fit in well to active unit life. He will, however, become dispirited and depressed if he is not kept busy and if he is not able to pursue to the full his sporting interests, such as playing rugby football and cricket. In short, he will do well in units that lead an active life from the point of view both of training and of sport and serve well under an officer who leads him with firmness and understanding; on the other hand, he will probably go to pieces much quicker than a BOR[85] would if he is employed in a relatively inactive capacity and given little opportunity for sport. The Indian and part-European are traditionally individualists and, therefore, likely to do adequately in the sort of job that would be unsuited to the Fijian.

13. Everyone in the Colony of Fiji will be watching with interest the reactions of the first batch of recruits to life in the British Army, and these reactions will, as I have mentioned above, constitute an important factor in assessing potential recruitment in the future.

Provision of Fiji Battalion

14. Leading Fijians, eg Ratu Pennia (sic), the Deputy Secretary for Fijian Affairs, Ratu Edward, Commissioner for the eastern Division, and the Government of Fiji are very keen that the idea is is given careful consideration of a Fiji Battalion's being formed and provided as a permanent contribution to the British Army. They visualise an agreement similar in some ways to that which exists between the British Government and the Government of Nepal,

---

85 Probably refers to British Other Ranks—author.

which provides a permanent contingent of Gurkhas. They consider that it would be possible to provide a battalion for service anywhere in the world, that day-to-day replacements would not present difficulty and that the battalion could be replaced by another every few years. The main attractions from the Fijian point of view to this idea are, first, that the Fijians would be kept together as a large group much as they are in their traditional communal system of living and, second, that the soldiers who comprised the battalion would be away from the Colony for only a matter of a few years rather than, as under the present system of recruitment, for over 20 years or even for good. Although I explained that I thought the whole of this question had been considered in England I undertook to raise the matter again. The Fijians certainly feel strongly about it. The Indians in Fiji do not seem to be especially interested in the idea and appear to be satisfied with the present system of recruitment.

The Indian, however, is essentially an individualist rather than a communalist and in any case does not, understandably, possess the fervent loyalty to the Crown of the Fijian.

Recommendations for any future visit

15. Since the team's visit to the Colony was the first which has been undertaken, much time was spent breaking new ground; I feel if subsequent visits are to take place much could be done beforehand to streamline procedures and thus shorten the time the team has to spend there. In the first place, before the team goes to Fiji, either the War Office and the Colonial Office or the OC team and the Fijian Government should work out in detail how and where the team is going to operate. Full publicity should be given to the agreed modus operandi before the team reaches the Colony in order to avoid political repercussions after the team gets there. Delays in getting recruits away raise administrative problems and are likely to create political ones; as the Fiji Government is in the position to make a fairly reasonable estimate as to the extent of the response, it is desirable that arrangements for embarking recruits are more than tentatively made at a very early stage.

16. The financial aspect of the team's work raised many problems, and

much more should be done in the future to anticipate them before a team goes to Fiji. In this connection, the Accountant-General, who proved most helpful and took an increasing part in paying bills and checking estimates for the team, would probably be prepared to undertake such commitments in the future from the start.

Summary of main conclusions

17. Relationships with the Government of Fiji developed amicably and productively.

18. Although at first restricting the number of recruits to be taken away to 100, the Governor subsequently agreed to raise it to 200.

19. If the need should arise, the Governor agrees in principle to consider the possibility of a recruiting campaign's taking place in about a year's time similar to the one that has just been completed.

20. The 200 male recruits, whatever their race, are well educated and potentially good soldiers.

21. The Fijians are very conscious of the fact that they ceded their home to Britain and for this reason alone the Fijian recruits cannot be regarded in the same light as men from other Colonies.

22. The Fijian is traditionally used to a disciplined community life and is a keen sportsman. The Fijian recruit should, therefore, do well if he is kept active at both work and sport but he is likely to deteriorate quickly if he is not.

23. The Fijians and the Government feel that the question of the provision of a Fiji Battalion along lines similar to those of the Gurkhas should be given further consideration.

24. If another recruiting team visits Fiji, all aspects of its administration and method of operating should be planned in detail before it arrives.

(Signed)

Major RASC

(G.H. Worsley)

21 November 1961

Reunion, over fifty years on; David Whey (left) and Subramani Naidu, Caloundra, Queensland, 2013. Photo: author

Selected Bibliography and References

Adams, Cindy, *Sukarno - an autobiography*, Bobbs-Merrill Company, 1965.

Angus, Beverley M., *My Colonial Fiji*, Trafford Singapore, 2013.

Bain, Kenneth, *Treason at 10,* Hodder & Stoughton, 1984.

Bayly, Christopher & Harper, Tim, *Forgotten Wars—The End of Britain's Asian Empire*, Penguin, 2007 p. 522.

Beale, Pat, *Operation Orders - the Experience of a Young Australian Army Officer 1963-70*, Australian Military History Publications, 2003.

Berwick, Sam, *Who's Who in Fiji*, Berwicks Publishing House, Suva, 1990.

Cole, Roger & Belfield, Richard, *Operation Storm*, Hodder & Stoughton, 2011.

Cosgrove, Peter, *My Story*, Harper Collins, 2006, pps. 311-312, Fijians in East Timor 'warriors with the voices of angels.'

Crosby, Ron, *NZ SAS—The First Fifty Years*, Penguin Viking, photograph and reference to Ponijase, pps. 249 & 260.

Cyclopaedia of Fiji 1907, reprinted 1984, Museum of Fiji.

Davies, Barry, *Heroes of the SAS*, Virgin Books, 2000.

Dean, Eddie & Ritova, Stan, *Rabuka—No Other Way*, The Marketing Team International, Suva, 1988.

Deeds, W.F, *Brief Lives*, Macmillan, 2004.

Dickens, Peter, *SAS - The Jungle Frontier*, subtitled '22 Special Air Service Regiment in the Borneo Campaign,1963-66,' Published 1983 by Arms and Armour Press, Lionel Leventhal Ltd, 2-6 Hampstead, High Street, London NW3 1QQ.

Farran, Roy, *Winged Dagger*, Collins, 1948, Arms and Armour Press, 1986.

Garvey, Sir Ronald, *Gentleman Pauper*, Anchor Publications, 1984, ISBN 0 948016 02 7.

Gatty, Ronald, *Fijian-English Dictionary*, Oceania Printers Fiji, 2009.

Geraghty, Tony, *Who Dares Wins*, subtitled 'The Story of the SAS 1950 -1980', Fontana/Collins 1981. Several references to Laba and one to 1 FIR.

Hodge, Dino, *Don Dunstan: Intimacy and Liberty - a political biography,* Wakefield Press, 2014.

Jeapes, Tony, *SAS Secret War*, Harper Collins 1996, pps. 126 & 128, May 1971 refs to Cpl 'Mule Gilairi.'

Kemp, Anthony, *The SAS - The Savage Wars of Peace - 1947 to the Present*, John Murray 1994, ISBN 0-7195-5044-0. References to 'several' unnamed Fijians serving with KMS in Sri Lanka and 'a couple' with David Stirling's KAS countering rhino poaching in Africa (pps. 201 & 204).

Kennedy, Michael Paul, *Soldier I SAS*. References to Laba, Sek, Valdez, Tom and Fred on pps. 37-38, 60, 63-64 (cannibalism), 67-69, 83, 85, 95-96, 119-120 (Belfast), 173, 200 (TKM), 208 (Sek, Jim & Fred in Falklands), 228 and 232.

Lal, Brij V, *Broken Waves - A history of the Fiji Islands in the twentieth century,* University of Hawaii Press, 1992, pps. 71, 267, 274, 277, 292 & 295 in particular ('Things Fall Apart').

Lal, Brij V, *Chalo Jahaji—on a journey through indenture in Fiji*, ANU Press 2012, ISBN 9781922144607.

Liava'a, Christine, *Qaravi Na'I Tavi: They Did Their Duty Soldiers from Fiji in the Great War*, ISBN 978 1 877332 623.

Lowry, Robert, *Fortress Fiji - Holding the Line in the Pacific War 1939-45* 2006.

Macintyre, Ben, *SAS: Rogue Heroes*, Viking/Penguin 2016.

Mackinnon, Marsali, *The Fiji Oral History Part 1: Part-Europeans and Europeans, 1998-99*. Pacific Manuscripts Bureau, Australian National University, ref. AU PMB MS 1235.

Maddocks, Sir Kenneth, *Of No Fixed Abode*, The Wolsey Press 1988, ISBN 0 9513895 0 5.

Michener, J.A and Day, Grove A, *Rascals in Paradise*, Secker and Warburg, 1957.

Morgan, Robin and Leve, Ariel, *1963 - The Year of the Revolution*, Harper Collins/It Books, 2013, ISBN 978 0 06 212044 1.

Murray, John, *The Minnows of Triton - Policing, Politics, Crime and Corruption in the South Pacific Islands* 2010.

Nandan, Satendra, *The Wounded Sea*, Sydney: Simon and Schuster, 1991.

Naughtie, James, Transcript of *The New Elizabethans,* episode on Talaiasi Labalaba

Nogueira, Thais, FCO website blog of 20 Feb 2015 on 'Speakers Corner' blog.

Palmer, George, *Kidnapping in the South Seas*, 1871 Facsimile edition published by Penguin, 1973.

Paton, Frank H.L, *Patteson of Melanesia. A brief life of John Coleridge Patteson, Missionary Bishop*, S.P.C.K [1930].

Prasad, Rajendra, *Tears in paradise: - unveiled: suffering and struggles of Indians in Fiji 1879-2004*, Glade Publishers, Auckland, 2004, ISBN-10: 0-473-11456-9.

Purdon, Corran, *List the Bugle*, Greystone Books, 1993.

Ravuvu, Asesela, *Fijians at War 1939-45*, Institute of Pacific Studies, USP 1988.

Ross, Hamish and Marafono, Fred *From SAS to Blood Diamond Wars*, Pen & Sword Military, 2011

Sandford, Christopher, *The Rolling Stones*, Simon & Schuster, 2012 (Ch 2, pps. 7-8).

Scarr, Deryck, *Ratu Sukuna - Soldier, Statesman, Man of Two Worlds*, Macmillan Education Ltd, 1980, p. 141.

Scott, Owen, *Deep Beyond the Reef*, Penguin, 2004.

Sharpham, John, *Rabuka of Fiji*, Central Queensland University Press, 2000, ISBN 1 875998 69 1.

Southwicke, Grahame, *Hard Day at the Office*, 2011, ISBN 978-982-98066-1-1.

Spate, O.H.K, *The Fijian People: Economic Problems and Prospects*, Colonial Paper No.13 of 1959, published by the Legislative Council of Fiji.

Stone, David, *Cold War Warriors*, Leo Cooper, 1998.

Teaiwa, Teresia, *What Makes Fiji Women Soldiers? Context, Context, Context,* Intersections: Gender and Sexuality in Asia and the Pacific Issue 37, March 2015.

Theroux, Paul, *The Happy Isles of Oceania: Paddling the Pacific*, p. 244 - reference to martial qualities of Fijian soldiers in WWII.

Thomson, Peter, *Kava in the Blood*, Tandem Press, 1999.

Tillotson, Michael, *Dwin Bramall—the authorised biography of FM the Lord Bramall*, Sutton Publishing, 2005.

Tuivaga, Sir Timoci Uluiburoto, KT, CF, self-published memoir, 2014.

Usher, Sir Len, *Letters From Fiji 1987-1990*, *Fiji Times* Ltd., 1992.

War Office Files in The National Archives, WO32/19455, *Army Recruiting in the Fiji Islands*, WO 32/20374, *Proposal for Recruitment of Personnel from Commonwealth and Colonial Territories*, WO 32/19260, *Overseas Recruitment for the British Army*.

Warner, Philip, *The Special Air Service*, William Kimber & Co. Ltd., 1971-2.

Waterhouse, Jill et al, *Canberra - Early Days at the Causeway*, ACT Museums Unit, Canberra, 1992.

Weddell, Howard, *Soldiers From the Pacific: the Story of Pacific Island Soldiers in the New Zealand Expeditionary Force in World War One*, Defence of New Zealand Study Group, 2015.

White, Rowland, *Storm Front*, Bantam Press, 2011. Innumerable references to Jim, Tak and Laba.

Wicks, David and Wilson, Simon, Destination: Malaya - a history of 2 Field Troop Royal Australian Engineers 1963–1965, ISBN 0646426265, Chapter 3: Thailand and Operation Crown.

Wiggins, Howard, *Changing Power Relations Between the Middle East and South Asia* in *Geopolitics of the Indian Ocean*, University of California Press, 1977.

Yasa, M.M.K, *Na Tawa Vanua*, a play about the first settlement of Fiji, 1983, subsequently reprinted in Feb. 1988, Sept. 1992 and Feb. 2003. Published and distributed by Textbook Wholesalers Ltd. *Of Baluka and Nibong Palm*, Pasifika Education Centre, 2009.

INDEX

Names marked with an asterisk hereunder are those mentioned in the *Fiji Times* of 6 November 1961 who did not actually leave Fiji for the UK, for whatever reason. They are not referred to elsewhere in this book. This group is not to be confused with the twenty-two names on the recruiting team's original list, which the Governor vetoed as too important for Fiji's immediate development to be released to the army.

www.ingramcontent.com/pod-product-compliance
Lightning Source LLC
Chambersburg PA
CBHW060038100426
42742CB00014B/2626